MODERN
PROJECT
MANAGEMENT

MODERN PROJECT MANAGEMENT

Successfully Integrating Project Management Knowledge Areas and Processes

NORMAN R. HOWES

AMACOM

American Management Association

New York • Atlanta • Boston • Chicago • Kansas City • San Francisco • Washington, D. C.
Brussels • Mexico City • Tokyo • Toronto

Special discounts on bulk quantities of AMACOM books are
available to corporations, professional associations, and other
organizations. For details, contact Special Sales Department,
AMACOM, a division of American Management Association,
1601 Broadway, New York, NY 10019.
Tel.: 212-903-8316. Fax: 212-903-8083.
Web site: www.amacombooks.org

This publication is designed to provide accurate and authoritative information in regard to the subject matter covered. It is sold with the
understanding that the publisher is not engaged in rendering legal,
accounting, or other professional service. If legal advice or other expert
assistance is required, the services of a competent professional person
should be sought.

Microsoft Access, Microsoft Explorer, Microsoft Excel, and Microsoft Project are registered
trademarks of Microsoft Corporation.

The term and program Modern Project is copyrighted by Norman R. Howes.

Library of Congress Cataloging-in-Publication Data

Howes, Norman R.
    Modern project management : successfully integrating project management
  knowledge areas and processes / Norman R. Howes.
      p. cm.
    Includes bibliographical references and index.
    ISBN 0-8144-0632-7
    1. Industrial project management.   I. Title.

  HD69.P75 H69   2001
  658.4'04—dc21   00–045108

Printing number

10   9   8   7   6   5   4   3   2   1

Contents

List of Illustrations

Preface

The purpose of this book is to describe how some of the most talented modern project managers manage projects, why they do it the way they do, and what types of computer tools they use to do it. Included with this book is a project management toolset called *Modern Project* that provides tools for doing all the project management tasks discussed in this book. It can be installed on a personal computer and used to help you learn about project management or to manage real-world projects.

While project management is practiced as a sophisticated profession in some companies, it is still, unfortunately, misunderstood in others. Even where project management is practiced professionally, the theory behind it is often misunderstood, causing it to be practiced mechanically, rather than artistically. Modern project managers need sound management skills, as they always have. But the current generation of project managers requires theoretical and technical skills that were virtually unknown not long ago and that are continually growing more complex.

A significant percentage of project managers currently use technical tools in much the same way that professional investors use technical tools. Both of these professions have well-known performance measures that are used day in and day out to assist in making decisions regarding how to employ their resources. Just as two different investors using the same technical tools can get radically different results, two different project managers on similar projects, utilizing the same measures of performance, may get radically different results. Let us consider a typical example.

Two project managers on similar projects are using the earned value measure of performance to evaluate work packages and higher summary level aggregations of the work. They both know that earned value at any level of aggregation is computed by multiplying the budget for the component of work being considered by the "percent complete" for the component of work. But one of them gets accurate earned value measurements, and the other one gets misleading information. How can this be?

The problem is that the "budget" and the "percent complete" are concepts that have subtle meanings. Unless you are managing one of those extremely rare projects whose budgets never change, there is no such thing as a single budget. There are many artifices companies use to deceive themselves into believing there is a single budget for a project. But in reality there are multiple implicit budgets. There is, of course, the original budget that is part of the original project plan. Then there are multiple variations of this budget caused by change orders, quantification variances, productivity variances, and contingency draw-downs.

You might think you do not have all these things on your project, but chances are you have some of them. These budget modifiers are all explained in this book. But, for now, we simply point out that most project managers do not know how to tell a quantification variance from a productivity variance or whether quantification or productivity variances should be included in the budget that is used for earned value calculation.

Calculating the "percent complete" is equally if not more complex. There are many methods (referred to as *statusing methods*) that have been devised for calculating the percent complete for some aggregation of work. Most of these methods have their place for certain types of work and for certain situations. Many project managers do not know when to use which method and, on many projects, project control personnel do not apply the methods in a uniform or consistent manner.

The end result can be performance measures that do not measure performance meaningfully. Moreover, it is difficult to see this early in the project lifetime. As a project nears completion, it becomes obvious that improperly calculated performance measures are meaningless. But by then, it is often too late. The very tools you have used to guide you through the pitfalls of project management now appear to have betrayed you.

This book has been designed to provide you with the right balance of theory, methods, psychology, and practice to become an effective project manager the very first time you get the opportunity to manage something more than a ten-person project. For many professional project managers, gaining this ability comes hard. Moreover, there are many would-be project managers who have abandoned their attempts along the way. Effective project management on today's projects, where the emphasis is often on the rapid completion of the project, is not something that is learned entirely in the classroom or by reading a book. But having the right training and the right tools makes a big difference. The purpose of this book is to give you this experience.

Two common misconceptions about project management are: (1) that project management is primarily the project scheduling activity, and (2) that it is just general management of an organization, where that organization happens to be organized as a project, rather than as a division or department or some other component of an organization.

To be sure, project managers on large projects know how projects are scheduled, and they know how to read the various forms in which project schedulers cast their schedules. Moreover, they probably understand the purpose and meaning of the schedules better than the project schedulers do themselves. Project scheduling is only a detail of project management, and project managers on large projects hire others to handle these details for them, such as cost accountants, project administrators, project schedulers, and control package managers.

The misconception that project management is just general management where the organization to be managed happens to be organized as a project is more subtle. There are many similarities between general management and project management. Both of these professions have their own methods, techniques, and computerized systems. Being a master of one of these disciplines does not guarantee that an individual will be a success at the other. For a manager who is not familiar with the methods and techniques of project management, the first five chapters of this book are especially relevant.

It is the author's viewpoint that most project management training is unnecessarily disjointed, and so are most project management tools. One of the purposes of this book is to show that this need not be the case. Today, most project managers get their training either through company training programs or at short, intensive training conferences offered by training companies or professional societies, rather than through college courses. This book presents an integrated treatment of project management theory, methods, and tools that is simple and easy to remember. This book should be well suited for any of the previously mentioned training vehicles, especially corporate training programs or college-level classes.

The author hopes this book and the accompanying toolset will contribute to a better understanding of how to manage projects and how to utilize automated project management tools. While this toolset is covered by copyright, the author and the publisher give you, the reader, the right of unrestricted usage for his or her own use. For instance, you are free to try to use the toolset to manage a real project. They do not, however, give the reader the right to sell this toolset or modified versions of this toolset.

Finally, the author wishes to thank Lance Barlow and Douglas Tiner for our long association and for the many enlightening conversations we have had over the years. Several of the ideas contained in this book are directly or indirectly attributable to these two long-term project managers. They are among the finest the author has ever met.

Norman R. Howes
Alexandria, Virginia

How to Use the CD

Before using the programs on the CD, you should read and understand the license contained in this book or read the file on the CD titled License.doc.

The files on the CD of the form xxx97.mde can only be executed by using Microsoft Access 97. The files of the form xxx2K.mde can only be executed by using Microsoft Access 2000. You will need to have one of these versions of Microsoft Access to execute these files.

The version of the desktop project management toolset that is distributed with this book is implemented as a Microsoft Access application. As such, it is packaged together with a database. Each of the files of the form example97ChaptX.mde or example2KChaptX.mde is an Access database that contains the Modern Project toolset. The databases in these files represent snapshots of what the example project database should look like at the end of Chapter X, where X is a chapter number. The files of the form example97.mde and example2K.mde contain an empty database that will be used to construct the example project that is used throughout this book.

In order to use the files on the CD, you will need to copy them onto a hard drive or a diskette. After you have done so, you may need to change the "read only" attribute of the Access files. For instance, if you use Microsoft Windows Explorer to copy the file from the CD to your disk drive, it will set the read only attribute to "true" since the CD is a read only file. This will prevent you from entering new data into the example97.mde and the example 2K.mde files.

To change the read only attribute to "false," first open the file using Access. Then click on the "File" control button on the menu bar at the top of the Access window. Next, select the "Database Properties" option. This will cause the Properties window to appear. Make sure the Properties window is displaying the "General" properties. If not, click on the "General" tab at the top of the window. Now look at the "Read only" attribute. If it has a checkmark in the box in front of it, click on the box to remove the mark. Finally, click on the "OK" control button at the bottom of the Properties window. You should now be able to write data into the file.

The file on the CD named example.mpp is a Microsoft Project 98 schedule file. It contains the example schedule used in Chapter 7 of this book that demonstrates the automated interface between Microsoft Project and Modern Project. You will need to have a version of Microsoft Project 98 to run this program. However, it is not essential to an understanding of Chapter 7 to actually execute this example schedule. It is intended primarily as an exercise in tranferring scheduling dates from Microsoft Project into the Modern Project database.

The file on the CD named example.html is an intermediate file that is produced during the process of moving scheduling dates between Microsoft Project and Modern Project. You can look at this file with a browser to see how the schedule dates are contained in a Microsoft Project HTML export file.

MODERN
PROJECT
MANAGEMENT

Chapter 1

Introduction

M odern project management is a well-understood discipline that can produce predictable, repeatable results. The methods of modern project management are highly analytic, usually requiring automated tools to support them on large projects. Like most other disciplines, it is learned through both practice and study. Since this chapter is an introduction, it is fitting that we explain how we will be using the term *project management*. Project management encompasses many different skills, such as understanding the interdependencies among people, technologies, budgets, and expectations; planning the project to maximize productivity; motivating others to execute the plan; analyzing the actual results; and reworking and tuning the plan to deal with the realities of what really happens as the project is executed.

While all these topics are covered in some detail in the book, the focus is on the theory and techniques project managers use to plan and control projects. So, when we use the term *project management* in this book, we often use it in this more specific sense. Several books on project management have already been written that deal with the organizational and team-building aspects of project management. Our intent is not to duplicate this work but rather to fill a gap in the presentation of the theoretical and practical aspects of project management. To a large extent, modern project management theory and methodology (the practical aspect) take into consideration the psychological and motivational aspects of project management and are designed to communicate the standards and measures that project management is using to the project workforce.

Also, several current books on project management deal extensively with requirements development and requirements specification. In the Information Technology (IT) field in particular, requirements specification has essentially become a profession in its own right. In order to keep this book relatively small and accessible, we have chosen to largely omit this aspect of a project and just assume that the requirements for the project have been adequately defined and documented. For many first-time project managers, the projects they will be managing will be small to medium in size. While project requirements development and specification are always important, they are often straightforward. It is usually on larger projects that requirements development and specification become complex. There is some discussion of requirements in Chapter 10 as they relate to rescuing a failing project. If you are trying to learn about project management for a large project, you should take a look at that material as you read Chapter 2 or consult a book on requirements engineering.

In this book we differentiate between general management and project management. While project management shares many of the concerns and methods of general management, project management is different from general management in essential ways. Project management is not to be confused with "management" in the sense of supervising workers, although many project managers perform that function. Whether project managers are supervisors or not often depends on an organization's structure.

In companies that are organized around the "matrix management" model, project managers may not have supervisory responsibilities. In such organizations, supervision is usually delegated to discipline managers, such as engineering managers, programming managers, and quality control managers. In companies that are organized around the "project" model, project managers supervise the personnel that work on their project. In either case, the issue of who does the supervision does not concern us here. Instead, we focus on the methods project managers use to plan, estimate, monitor, and ultimately control projects for which they have performance responsibility, whether or not they directly supervise the project personnel.

We now turn to presenting some examples of project management tools to convey a little of the flavor of modern project management methods and to provide some motivation for the need for these methods. These examples are the only "introduction" the reader will get, and it is not too important that the reader understand these examples in any depth at this point. Several existing project management books give extensive introductions as to what project management is, how it fits into the organization of an enterprise, and the challenges that face the project manager. Again, our reason for omitting such an approach is to keep the book small and easy to use, that is, to get the reader into project management as quickly as possible. The book is designed to unfold the topics of project management in the order in which the new project manager will need them. The explanation of the concepts occurs simultaneously with the introduction of the concepts throughout the book, rather than in a lengthy introduction.

We will not attempt to define the terms that appear in this introduction, saving that for the chapters that lie ahead. The inexperienced reader (inexperienced in terms of project management) should not be concerned if he or she does not understand the meaning of any new terms that might be encountered. The intent is to convey some of the spirit of modern project management. At this point, new terminology should just be accepted naïvely. Even with a naïve interpretation, it is likely that the uninitiated will still capture the spirit of the subject.

Figure 1-1 shows a typical project management chart, called the *Earned Value Report*. To the untrained eye this chart

Figure 1-1. Earned Value Report.

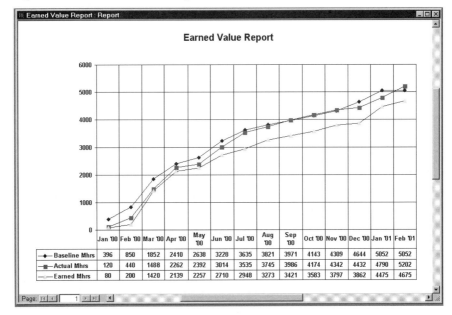

may appear interesting, but to the experienced project manager it speaks volumes about the current situation that exists on the project that this chart depicts. It gives the experienced project manager a summary of how the project is being managed and the information needed to begin the process of isolating problems and finding solutions.

On this chart there are three "curves" (graphs). They are labeled *baseline man-hours, actual man-hours,* and *earned man-hours.* The baseline man-hour curve expresses how much labor project management intends to expend and how this labor will be expended over time. The actual man-hour curve expresses how labor is actually being expended on the project. The actual man-hour curve is an accumulation of labor expended to date, plotted against time.

These two curves together tell a lot about a project overall. If the two curves are very close together, then we know that the project is expending labor-hours at about the same rate as called for in the plan. If these two curves diverge significantly at any point in time, then we know that during that period, labor was not being expended as planned. But these two curves do not tell the whole story. It is possible that labor is being expended as planned but little is being accomplished. The third curve, the earned man-hours curve, completes the picture.

The earned man-hour curve on the chart in Figure 1-1 is a special case of a more general concept called *earned value*, which is discussed in Chapter 4. Earned value is a measure of what has been achieved (earned). Earned value is an expression of worth and as such can be expressed in various ways. It can be expressed in dollars or in the amount of labor needed to create this worth. It is frequently the case that the client is more interested in the dollar value of the achievement, whereas the project manager is more interested in the labor-hour value of what has been accomplished, because labor-hours are what the project manager directly controls (primarily). And, on most projects, labor-hours account for more than half the cost of a project.

Earned value is calculated by a simple formula. It is the *percent complete* multiplied by the budgeted (planned) value of the project. Earned value is a measure of accomplishment that can be applied equally well to a single task within a project, a group of tasks, or the total project. For example, if the budgeted value of the project is 100,000 labor-hours or $8 million, and the project is 50% completed, then the earned labor-hours are 50,000 and the earned value is $4 million.

In the chart in Figure 1-1, the baseline (budgeted) labor-hours curve and the actual labor-hours curve are close together. This means that the rate of expenditure of labor-hours is very close to the estimated rate of expenditure envisioned in the budget. If the actual labor-hours curve is below the baseline labor-hour curve, then we know the labor-hour expenditure is less than what was planned. On the other hand, if the actual labor-hour curve is above the baseline curve, we know that the rate of expenditure is greater than what was anticipated in the budget. In Figure 1-1 we also notice that the earned labor-hours curve is trailing somewhat below the baseline labor-hours and the actual labor-hours curves. This indicates that the actual accomplishment on the project is a little less than anticipated in the project plan.

Some of the charts and reports discussed in this book, like the Earned Value Report, keep the project manager informed about the "health" of the project. Other reports provide capabilities for the project manager to review the plan (e.g., the budget and the schedule) for the project. The report shown in Figure 1-2 is titled *WBS Listing*, where WBS stands for *Work Breakdown Structure*. The WBS for a project is one of the fundamental concepts of project management.

The WBS depicts how the work of the project is subdivided into individual components. The WBS is more than just a list of tasks within the project. It is a hierarchical structure that depicts how the work is organized. It shows how the overall project is subdivided into lower-level components called *control packages* and how these control packages (there can be several layers or levels of them) are finally subdivided into *work packages*. Work packages are the lowest level of decomposition of the work that the project manager manages. They contain the individual tasks that are scheduled by the scheduling system.

Let us consider the first line item on this report. The first line item is the control package at hierarchy position "0." It represents the total example project that we will be considering in later chapters. The description of this control package is "5000 SF Building," since the example project we will be considering in this book is the construction of a 5,000-square-foot (SF) building. The second line item on the report is what is called the detail line item for control package "0." The detail line item for a control package on this report gives the budget quantities for the three budgets, titled "Original Budget," "Client Budget," and "Control Budget." It also shows the budget quantity for the "Forecast." As is explained in Chapter 2, budgets can be measured in dollars, in quantities, and in the

Figure 1-2. WBS Listing.

WBS Listing

WBS Position	*Package ID*	Active Indicator	*Description*	*Unit of Meas.*	Original Qty	Client Qty	Control Qty	Forecast Qty
0	*Example Proj*		*5000 SF Building*	*SF*	5000	5000	5000	5000
1	*Foundation*		*Construct Foundation*	*CY Concrete*	290	290	319	319
1.1	*Siteprep*		*Site Preparation*	*SF Land*	20000	25000	25000	25000
1.2	*Forms*		*Forms Installation & Removal*	*SF Forms*	750	750	750	750
1.3	*Rebar*		*Rebar, Mesh & Anchors*	*LBS*	1000	1000	1000	1000
1.4	*Concrete*		*Concrete Pour, Cure & Finish*	*CY Concrete*	290	290	319	319
2	*Structure*		*Build Structure*	*SF*	5000	5000	5000	5000
2.1	*Frame*		*Framing & Misc. Carpentry*	*LF Lumber*	20000	20000	20000	2000(
2.2	*Sheetrock*		*Sheetrock Tape, Bed & Float*	*SF Sheetrock*	10000	10000	10000	10000
2.3	*Roofing*		*Roofing*	*SF Roofing*	6000	6000	6000	6000
2.4	*Painting*		*Painting*	*SF Surface*	10000	10000	10000	10000
3	*Systems*		*Systems*	*EA*	3	3	3	3

Saturday, February 05, 2000 *Page 1 of 2*

amount of labor to accomplish the project. In the WBS Listing, only the quantity budgets are shown.

The reader may find it strange that there is more than one budget on a project. This has to do with the way change control and variance tracking are handled on the project. The forecast for the project can be viewed at this point in the naïve sense of the word, that is, what we think the final quantity will be when the project completes. When the project finally completes, we may have something other than a 5,000-square-foot building. The client may decide to expand the building by another 1,000 square feet for some reason during the project lifetime, and what we end up with may be a 6,000-square-foot building. But, at the beginning of the project, this cannot be foreseen. Changes like this often occur on projects, and for that reason there is another budget called the "Client Budget."

In addition to client-introduced changes, there may be changes in the quantity budget because the quantities were not estimated correctly originally. This gives rise to the "Control Budget." This is a corrected version of the budget that the project manager manages to. The client may or may not be responsible for paying for all of what is included in the control budget, depending on the terms of the contract (if there is a contract for the project).

Finally, projects are not always executed with the same productivity that was originally estimated. This gives rise to the "Forecast." All of these concepts are defined carefully in the next two chapters. It is not important that you understand the details at this point. The idea here is to get a feeling for how the work of a project is subdivided into major components called control packages, how these control packages have various budgets, and how these budgets change over time.

After the total example project control package in Figure 1-2 comes control package "Foundation" that is at hierarchy position "1." The foundation control package is a major component of work for the example project. Notice that the foundation control package has a different unit of measure from the total project. Whereas the project is measured in square feet, the foundation control package is measured in cubic yards (CY) of concrete, that is, by the amount of concrete used to complete the foundation.

From Figure 1-2 it can be seen that the WBS Listing of packages is much like the table of contents of a book. Notice that the control package "Structure" is at hierarchy position 2 and "Systems" at hierarchy position 3. Next, notice that the control package "Foundation" contains the work packages "Siteprep" at hierarchy position 1.1, "Forms" at hierarchy position 1.2, "Rebar" at hierarchy position 1.3, "Concrete" at hierarchy position 1.4, and so on.

The WBS Listing represents how the work unfolds in much the same way that the table of contents of a book represents how a book unfolds into chapters and sections and subsections. In addition to showing the structure of the program manager's plan for accomplishing the work, the WBS Listing also provides a brief description of each package in the WBS hierarchy.

The project management theories, methods, and tools discussed in this book have a fundamental relationship to the project WBS: project management concepts that hold at the lower-level packages can be "rolled up" to higher levels of summarization (the control packages) and eventually to the "top-level" summarization, that is, the whole project. This rollup is a form of aggregation that holds for both values (amounts) and concepts.

Figure 1-3 shows how such a rollup occurs. The report shown in Figure 1-3 is called the *Budgeted Cost Listing*. This is a report that expresses how the cost budget for a project is distributed over the various control packages and work packages of the project. Notice that it is organized around the same WBS hierarchy structure that we just discussed.

In addition to these capabilities, there are a variety of other functions the project manager needs help with. This book discusses the tools the project manager needs to assist with these functions. For instance, the project manager has access to tools

Figure 1-3. Budgeted Cost Listing.

Budgeted Cost Listing

Hierarchy Position	*Package ID / GL Account*		*Original Budget*	*Client Budget*	*Control Budget*	*Forecast*
0	*Example Proj*		$88,467	$91,027	$97,898	$106,298
1	*Foundation*		$88,467	$91,027	$97,898	$106,298
1.1	*Siteprep*		$19,760	$22,320	$22,320	$30,720
	601	Direct Labor	$12,000	$13,000	$13,000	$20,200
	603	Supervision	$2,400	$3,600	$3,600	$4,800
	605	Sub-contract labor	$1,760	$1,760	$1,760	$1,760
	651	Equipment	$3,000	$3,300	$3,300	$3,300
	652	Equipment Consumables	$600	$660	$660	$660
1.2	*Forms*		$9,700	$9,700	$10,670	$10,670
	601	Direct Labor	$6,800	$6,800	$7,480	$7,480
	603	Supervision	$1,800	$1,800	$1,980	$1,980
	632	Construction Materials	$1,100	$1,100	$1,210	$1,210
1.3	*Rebar*		$26,627	$26,627	$29,290	$29,290
	601	Direct Labor	$17,600	$17,600	$19,360	$19,360
	603	Supervision	$3,600	$3,600	$3,960	$3,960
	631	Permanent Materials	$4,800	$4,800	$5,280	$5,280
	632	Construction Materials	$627	$627	$690	$690
1.4	*Concrete*		$32,380	$32,380	$35,618	$35,618
	601	Direct Labor	$9,200	$9,200	$10,120	$10,120
	602	Indirect Labor	$1,800	$1,800	$1,980	$1,980
	631	Permanent Materials	$18,000	$18,000	$19,800	$19,800
	632	Construction Materials	$900	$900	$990	$990
	651	Equipment	$2,480	$2,480	$2,728	$2,728

Wednesday, August 04, 1999 ***Page 1 of 2***

for tracking progress on the project, for keeping track of changes as the project matures, for calculating productivity, and for scientifically forecasting the end results of the project.

All of these capabilities are discussed in the following chapters. But before we get into any project management discussions, it is worthwhile discussing how projects should begin. How projects come into existence plays a key role in whether a project will be successful. Projects are started up for innumerably many different reasons and in innumerably many different situations. Why they come about is not so important as how they come about. Here we are talking about projects that organizations undertake. Projects of individuals come and go without affecting anyone but the individual who undertook them. But organizational projects affect not only those who execute the project but those who finance the project and those who count on the project's being successfully executed.

Projects should come into existence with a clearly documented purpose. Even if the project is an exploratory research effort, there should be specific problems or issues that the project seeks to address. This definition of purpose should take the form of a statement of what will constitute the work of the project. The definition of a project's purpose is often called a project's *statement of work*. A statement of work is not a project plan. (How to develop a project plan is explained in detail in Chapter 2.) A statement of work focuses on what will be done, not how it will be done. The project plan focuses on how to accomplish the work; the statement of work focuses on what is to be done.

For large developmental undertakings, there may be sequential projects, first to study the feasibility of such an undertaking, then to design whatever it is to be developed, and finally to produce whatever it is that is being undertaken. Often, there are periods of time in between these individual projects to allow management of the organization to understand the findings of a previous stage before a subsequent stage is allowed to begin. This gives management the opportunity to abort the undertaking at specific points if the work is not proceeding as originally conceived.

On large, government-sponsored undertakings, a collection of sequential or otherwise related projects like this is referred to as a program. In such cases, there should be a statement of work for the program. But the statement of work for the program is not a substitute for a statement of work for each project. The statement of work is meant to define not only the work to be undertaken but also the expectations of those who commission the project. It should be clear from the statement of work that the expected outcome is not only feasible but also likely if the project is executed effectively. For instance, a statement of work saying that the work of the project is to find a cure for cancer is not a legitimate statement of work.

Statements of work can take a variety of forms. Organizations that undertake projects frequently have their own procedures for producing a statement of work. We will not concern ourselves here with the format of such a statement. What is being emphasized is that such a statement should exist. Beyond a statement of work, there are other things that should often logically exist at the start of a project. If the project is for the purpose of constructing or developing something (e.g., a facility or a product), then a design upon which to base a plan for constructing or developing upon should exist. If the project is to produce a design, then there should exist a requirements specification, or conceptual diagrams or architectural sketches that sufficiently characterize what is to be done. Otherwise, the project manager or project team cannot develop a project plan that is firmly grounded in reality.

In Chapter 2, we explain how to develop a project plan. We explicitly assume that a statement of work for the project exists, together with all other necessary documents, such as specifications, designs, or drawings, upon which to base a project plan. The emphasis of this book is on the theory, methods, and tools of project management. Many books have been written on how to write requirement specifications and on various design methodologies for producing designs. These subjects are beyond the scope of this book. In comparison, there have been far fewer attempts at explaining the theory, methods, and tools of project management. We therefore concentrate on where we feel that we can make a contribution.

Chapter 2

Project Planning

The author has described project management in a number of papers, talks, and classes during the past twenty years. Two of these papers summarized the methods of project management. The first, titled *Project Management Systems*, appeared in the *Journal of Information and Management*. The next, titled *Managing Software Development Projects for Maximum Productivity*, appeared in *Transactions on Software Engineering*. The later paper was republished in 1988 in the book *Software Engineering Project Management*, edited by Richard Thayer. The first paper deals with project management methods in general, while the second, which is somewhat more detailed, deals with project management for software development projects.

Those papers introduced a decomposition of project management into two separate but related parts: *project planning* and *project execution*. Each of these parts consists of five activities. Project planning consists of:

1. Subdivision of work
2. Quantification
3. Sequencing of work
4. Budgeting
5. Scheduling

Project execution consists of:

1. Cost accounting
2. Progress measurement

   3. Variance tracking and change control
   4. Performance evaluation
   5. Productivity measurement

   In this chapter we devote considerable space to explaining the activities of project planning and how to use the desktop computer tools provided with this book to do project planning. In later chapters we discuss project execution, which in a way is the easier part, and how to use these desktop tools for project control.

   In this chapter, a concise definition or description of each of the five activities of project planning is given. Also included is a discussion of the rationale for these activities, presented within the framework of business practices. These practices have proven essential in the consistent application of the methods of modern project management and in the establishing of credibility between a project manager and the project manager's client(s). They exist to ensure that the project management team understands the client's objectives, their responsibilities, and the need for consistent and continuing planning and control. Furthermore, their consistent application ensures that the results of the methods embodied in the practices are repeatable.

2.1 Subdivision of the Work

The essential idea behind project planning is the subdivision of the work into manageable pieces. These pieces are called *work packages*. For this reason, subdivision of the work is often referred to as "packaging the work." Work packages are elements of work that are small enough that the responsibility for performing them can be assigned to a single individual. This does not mean that individual actually performs all the work of the work package. Indeed, the person responsible for a work package may be a manager who assigns the work to others. But the fact that each work package has a single individual who has performance responsibility is a fundamental concept in project management.

Each work package is individually estimated and scheduled. Specifically how this is done is explained later in this chapter. In this section it suffices to assume that since the work packages are conceptually "small," it is always possible to easily estimate accurately how much time and money it will take to complete each work package. Another useful assumption, which needs to be enforced as a policy, is that each work package is of short duration. Projects always have *reporting periods*. The reporting period may be a week or a month or any other convenient time period that is useful for a specific project. At the end of each reporting period, the status of each active work package is reported, together with the actual cost and labor-hours expended to date on the package. The assumption that a work package is of short duration means that it spans at most a few reporting periods.

The total cost of the project at any point in time and the status of the project are derived from the expenditure and status information for each work package. Specifically how this is done is explained in Chapter 3. The subdivision of the work is important in project management because it facilitates the management of the work, it facilitates the estimation of the amount and cost of the work, and it provides a means for calculating the cost and status of the project at any point in time.

There is a specific method for arriving at what the work packages should be. Rather than dividing the work into the individual tasks that will appear in the project schedule and later gathering the tasks together into packages as advocated by some, we prefer to proceed in a "top-down" fashion. This top-down approach reflects the way the overall work will proceed. Usually, there is a specific way the work is conducted on a project. For example, if the project consists of building a ten-story building, one would not expect to begin building the tenth story first, before the foundation was laid and the lower nine stories were constructed.

In order to facilitate our thinking about project management, we now introduce an example project that has been devised to be extremely simple. We will use this example project in what follows to explain project management concepts and how to use the project management tools furnished with this book. This example project is not intended to be entirely realistic; rather, it was designed to be simple, yet realistic enough to be useful. The example project is to build a small, 5,000-square-foot building.

In order to build this building, it will be necessary first to construct a foundation, then to build the structure, and finally to install the plumbing system, the electrical system, and the heating and air-conditioning system. Consequently, we first subdivide the project into three subcomponents that we will call the *foundation* component, the *structure* component, and the *systems* component. In fact, we introduce some new terminology here for distinguishing the components of our subdivision. We call these components *control packages*, as opposed to work packages. The reason for this is that they are too large to be work packages; yet they are meaningful components both conceptually and, later, for project control. So we will have control packages that we will refer to as "Foundation," "Structure," and "Systems." We can represent this hierarchically as shown in Figure 2-1.

Figure 2-1. Subdivision of example project into control packages.

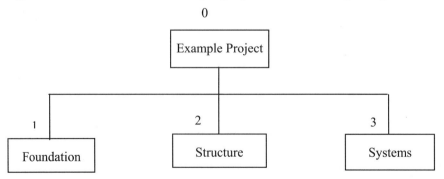

Notice that the hierarchy positions of these control packages are labeled 1, 2, and 3. Notice also that we are treating the whole project as a control package, which is at hierarchy position "0." We have given a name to the "top-level" or total project control package, namely "Example Project." It is customary to label control packages this way.

Next we subdivide these control packages further. For example, we subdivide the Foundation control package into four new packages that we label 1.1, 1.2, 1.3, and 1.4. This is the same way that sections in a document are often labeled. These labels are called the *package identifiers* or *package IDs*. They are used to show how the work content unfolds in much the same way that sections in a book show how the content of the book unfolds. Continuing our subdivision of these control packages, we subdivide control package 1 (Foundation) into these packages:

    1.1 Site Preparation
    1.2 Forms Installation & Removal
    1.3 Rebar, Mesh, & Anchors
    1.4 Concrete Pour, Cure, & Finish

Similarly, we subdivide control package 2 into these packages:

    2.1 Framing & Misc. Carpentry
    2.2 Sheetrock Tape, Bed, & Float
    2.3 Roofing
    2.4 Painting

And we subdivide control package 3 into these packages:

    3.1 Plumbing
    3.2 Electrical
    3.3 HVAC (Heating, Ventilation, and Air-conditioning)

This finer decomposition of the work content is shown in Figure 2-2. For the purpose of keeping the example small, we

Figure 2-2. WBS for example project.

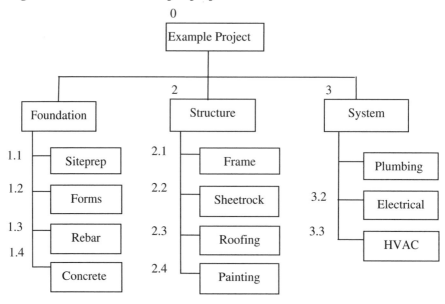

assume that we have now decomposed the work far enough for the needs of project planning and control. In other words, we believe that these latest packages are small enough to be work packages. We could have had additional levels of control packages between the top-level control package and the work packages, but, for the sake of simplicity, the example project stops here. In what follows we will refer to any of these packages as control packages but to only the lowest-level packages (e.g., 1.1, 1.2, 1.3) as work packages. This structure of control packages we have just described for the example project is referred to as the *Work Breakdown Structure* or simply the *WBS*, for the project. The hierarchical diagram in Figure 2-2 represents the example WBS.

There are other meaningful subdivisions of the work besides the work breakdown structure. Subdividing the work by discipline (craft) may be useful for supporting monthly labor reporting; for example, electrical or carpentry or masonry activities could be grouped together. It is often necessary to have the work subdivided by organizational structure (e.g., by division, department, or section). These organizational subdivisions are so common that they are often given the name *Organizational Breakdown Structure* or *OBS*.

It is also standard practice to subdivide the work by cost codes to support cost accounting and by general ledger codes to support general accounting or tax form preparation. Such subdivisions are often referred to as *cost breakdown structures*. Finally, in many industries, especially those that do business with the federal government, the work may need to be broken down along product lines, such as the various subsystems of an overall system (e.g., the avionics subsystem and the flight control system of an aircraft). Such subdivisions are referred to as *product breakdown structures*. The military, as we see in Chapter 8, refers to these product breakdown structures as work breakdown structures.

Whatever the need for these additional subdivisions of work, it is important that they be related in a meaningful way to the WBS. In the example project we will consider three different subdivisions. In addition to the WBS, there will be a cost breakdown based on General Ledger (GL) codes and an organizational breakdown structure. The discussion in the following sections and chapters shows how these additional subdivisions are supported in the Modern Project toolset provided with this book.

The way we relate the cost breakdown structure to the WBS is explained in Section 2.5. The way we relate the OBS to the WBS is via a second (or alternate) hierarchy. This is explained in Chapter 6. The OBS hierarchy will have the same work packages as the WBS but different control packages above the work package level in the OBS hierarchy. The reason this is possible is because of our rule that work packages be small enough to be assigned to a single person. Since each person is a member of some section or department or division, the work packages assigned to a person in a given organizational unit will be considered to belong to the control package that represents this organizational unit in the OBS hierarchy diagram.

There is one more thing that should be mentioned about the WBS. Even if a client requires that his or her WBS be a product breakdown structure or an OBS, our policy will still be to subdivide the work in the manner in which it is to be done and to utilize alternate reporting hierarchies to provide the client with his or her required reports. Subdividing the work in the manner that it will actually be accomplished provides project management and assisting departments with the best understanding of how to accomplish the project's objectives. The importance of subdividing the work in the way it will actually be performed cannot be overemphasized. If the WBS does not reflect the way in which the work will actually be done, the WBS is not really useful to the project manager as a communications and control mechanism.

By accommodating multiple subdivisions of the work (e.g., the OBS) via multiple hierarchies, which collectively will be referred to as *reporting hierarchies*, these desktop tools allow a project to provide all the components of an organization with reports about the project that are meaningful for them. Essentially, these alternate reporting hierarchies provide *alternate views* of the project that are meaningful to different organizations. Each of these reporting hierarchies will possess the same set of work packages. They will differ only in the way the control packages above the work packages are organized. It should be noted that not all of these alternate reporting hierarchies will have the same number of levels. A WBS is often expected to have more levels than an OBS, but there can be exceptions to this rule. Finally, it should be noted that, even within the WBS, each branch of the WBS should not be expected to have the same number of levels. Some parts of the work may naturally be expected to be more complicated than other parts, and this may be reflected in the WBS by branches with unequal numbers of levels of control packages before work packages are encountered.

2.2 Quantification of the Work

The next step after subdividing the work is quantification of the work. Quantification of the work consists of assigning an appropriate *unit of measure* to each control package and then assigning a *quantity* to the work content of the package that quantifies the amount of work in the package in terms of its unit of measure. The way this is done requires some explanation. We first discuss how it is done for work packages. The work content of a work package is further subdivided into *tasks* or *activities*. The terms *task* and *activity* are interchangeable in this book. These individual tasks are the things that are eventually scheduled, usually with an automated scheduling software package. This produces a *start date* and an *end date* for each task. But this is not our concern at the moment. The important thing to understand just now is that each task needs to be assigned a unit of measure.

It is the responsibility of the work package manager to subdivide the work packages for which he or she is responsible into appropriate tasks. It is also this manager's responsibility to quantify and estimate these tasks. Suppose the work package manager for the "Siteprep" work package, after careful consideration and perhaps consultation with those who will actually perform the work, decides to subdivide the work package into four tasks, say:

Task 1: Clear and Grub the Site
Task 2: Remove Excess Earth
Task 3: Grade the Site
Task 4: Excavate for a Foundation

The unit of measure for Task 1 might be "square feet," since the site that is to be prepared for the structure is likely to be measured in square feet. On the other hand, the unit of measure for Task 2 might be "cubic yards," since earthmovers usually estimate the amount of earth to be removed in cubic yards of earth. On the other hand, if the project is a computer software development project and the activity is to write a computer program, the unit of measure might be "source lines of code." If the activity is to write a chapter of a book, the unit of measure might be "pages."

First-time project managers are often faced with the claim from some member of the project team to whom a task has been assigned that this type of work has never been done before and so there is no known unit of measure for this task. This often happens on research or development projects. While this is never really the case, it is often easier for the project manager to just assign this task the unit of measure called *each* (abbreviated "EA"), rather than argue about it. Then a quantity of 1 can be assigned to the task in the EA unit of measure. This means that this task is considered as a single unit.

The effect on the overall project of doing this occasionally is not usually great, since work packages are assumed to be of short duration and, therefore, so are tasks. But, as the reader will see in Chapter 3, assigning a unit of measure of EA will curtail the options for a work package manager to take partial credit for work in progress on the periodic status reports. This can cause the task leader to appear not to be making progress until the task is completed. This usually leads task leaders to wish they had taken time to quantify their tasks correctly in the first place. For the project manager, this is not a problem. Most project managers prefer a conservative approach for claiming credit for work in progress, anyway, and assigning a task a unit of measure of EA is extremely conservative. Task leaders do not get credit for any task until it is completely finished when the unit of measure is EA.

Some experienced project managers force this type of quantification uniformly on their project to maintain a conservative progress measurement policy. But we consider this an extreme measure that should be avoided. The reason is that better cost and manpower estimates can be made if the work packages are quantified meaningfully. An old saying among project managers and cost estimators is: "If the work can't be quantified, it can't be estimated." It is important for project team members to understand this and to do their best to produce a meaningful quantification.

After each task in a work package has been quantified, the work package itself needs to be quantified. Again, the responsibility for the quantification of a work package rests with the work package manager. And again, quantification of a work package involves selecting an appropriate unit of measure for the package and an appropriate quantity for the package expressed in this unit of measure. Often, it is the case that the unit of measure for a work package is the same as the unit of measure for one of the tasks within the work package.

For instance, the Siteprep work package in the example project, as we will see in Section 2.3.3, has Tasks 1 and 3 with a unit of measure of Square Feet (SF) and Tasks 2 and 4 with a unit of measure of Cubic Yards (CY). We will also see in Section 2.3.3 that the unit of measure chosen for the Siteprep work package is SF, rather than CY or some other measure. This reflects the belief of the work package manager that quantifying the Siteprep work package is best done via SF, as opposed to CY or some other measure. In a case like this, it is sometimes said that among the units of measure for the tasks, SF is the *dominant* unit of measure, since it determines the unit of measure for the package.

Unlike quantification of work packages, quantification of control packages above the work package level is the responsibility of the project manager. Quantification at this level does not affect the progress and performance measures that are based on the status information at the work package level. Nonetheless, it is important that the project manager or the project manager's staff select meaningful quantifications for the summary level control packages. This enables those reading reports to relate the progress measures at summary levels to something intuitively meaningful.

For instance, we will see in the WBS Listing report (Figure 2-6) that the unit of measure for the summary level "Foundation" control package is CY (of concrete). If a progress report shows this control package is 50% complete, the reader of the report can relate this to the 290 CY of concrete quantification for the package and envision that about 145 cubic yards of concrete has been poured so far.

2.3 Using Modern Project© to Create a WBS

Before moving on to a discussion of sequencing the work, we first cover how to enter a work breakdown structure into the project database. A desktop toolset called *Modern Project* is included with this book. In order to run the tools provided in this toolset, it is necessary for you to have Microsoft Access 97, or a later version, such as Access 2000, installed on your computer. Modern Project is a learning aid intended to demonstrate how a set of desktop tools can support the project management techniques covered in this book. Modern Project has been tested on the example project described in the book but has not been subjected to exhaustive testing. Neither the author nor the publisher takes any responsibility for the correct operation of this toolset. It is intended to be useful on projects on which it is used, but the reader must understand that it is to be used at his or her own risk.

There is a file on the electronic media provided with the book that you need to copy to one of your disk drives. If you are using Access 97, then the file is the one named *example97. mde*. If you are using Access 2000, then the file is the one named *example2K.mde*. For simplicity, we will just use the filename *example.mde* in what follows instead of repeatedly distinguishing between the two. Example.mde is a database that will eventually contain the example project data that will be used throughout the book to illustrate project management concepts and the use of Modern Project.

After you have saved the file example.mde to your disk drive, you may need to change the *read only* attribute. For instance, if you use Microsoft Windows Explorer to copy the file from the CD to your disk drive, it will set the read only attribute to "true" since the CD supplied with the book is a read only medium. This will prevent you from entering any data into the example database until you change the read only attribute to "false."

To change the read only attribute to false, first open the file with Microsoft Access. A window should appear that looks like Figure 2-3. Now click on the **File** control button, and select the **Database Properties** option by clicking on the option's entry in the File menu that dropped down. This will cause the *Properties* window to appear. Make sure the Properties window is displaying the *General* (properties) with *Attributes:* showing at the bottom of the window. If not, click on the **General** tab at the top of the Properties window.

Now look at the "read only" attribute. If it has a checkmark in the box in front of it, click on the box to remove the checkmark. If there is no checkmark in the read only attribute box, there is nothing to change. Next, click on the **OK** control button at the bottom of the Properties window. You should now be able to write data into the example database. You will begin learning how to do this shortly.

If you do not have either Microsoft Access 97 or Microsoft Access 2000 installed on your computer, it should not interfere with your ability to understand the project management methods, philosophy, and tools discussed in this book. During the past three decades, many project managers have used these methods and policies manually, without the aid of a computer. On large projects this requires a considerable staff, but it has been done and continues to be done.

Packaged within example.mde is the Modern Project toolset. When you open example.mde with Microsoft Access the *Main Menu* for the Modern Project toolset will be displayed as shown in Figure 2-3. Assuming you have one of these versions of Microsoft Access available on your computer, start it up and open the example database (example.mde). Your computer screen should now look like Figure 2-3.

2.3.1 Entering WBS Information

Now *select* (click your left mouse button on) the **WBS Entry/ Edit Tool** button on the left side of the Main Menu. This will cause the WBS Entry/Edit tool to start and display a WBS Edit/ Entry form on your computer screen that looks like Figure 2-4.

The WBS information to be entered is shown in Figure 2-5. The far-left column of Figure 2-5 is labeled *Hierarchy Position*. Each control package in the WBS hierarchy has a position within the hierarchy, as previously discussed. The control package's *hierarchy position identifier* tells what that position is. We have already discussed how these identifiers were chosen for the example project. We chose to label these control package

Figure 2-3. Main menu for the Modern Project toolset.

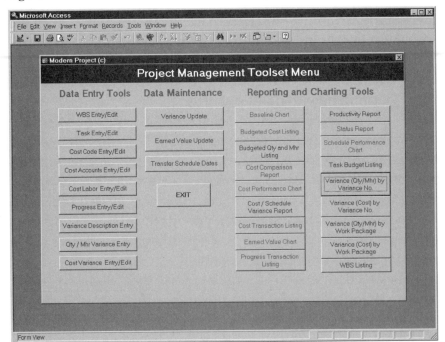

Figure 2-4. The WBS Entry/Edit Tool.

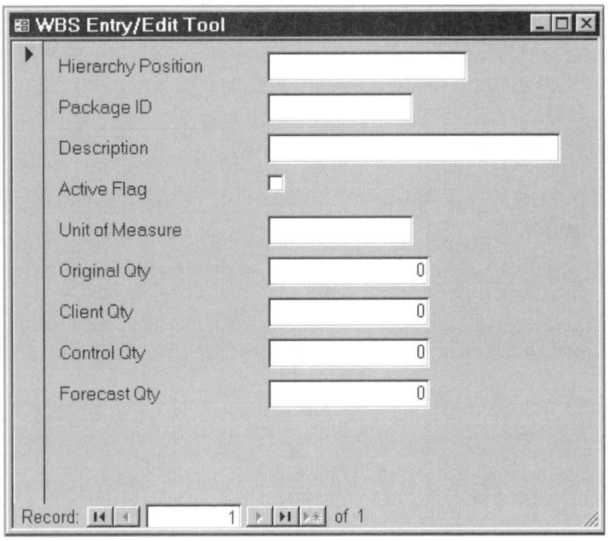

hierarchy position indicators as 0, 1, 2, 3, 1.1, 2.1, 3.1, and so on. But we could have used a scheme like 0, 1, 2, 3, 1–1, 2–1, 3–1, and so on, employing dashes between the numbers instead of dots (periods).

Unless you have some compelling reason to adopt a numbering scheme other than the one described for the example project, it is recommended that you adopt the scheme in the book, since the tools in the toolset have been tested only using the numbering scheme of the example project. The reports may still work if one does not depart too far from the hierarchy labeling scheme presented in the book. But they have not been systematically tested on any other scheme.

It is preferable to avoid having more than six or seven packages under a given summary level control package, but it is possible to have more. There have been studies that indicate our comprehension of hierarchies diminishes when more than six hierarchy elements exist under a single parent hierarchy element. The reporting tools provided with this book have not been tested with more than nine packages under a single *parent package* at the next level up in the hierarchy.

Figure 2-5. WBS data to be entered for the example project.

Hierarchy Position	Package ID	Description	Active Flag	Unit of Measure	Original Qty
0	Example Proj	5000 SF Building	Yes	SF	5000
1	Foundation	Construct Foundation	Yes	CYC	290
1.1	Siteprep	Site Preparation	Yes	SF	20000
1.2	Forms	Forms Installation & Removal	Yes	SF	750
1.3	Rebar	Rebar, Mesh & Anchors	Yes	LBS	1000
1.4	Concrete	Concrete Pour, Cure & Finish	Yes	CYC	290
2	Structure	Build Structure	No	SF	5000
2.1	Frame	Framing & Misc. Carpentry	No	LF	20000
2.2	Sheetrock	Sheetrock Tape, Bed & Float	No	SF	10000
2.3	Roofing	Roofing	No	SF	6000
2.4	Painting	Painting	No	SF	10000
3	Systems	Systems	No	EA	3
3.1	Plumbing	Plumbing	No	EA	10
3.2	Electrical	Electrical	No	EA	50
3.3	HVAC	Heating, Ventilation & AC	No	EA	2

We note that the hierarchy position field (in the database) is a "text" field. Thirty characters have been allocated in the database for this hierarchy position identifier for each control package. So, if we never expect to have more than nine packages with the same parent control package (e.g., 3.1.0 through 3.1.9 under package 3.1), it is possible to have up to 15 levels in our WBS. Or, if we expect to have 10 or more packages with the same parent control package, (e.g., 13.07.01 through 13.07.23 under package 13.07), then 30 characters is only enough space for WBS hierarchies with up to six levels.

Consequently, it should be possible to have WBS hierarchies that are "very wide" if they are not too "deep," but, again, the reporting tools have not been tested on such hierarchies.

The *Package ID* column of Figure 2-5 contains the names (identifiers) of each control package, and the *Description* column contains a description of the control package. Thereafter comes a column for the package's *Active Flag*, which we have not yet discussed. The fifth column contains the *Unit of Measure* for each control package, which has already been discussed at length.

The sixth column contains the quantifications of each control package in the chosen unit of measure for the control package. This column is labeled *Original Qty*, which refers to the *original quantity budget*. The term *quantity budget* is interchangeable with the term *quantification*, which we discussed in the previous section. In fact, the terms *original quantity budget*, *original budget quantity*, and *original quantification* are all equivalent terms.

Let us now discuss the meaning of the *Active Flag* column of data. All the control packages in a WBS are considered to be either "open" or "closed." If a control package is open, then the *Active Flag* column contains a YES. When entering a YES value in the *Active Flag* field of the data entry form, just click on the field box, and a check mark will appear. This indicates a value of YES. Otherwise, it contains a NO. The meaning of a control package's being *open* is that actual expenditures can be charged to that control package. By this is meant that if a control package is a work package and the package is open, then actual expenditures can be charged to the package. If, instead, the control package is a summary level control package and it is open, then it is okay to have open work packages under this control package in the hierarchy.

The purpose of open and closed packages is to allow the project manager to control the available charge numbers on the project. It may be the case that the entire project is planned and budgeted in the beginning. But, since work cannot usually begin on all work packages at the same time, the project manager can specify which work is acceptable at a given point in time. This prevents the work package managers from making charges to work packages that are not actually being worked on or are not yet authorized to be worked on. Generally, workers will not try to charge to invalid charge numbers as it may interfere with their getting paid for their time spent working.

You can now begin entering the data in Figure 2-5 into the WBS database, using the WBS Entry/Edit Tool. As you enter the *Original Qty* for each control package, you will notice that there are some other text boxes, titled *Client Qty*, *Control Qty*, and *Forecast Qty*. The concepts of Client Quantity, Control Quantity, and Forecast Quantity are explained in Chapter 3. Do not be concerned with the absence of data for these additional budgets and the forecast at this time. Just enter the Original Qty amount for the Client Qty, for the Control Qty, and for the Forecast Qty. In Chapter 3 we will make changes to these quantities as we explain their meanings.

You can move around within the WBS Entry/Edit form by either moving the cursor (with the mouse) into one of the data element entry boxes and clicking on the left mouse button or by using the **TAB** key to move to the next box. After you have entered all data elements into the form for one of the control packages, the data elements will be recorded in (written to) the database when you move to another WBS control package.

Moving to the next control package (or a new control package) is done by (left) clicking on the **Forward** button at the bottom of the form. The **Forward** button is the control button just to the right of the text box titled "Record." Similarly, there is a **Back** button immediately to the left of the text box. There are also buttons to move to the first control package record, to move to the last control package record that has been entered, and to create a new control package record. You will be able to figure out which ones are which by experimenting with these additional buttons. You do not have to click the new control package button to move to a new control package when you are entering control package information. By simply clicking on the forward button, you will automatically be given a new blank control package record.

If you accidentally enter a control package incorrectly into the database, you can edit it later by returning to the record using the **Forward** and **Back** buttons or by entering the record number in the *Record* field at the bottom of the form. You can delete a record entirely by first returning to the record and then clicking on the **Edit** button at the top of the Access window and then selecting the **Delete Record** option. When you do this, Access will present you with another window that asks you to confirm that you really want to delete this record and warning you that once you delete it the deletion will be final. If, after the warning, you still want to delete the record, click on the **Yes** button, and the record will be deleted.

After you have finished entering the WBS information into the database, you should close the WBS Entry/Edit tool by (left) clicking on the "X" in the upper right corner of the tool.

2.3.2 The WBS Listing Report

We are now in a position to produce the example project's first report, namely the *WBS Listing* report, as shown in Figure 2-6. To display this report, left click on the **WBS Listing** button in the "Reports and Charts" section of the Main Menu. You should now see a copy of the report appear in a *report window*. You can print the report by left clicking on the **File** button at the top of the screen and selecting the **Print** option that appears in the *file menu*. What you get should look like Figure 2-6.

The WBS Listing report shows how the work of the project is subdivided into control packages and the hierarchical structure that depicts how the work is organized. The WBS Listing represents how the work unfolds in much the same way that the table of contents of a book represents how the book unfolds into chapters and sections and subsections. The example project itself is depicted in this Listing by the top-level control package at hierarchy position 0 and contains the control packages "Foundation" at position 1, "Structure" at position 2, and "Systems" at position 3 (which appears on the second page of the

Figure 2-6. WBS Listing.

WBS Listing

WBS Position	*Package ID*	*Description*	*Unit of Meas.*		
	Active Indicator	Original Qty	Client Qty	Control Qty	Forecast Qty
0	*Example Proj*	*5000 SF Building*	*SF*		
		5000	5000	5000	5000
1	*Foundation*	*Construct Foundation*	*CYC*		
		290	290	290	290
1.1	*Siteprep*	*Site Preparation*	*SF*		
		20000	20000	20000	20000
1.2	*Forms*	*Forms Installation & Removal*	*SF*		
		750	750	750	750
1.3	*Rebar*	*Rebar, Mesh & Anchors*	*LBS*		
		1000	1000	1000	1000
1.4	*Concrete*	*Concrete Pour, Cure & Finish*	*CYC*		
		290	290	290	290
2	*Structure*	*Build Structure*	*SF*		
		5000	5000	5000	5000
2.1	*Frame*	*Framing & Misc. Carpentry*	*LF*		
		20000	20000	20000	20000
2.2	*Sheetrock*	*Sheetrock, Tape, Bed & Float*	*SF*		
		10000	10000	10000	10000
2.3	*Roofing*	*Roofing*	*SF*		
		6000	6000	6000	6000
2.4	*Painting*	*Painting*	*SF*		
		10000	10000	10000	10000

Thursday, January 13, 2000 *Page 1 of 2*

WBS listing, which is not shown in Figure 2-6). Similarly, control package "Foundation" contains the work packages "Siteprep" at hierarchy position 1.1, "Forms" at position 1.2, "Rebar" at position 1.3, and "Concrete" at position 1.4, and so on.

2.3.3 Entering Task Data

Now let us turn our attention to entering task quantification data for the work packages we have already entered into the database. On real projects, tasks are quantified in terms of the amount of work and the amount of materials and equipment necessary to complete them. The present volume does not deal with quantification of the materials used in task work or provide a desktop tool for this capability. There are many projects in which material quantification is not a significant part, for example, the development of a software system or the reengineering of office processes. Consequently, for many projects, materials quantification does not play a significant role. For other projects, such as construction projects, materials and equipment management plays a very significant role. The underlying principles of materials quantification are similar to work quantification that has already been discussed, but materials and equipment management are beyond the scope of this book.

Moreover, companies that engage in projects with a large materials component usually already have centralized materials management systems that they require to be used on their projects. These systems attempt to optimize materials purchasing through consolidation of purchases across project boundaries. For these reasons we do not cover materials management in this book.

In what follows, the terms *activity* and *task* are interchangeable. The task data to be entered into the database are shown in Figure 2-7. So far there are only four open work packages, namely the Siteprep work package, the Forms work package, the Rebar work package, and the Concrete work package. Tasks for work packages that are not yet open could be entered at this time, but to keep the amount of data entry at a minimum right now, only tasks for these open packages are included in Figure 2-7.

For instance, the Siteprep work package includes four activities, namely clearing the site for the structure to be built (the Clear & Grub task), earth removal to smooth out the site (the Earth Removal task), grading the site (the Grading task), and excavating for the foundation (the Excavation task). These four activities are denoted by Tasks 1 through 4 within the Siteprep work package, as shown in Figure 2-7.

The unit of measure for the "Clear & Grub" task is Square Feet (SF), and the quantity is 20,000. This indicates that there is a 20,000-square-foot plot of ground that has to be cleared so that a suitable site can be prepared for raising the building structure. The unit of measure for the "Earth Removal" task is Cubic Yards (CY) of earth, and the quantity is 480, so there are 480 cubic yards of earth to remove in order to prepare the site for building.

Figure 2-7. Task data to be entered.

Package ID	Task ID	Description	Unit of Measure	Original Qty
Concrete	1	Pour Concrete	CYC	290
Concrete	2	Cure Concrete	CYC	290
Concrete	3	Finish Concrete	SF	5080
Forms	1	Forms Installation	SF	750
Forms	2	Forms Removal	SF	750
Rebar	1	Rebar Installation	LBS	760
Rebar	2	Mesh Installation	LBS	140
Rebar	3	Anchor Bolts	LBS	100
Siteprep	1	Clear & Grub	SF	20000
Siteprep	2	Earth Removal	CY	480
Siteprep	3	Grading	SF	20000
Siteprep	4	Excavation	CY	260

The third column in Figure 2-7 is labeled *Description,* and the entries in this column are brief (30 characters or less) descriptions of the nature of the task. The fifth column of Figure 2-7 is labeled *Original Quantity.* It has the same meaning as the original quantity for a work package or control package in the WBS, but this time at the task level rather than at a package level.

You will use the *Task Entry/Edit* tool to enter this task information into the example database. To activate this tool, click on the tool button labeled **Task Entry/Edit** on the Main Menu. It should look like the form shown in Figure 2-8. For each task, you first enter the name of the work package it belongs to in the Package ID field. Then you enter the task identifier in the Task ID field. Entering data into this form is entirely analogous to entering information into the WBS Entry/Edit form with which you are already familiar.

In the example project, the task identifiers are simply numbers. For the Siteprep work package they are the numbers 1 through 4. You are not limited to using numbers for the task identifiers. But it is often convenient to do so. Notice that the task identifiers do not have to be unique. For instance, in the

Figure 2-8. The Task Entry/Edit Tool.

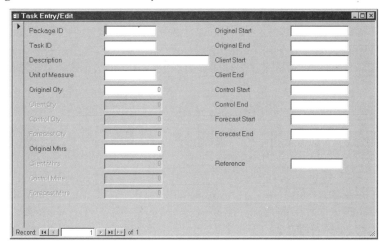

example, all of the work packages have a task number 1. However, the task identifiers must be unique within a work package.

After entering the identifying information for a task, the description of the task needs to be entered in the Description field, and the unit of measure and the quantification for the task needs to be entered in the Unit of Measure and Original Qty fields respectively.

You will notice that you are prohibited from entering data into the Qty and Mhr fields for the Client and Control budgets and for the Forecast. The reason for this is that the Change Control and Variance Tracking tools within Modern Project control the values of these other budgets. These are explained in the next chapter.

2.3.4 The Task Budget Listing Report

We are now in a position to display (or print out) another report, called the *Task Budget Listing*. The Task Budget Listing report is displayed or printed the same way the WBS Listing is displayed or printed. To display the report, click on the **Task Budget Listing** button on the Main Menu. What you see should look like Figure 2-9.

The data displayed in this report are the budgeted (estimated) quantities for each task. You will notice that the budgeted man-hours are all zero at this time because we have not yet estimated the work. At this point in the example project (which we assume to be the beginning of the project), the budgeted quantities are the same for each of the budgets and the forecast because no changes to the project plan have yet occurred. Later it will be shown how to enter change information into the database that will cause these budgeted quantities and man-hours to be updated and thus possibly end up different for each budget type.

Figure 2-9. The Task Budget Listing.

Task Budget Listing

Package / Task ID		--- Original --- Qty	Mhrs	---- Client ---- Qty	Mhrs	--- Control --- Qty	Mhrs	--- Forecast -- Qty	Mhrs
Concrete									
1	***Pour Concrete***			***CYC***					
		290	0	290	0	290	0	290	0
2	***Cure Concrete***			***CYC***					
		290	0	290	0	290	0	290	0
3	***Finish Concrete***			***SF***					
		5080	0	5080	0	5080	0	5080	0
Forms									
1	***Forms Installation***			***SF***					
		750	0	750	0	750	0	750	0
2	***Forms Removal***			***SF***					
		750	0	750	0	750	0	750	0
Rebar									
1	***Rebar Installation***			***LBS***					
		760	0	760	0	760	0	760	0
2	***Mesh Installation***			***LBS***					
		140	0	140	0	140	0	140	0
3	***Anchor Bolts***			***LBS***					
		100	0	100	0	100	0	100	0
Siteprep									
1	***Clear & Grub***			***SF***					
		20000	0	20000	0	20000	0	20000	0
2	***Earth Removal***			***CY***					
		480	0	480	0	480	0	480	0
3	***Grading***			***SF***					
		20000	0	20000	0	20000	0	20000	0
4	***Excavation***			***CY***					
		260	0	260	0	260	0	260	0

Friday, January 14, 2000 ***Page 1 of 1***

2.4 Sequencing the Work

The next step in developing a project plan, after subdividing the work into packages and quantifying those packages, is to sequence the individual tasks within the work packages. Sequencing the work is not scheduling, and it is probably a mistake to try to sequence and schedule the work simultaneously. Nevertheless, sequencing the work and scheduling the work are related planning steps, and some find them hard to conceive of when separated from each other. Both are necessary to produce a *schedule* for the project.

By a schedule for the project is meant a set of *start* and *end* dates, one pair for each task, each work package, and each control package. The schedule is used not only to control when individual pieces of work are started, but also to "time-phase" the labor-hour budget to produce a *project plan,* which is often referred to as the *project baseline.* Time phasing the budget is a powerful mechanism for project monitoring and control, as will be explained in Chapter 3.

One should think of sequencing the work as the creative, mental process involved in producing the project schedule and of project scheduling as the mechanical part of producing the actual collection of start and end dates for each of the tasks, work packages, and control packages. For projects of any significant size, project scheduling is usually done with the help of an automated project scheduling tool.

Automated scheduling tools have been available for more than three decades. But none of these tools has ever been capable of figuring out how the tasks of a project relate to each other. Humans have to figure that out and tell the scheduling tools. Thereafter, the scheduling tools can perform the laborious computations to compute the "optimal" set of start and end dates for the project. "Optimal" here can take on various meanings for different projects. The project team must also define just what optimal means to the automated scheduling tool. This is discussed in more detail in Chapter 7.

Sequencing the work involves determining the *order* in which the tasks will be accomplished. This means that the project team needs to know which tasks precede which other tasks. Ordinarily, the order in which the tasks will be accomplished is what is known as a *partial order* in mathematics. This means that there is no *sequential ordering* of all the tasks in such a way that only one task is executed at a time. Instead, the ordering among tasks is one where several tasks can proceed in parallel. Some tasks are dependent on other tasks and cannot be started until the other tasks are completed. Other tasks are independent of one another and can proceed in parallel with each other or, one can precede another, but it does not matter in which order.

Sequencing the work refers to this process of determining this (partial) ordering of the individual tasks within the project. Project team members usually make use of diagramming techniques to assist them in discovering this ordering. For many projects this ordering is almost self-apparent, but on others it is subtle, and it sometimes takes clever engineering to produce a "good" sequencing of the work. This is because the techniques and methods used to accomplish certain tasks can affect the level of difficulty of performing other tasks. For instance, if one method of accomplishing a task A is used, it may be better for A to precede task B, whereas if another method of accomplishing A is used it may be better for B to precede A.

The diagrams that project team members use to assist in discovering the sequence of work have historically fallen into two categories, namely *arrow diagrams* and *precedence diagrams*. Arrow diagrams were more popular many years ago because of limitations in scheduling algorithms and computational resources that existed then. Older scheduling tools tended to illustrate the schedules they produced by arrow diagrams, and so project personnel became accustomed to thinking in terms of arrow diagrams.

Today, precedence diagrams are more widely used, as they are more flexible and generally more comprehensible in representing the sequence of work. In a precedence diagram, the ordering of the work is represented as a "network" of nodes interconnected by lines or arrows. Each node in this network represents a task. The connecting lines (or arrows) represent which nodes (tasks) precede which other nodes. In arrow diagrams it is the other way around. The interconnecting lines represent the tasks, whereas the nodes represent the relationships between tasks.

An example of a precedence diagram is given in Figure 2-10. If two nodes, say A and B, are connected by a line and A lies to the left of B in the diagram, then A is considered to *precede* B. In this case, A and B are said to have an *end-to-start* dependency. Things are not always this simple. There are other types of dependencies between two tasks A and B that can occur, such as *start-to-end* dependencies, *start-to-start* dependencies, and *end-to-end* dependencies. Precedence diagrams are well suited for representing these other types of dependencies.

Figure 2-10 represents a fragment of a precedence diagram for the tasks that appear in Figure 2-7. The relationship between the Clear & Grub task and the Grading task is a simple end-to-

Figure 2-10. An example of a precedence diagram.

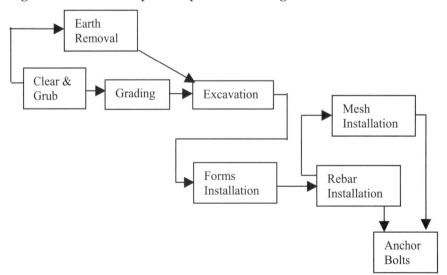

start relationship, that is, the Grading task cannot start until the Clear & Grub task is finished. However, the relationship between the Clear and Grub task and the Earth Removal task is what is called a start-to-start relationship. This means that the Earth Removal task can begin (a certain fixed *lag* time) after the Clear & Grub task starts.

The relationship in Figure 2-10 between the Mesh Installation task and the Anchor Bolts task is an example of a finish-to-finish relationship. What this means is that the Anchor Bolts task must finish within a fixed lag time after the Mesh Installation task finishes. There is no example of a start-to-end relationship in Figure 2-10. A start-to-end relationship between tasks A and B is one in which task B must finish within a fixed time after task A starts. Start-to-end relationships are not as common as the other types of relationships. Nonetheless, they occur occasionally on many projects.

Sequencing the work is ordinarily an iterative process. It is often undertaken by a group of project team members on large projects. Precedence diagrams are constructed and then reviewed and discussed among the group. An automated scheduling tool is often helpful in generating these work sequencing diagrams. But, just because a scheduling tool is used, we should not confuse these sequencing diagrams with a project schedule, even if they are used in such a way as to produce (putative) start and end dates for the individual tasks.

It is not unusual for construction of work sequencing diagrams to cause the project management team to rethink the very nature of some of the work packages and tasks. In fact, it is a process that often helps validate the subdivision of work. It is often found that problems in the sequencing of the work can be solved by changing the decomposition of the work into different work packages and tasks. Changes in the subdivision of work leads to changes in quantifications, which in turn leads to changes in the sequencing. This is not a never-ending process, however. Usually, one or a few iterations serve to produce a meaningful sequencing of the work. Such a sequencing gives confidence to the project manager that the work is really subdivided in a manner that can be executed in a timely fashion.

2.5 Budgeting (Estimating) the Work

The next step in project planning is to establish a project budget. To do this, an estimate of the labor-hours and the cost for each work package needs to be made. This is done by using the quantification of each task in each work package to estimate how many labor-hours are needed to complete that task. The sum of the labor-hours for each task in a work package is the number of labor-hours needed to complete the work package. Knowing the number of labor-hours needed to complete the work package (and the material and equipment needs), one can estimate the cost of the work package. This is called *detailed cost estimating*.

The cost estimate for a work package takes into consideration the fact that different types or grades of labor on the work package may have different labor rates. The cost estimate also takes into consideration the cost of material and equipment needed to complete the work package. How this is done will be explained shortly.

Many schemes have been proposed over the years to come up with estimates for a project, or even for all of the work packages, that avoids this level of detail in estimating. Of course, if a project is extremely similar to a previous project the same project team has already done, and if good historical records exist about the labor-hours and the costs of the previous project, then one could perhaps use this information to obtain a fairly accurate estimate of the labor-hours and the cost of the new project. In practice, this is rarely the case.

Many of the schemes for avoiding detailed cost estimating are based on the use of cost models for projects. Companies that perform certain types of projects regularly can be expected to gain some expertise in estimating and managing these types of projects. This often leads to the belief that the way to avoid the effort of detailed cost estimating and possibly even to get more accurate estimates is to collect statistics on these historical projects and to use them in some way to predict what the average costs will be on future projects of the same type. This works sometimes when there is little difference from one project to the next. But some advocates of this approach go so far as to propose using this historical statistical information to build a general estimating model that can be used to estimate the labor-hours and the cost of all future projects. For instance, B. Boehm's book *Software Engineering Economics* advocates using the COCOMO cost model for estimating software development project costs.

These estimating models rarely give consistently good results. The models' authors often claim there is evidence that they do. But experience with some of these models and with trying to verify the claims of their advocates has convinced the author that most of the claims are greatly exaggerated. These models usually do not take proper account of the highly diverse levels of experience and capabilities of the individual project team members, and it is they who execute the work packages. These team members, on the other hand, often know their own capabilities better than those who employ the models. And if these team members take part in the estimation of the work packages for which they are going to be responsible, they often give estimates that realistically fit their capabilities and experiences.

On the other hand, these cost-estimating models often involve terms with exponential parameters that are supposed to capture these subtle estimating relationships. The result is that these models are often unreasonably sensitive to small changes in these estimating parameters.

The project manager should always use judgment in accepting the detailed cost estimates of team members, and the process of approving the labor-hour and the cost budgets for each work package should involve a dialogue between the project team members who will be responsible for the work and the team members who will be responsible for project monitoring and control. On small projects, the only one doing project monitoring and control may be the project manager, and the dialogue may be between only the project manager and half a dozen other team members.

Some companies bid on projects before a project team is formed. In fact, it is often the case that these bids are done by marketing or "business development" teams. These bids must be based on some kind of estimate, and it is often the case that these business development teams are the ones that embrace these simple estimating models, rather than engage in detailed cost estimating. Business development teams can usually bring in experienced project management personnel to do the detailed cost estimating, but this increases the cost of bidding for a job.

In this book, the assumption is made that the project manager (or business development team) will opt for detailed cost estimating and that the members of the project team responsible for the work packages will be involved in producing the detailed cost estimates for the work packages. Detailed cost estimating is not difficult, but it does take time. Detailed cost estimating is, in fact, straightforward. Since each task has already been quantified, it is not surprising that an experienced team member can give a reasonably good estimate of the labor-hours it takes to complete such a task.

The labor-hour estimates for the tasks shown in Figure 2-7 appear in the *Original Mhrs* column of Figure 2-11. Since the example project is a hypothetical project, no great pains have been taken to ensure that these labor-hour estimates in Figure 2-11 are particularly realistic.

You can now enter these labor-hour estimates into their respective tasks using the Task Entry/Edit tool (shown in Figure 2-8), with which you are already familiar. The column labeled *Original Mhrs*, which stands for *original man-hours*, is the original labor-hour budget for each task. The terms *man-hours* and

Figure 2-11. Quantification and labor-hour estimates for tasks in
         Figure 2-7.

Package ID	Task ID	Description	Unit of Measure	Original Qty	Original Mhrs
Concrete	1	Pour Concrete	CYC	290	240
Concrete	2	Cure Concrete	CYC	290	40
Concrete	3	Finish Concrete	SF	5080	240
Forms	1	Forms Installation	SF	750	240
Forms	2	Forms Removal	SF	750	160
Rebar	1	Rebar Installation	LBS	760	240
Rebar	2	Mesh Installation	LBS	140	80
Rebar	3	Anchor Bolts	LBS	100	160
Siteprep	1	Clear & Grub	SF	20000	80
Siteprep	2	Earth Removal	CY	480	240
Siteprep	3	Grading	SF	20000	80
Siteprep	4	Excavation	CY	260	360

labor-hours are equivalent. In the case of man-hours, the term is used generically and does not literally mean work done by men. There does not exist a corresponding term *women-hours*. The classical notation of man-hours has been retained here because the classical abbreviation *mhrs* (man-hours) is well known, while a similar abbreviation for labor-hours is not.

These labor-hours can be added to their respective tasks by using the **forward** and **back** control buttons at the bottom of the Task Entry/Edit form to move through the database to locate a task. Then its labor-hours can be entered into the Original Mhrs field.

2.5.1 Using the Cost Accounts Entry/Edit Tool

Once the labor-hour estimates have been made for a work package, the cost for the work package can be estimated. Often, there is not just a single type of work conducted on a work package. For instance, there may be "direct labor" and "indirect labor" or possibly "subcontract labor." Each of these types of labor is usually billed at a different rate. Also, there may be large differences in compensation among workers on a given work package. Often, there may be a supervisory-level person conducting the work, with a number of less senior persons working for the supervisor. These different types of workers account for different labor rates.

Also, there are costs for a work package other than just labor costs. There may be materials costs, equipment costs, supply costs, maintenance costs, and so on. To make matters a little more complicated, the cost information for a project is often put to a different use than the labor-hour data. The project manager uses the labor-hour budgets to manage the work of the project, but the cost information is used to communicate with the client, for general accounting purposes, for tax determination, and for a host of other uses. For whatever uses are made of this information, it is customary to classify cost data by *cost accounts*. Often a company has multiple sets of cost accounts. One of these is the *General Ledger* (GL) chart of accounts. There may be a different chart of accounts for cost accounting, sometimes refered to as the *cost codes*.

In the Modern Project toolset supplied with this book, there is only one database for cost accounts, and it is assumed to be the GL chart of accounts for the example project. There is nothing to prevent you from using this capability for some other set of cost codes, since you will be the one defining the account identifiers, and you can assign GL account numbers to them or some other cost code account identifiers. There are actually two different entry/edit tools needed for entering cost information. One is used infrequently. It is the *Cost Code Entry/Edit Tool*. It is used only for entering the definitions of the Cost Account Identifiers. For the purposes of the example project we assume a very simple GL chart of accounts that is shown in Figure 2-12.

By now you know how to activate the data entry/edit tools listed on the Modern Project Main Menu. So click on the **Cost Code Entry/Edit** button, and you should see a form appear that looks like Figure 2-13.

This is the form you will use to enter the GL account codes shown in Figure 2-12. After you have entered these GL account codes and their descriptions, you will need to enter the cost estimates for each work package. You will need a different

Figure 2-12. Cost code descriptions for the example project.

Cost Account	Description
601	Direct Labor
602	Indirect Labor
603	Supervision
605	Sub-contract labor
631	Permanent Materials
632	Construction Materials
651	Equipment
652	Equipment Consumables

Figure 2-13. The Cost Code Entry Form.

entry/edit tool to do this. The cost estimates for a work package are indexed by the Cost Account identifiers (in this case GL codes), as shown in Figure 2-14. Notice that a given work package, say the "Concrete" work package, can have several cost accounts associated with it. Cost accounts 601 and 603 are different labor accounts, whereas accounts 631 and 632 are different materials cost accounts.

The cost estimates from Figure 2-14 are entered using the *Cost Accounts Entry/Edit* tool. To select this tool, click on the **Cost Accounts Entry/Edit** button on the Main Menu. A form like the one shown in Figure 2-15 should appear. You will notice that there are four fields that can be entered into this form, but there are only three categories of information in Figure 2-14. The additional field, Open Commitments, has not yet been explained. We will do that now, but for the model project there will be no open commitment data.

Open commitments are binding commitments to expend funds. For instance, when you place certain orders for materials, you may be required to sign a contract prior to shipment.

Figure 2-14. Cost estimates for the example project.

Package ID	Cost Account	Original Budget
Concrete	601	$9,200
Concrete	602	$1,800
Concrete	631	$18,000
Concrete	632	$900
Concrete	651	$2,480
Forms	601	$6,800
Forms	603	$1,800
Forms	632	$1,100
Rebar	601	$17,600
Rebar	603	$3,600
Rebar	631	$4,800
Rebar	632	$627
Siteprep	601	$12,000
Siteprep	603	$2,400
Siteprep	605	$1,760
Siteprep	651	$3,000
Siteprep	652	$600

Once the commitment is made the funds are "as good as spent," even if no invoice has yet been paid for the materials. The open commitment field is simply a place to record commitment information temporarily so that it will show up on reports, until the actual cost transaction has been entered, at which time the commitment needs to be removed. In this book we assume that the entry and removal of commitment information are done manually using the Cost Accounts Entry/Edit form (see Figure 2-15).

You should enter the cost (budget) data for these work packages now. Once the cost estimates have been entered for each work package, you can try out the budget reports provided with the toolset.

2.5.2 Budget Reports

The *Budgeted Cost Listing* report (Figure 2-16) displays the cost estimates for each control package. This is the report that proj-

Figure 2-15. Cost Accounts Entry/Edit form.

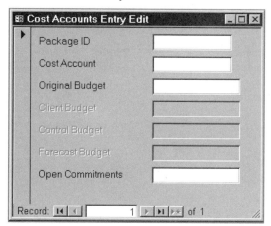

ect management uses to communicate the original cost estimate to the client. After this original cost estimate is approved by the client and by general management, it becomes known as the *Original Cost Budget*. The Budgeted Cost Listing report can be displayed by clicking the **Budgeted Cost Listing** button on the Main Menu.

Similarly, the *Budgeted Quantity and Man-Hour Listing* report (Figure 2-17) can be produced to obtain the labor-hour estimates for each control package above the work package level. This is the report that the project manager uses to communicate the original labor-hour budget to general management and perhaps to the client. After this original labor-hour estimate is approved, it becomes known as the *Original Man-Hour Budget*. The Budgeted Quantity and Man-Hour Listing report can be displayed by clicking on the **Budgeted Qty and Mhr Listing** button on the Main Menu.

After the original man-hour budget has been approved, it needs to be "time phased." This refers to a graphical representation of how the man-hour budget will be expended over time, as depicted in Figure 1-1. Time phasing is a process that "integrates" the budget data with the scheduling data to produce

(text continues on page 54)

Figure 2-16. Budgeted Cost Listing.

Budgeted Cost Listing

WBS Position	*Package ID / GL Account*		*Original Budget*	*Client Budget*	*Control Budget*	*Forecast*
0	*Example Proj*		$88,467	$88,467	$88,467	$88,467
1	*Foundation*		$88,467	$88,467	$88,467	$88,467
1.1	*Siteprep*		$19,760	$19,760	$19,760	$19,760
	601	Direct Labor	$12,000	$12,000	$12,000	$12,000
	603	Supervision	$2,400	$2,400	$2,400	$2,400
	605	Sub-contract labor	$1,760	$1,760	$1,760	$1,760
	651	Equipment	$3,000	$3,000	$3,000	$3,000
	652	Equipment	$600	$600	$600	$600
1.2	*Forms*		$9,700	$9,700	$9,700	$9,700
	601	Direct Labor	$6,800	$6,800	$6,800	$6,800
	603	Supervision	$1,800	$1,800	$1,800	$1,800
	632	Construction	$1,100	$1,100	$1,100	$1,100
1.3	*Rebar*		$26,627	$26,627	$26,627	$26,627
	601	Direct Labor	$17,600	$17,600	$17,600	$17,600
	603	Supervision	$3,600	$3,600	$3,600	$3,600
	631	Permanent Materials	$4,800	$4,800	$4,800	$4,800
	632	Construction	$627	$627	$627	$627
1.4	*Concrete*		$32,380	$32,380	$32,380	$32,380
	601	Direct Labor	$9,200	$9,200	$9,200	$9,200
	602	Indirect Labor	$1,800	$1,800	$1,800	$1,800
	631	Permanent Materials	$18,000	$18,000	$18,000	$18,000
	632	Construction	$900	$900	$900	$900
	651	Equipment	$2,480	$2,480	$2,480	$2,480

Saturday, January 15, 2000 *Page 1 of 2*

Figure 2-17. Budgeted Qty and Mhr Listing.

Budgeted Qty and Mhr Listing

WBS	*Package /*		*Unit of*	*---- Original ---*		*--- Client ----*		*--- Control ----*		*--- Forecast ---*	
Position	*Task ID*	*Description*	*Meas*	*Qty*	*Mhrs*	*Qty*	*Mhrs*	*Qty*	*Mhrs*	*Qty*	*Mhrs*
0	*Example Proj*	5000 SF Building	SF	5000	2160	5000	2160	5000	2160	5000	2160
1	*Foundation*	Construct	CYC	290	2160	290	2160	290	2160	290	2160
1.1	*Siteprep*	Site Preparation	SF	20000	760	20000	760	20000	760	20000	760
	1	Clear & Grub	SF	20000	80	20000	80	20000	80	20000	80
	2	Earth Removal	CY	480	240	480	240	480	240	480	240
	3	Grading	SF	20000	80	20000	80	20000	80	20000	80
	4	Excavation	CY	260	360	260	360	260	360	260	360
1.2	*Forms*	Forms Installation &	SF	750	400	750	400	750	400	750	400
	1	Forms Installation	SF	750	240	750	240	750	240	750	240
	2	Forms Removal	SF	750	160	750	160	750	160	750	160
1.3	*Rebar*	Rebar, Mesh &	LBS	1000	480	1000	480	1000	480	1000	480
	1	Rebar Installation	LBS	760	240	760	240	760	240	760	240
	2	Mesh Installation	LBS	140	80	140	80	140	80	140	80
	3	Anchor Bolts	LBS	100	160	100	160	100	160	100	160
1.4	*Concrete*	Concrete Pour,	CYC	290	520	290	520	290	520	290	520
	1	Pour Concrete	CYC	290	240	290	240	290	240	290	240
	2	Cure Concrete	CYC	290	40	290	40	290	40	290	40

Sunday, January 23, 2000

Page 1 of 2

what is often called the *project baseline*. This integrated budget and scheduling information, as shown in Figure 1-1, is also called the *project plan* or the *time-phased budget*. Consequently, time phasing cannot be done until a project schedule has been produced.

Time phasing is first calculated at the work package level and then "rolled up" to obtain the time phasing for all the control packages at higher levels in the WBS hierarchy. This "rollup" is more complicated than the rollup seen on the Budgeted Cost Listing or the Budgeted Quantity and Man-hour Listing because it involves the schedule dates for each task.

In order to *time-phase* an individual work package, one must first know when the work of the work package is to begin and end. This information is obtained from the project schedule, which is explained in the next section. One also needs to know how the labor-hour budget for the work package will be expended during this interval between the work package start date and the work package end date. In this book we assume that each task's budget is expended uniformly over the duration of each task. This is a good assumption if our rule that work packages are of short duration is observed. If there exist tasks with unusually long durations, this may not be a good assumption, but it can be corrected by subdividing the task into a number of tasks with short duration.

Modern Project uses the *linear spread method* to time-phase work packages. This means that the labor-hour budget is expended uniformly between the start date and the end date of each task. There are other, more complicated time-phasing techniques, but it has been found that there are few projects that really require them. For this reason they have not been incorporated into Modern Project.

2.6 Scheduling the Work

The difference between *work sequencing* and *scheduling the work* is the application of the estimated resources to the sequence of work. This is sometimes referred to as *resource scheduling*. Resource scheduling can often be a complex undertaking and is therefore dealt with in detail in Chapter 7. Only enough about the subject is presented here to enable the reader to understand the purpose of resource scheduling to complete this discussion of project planning and to familiarize the reader with how to enter schedule dates into the example database manually. This understanding will enable a reader who is already familiar with a particular automated scheduling package to use it and then to enter that scheduling system's dates into the Modern Project database manually. In Chapter 7 we present an automated scheduling interface between Modern Project and Microsoft Project that allows automated transfer of schedule dates into the Modern Project database.

After estimating the labor-hours and the costs of a project (including equipment and materials costs), the project manager must ensure that these *resources* are applied to the sequence of work. This last element of project planning is what establishes the *project schedule*. The previous four elements of project planning all lead to a specific estimate of the required resources to complete the project. However, adjustments are often necessary during resource scheduling.

For instance, on large projects done for external clients, the project managing organization may be competing with other firms for the project work. Depending on a number of factors, they may or may not have all the resources at hand at the time their bid is made to the client. They may be counting on hiring a substantial amount of the proposed labor force after the contract is awarded. The project management team making the bid will no doubt investigate the feasibility of hiring such a workforce and make estimates on how its aggregate *labor pool* will increase over time.

If it is found that the labor pool for some particular category of labor will not increase rapidly enough to allow the scheduling system to compute a schedule that meets the client's requirements, adjustments may have to be made to save time

elsewhere in the work. These adjustments may lead to ineffi-
ciently large labor pools for other categories of work in order
to force other work packages to complete earlier. This situation,
in turn, will cause labor to be utilized less efficiently than originally planned, which in turn will lead to larger labor estimates
for some control packages. This point will become clearer in
Chapter 7.

It is the project manager's responsibility to ensure that the
dates in the project schedule are in agreement with the contractual dates with either the client or the project manager's senior
management, or both, depending on the (contractual) relationship between project manager and client. This first project
schedule, developed by the project management team and
agreed to by the client, is called the *original schedule*. The original budget, time phased by this original schedule, is referred to
as the *original project plan*. The project manager has the responsibility of ensuring that these original contract dates are unchanged during project execution. Changes to the scope of the
work (that are client approved) will be reflected in another budget and schedule, referred to as the *client budget* and *client schedule*, which are explained in Chapter 3.

The time phasing of the original budget by the original
schedule is needed by the project manager to plan for the labor
requirements of the project and to control the expenditure of
labor-hours in the most efficient manner possible.

It is important to recognize the purpose of scheduling. Just
as budgeting is not project management, neither is scheduling.
Schedules give dates for when work should start and end but
do not guarantee that work will actually start and end on those
dates. By themselves, schedules give no insight into the success
of a project. The essence of managing a project is to understand
the interrelationship between the budget and the schedule and
to apply methods of performance measurement against this relationship. The interrelationship is the project baseline or project plan mentioned in the previous section. When the term
project plan is used in this way, one really means that it is a

concise representation of the (real) project plan, which is the accumulation of all budget and schedule data.

As a general rule of thumb, if there are more than 2,000 tasks or 500 work packages in a schedule, something is probably wrong. Scheduling at too detailed a level tends to create far too many work elements, which can cause the schedule to become unwieldy. In fact, scheduling at the work package level can be a viable alternative on large projects. In such cases, it is then possible to manage 2,000 work packages.

The author is familiar with attempts to schedule large projects with more than 30,000 tasks. These were heroic efforts, but they all ended in chaos. Just because you have an automated scheduling program to make scheduling more tractable does not mean this scheduling program will make your brain more capable. Human beings cannot deal with this degree of fragmentation in conceiving of an object or process. The number 2,000 may seem arbitrary, and in a sense it is, but experience has shown that it is a limit that usually should not be exceeded.

As previously mentioned, a common misconception is that project management is scheduling. The documentation of some scheduling systems tends to promote this misconception or to focus all of project management around scheduling. This gives a distorted view of the place of scheduling in the overall scheme of project management. One needs only to read the Microsoft Project 98 *User's Guide* to see an example of this. Project scheduling systems are often marketed as project management systems, which may account for this confusion. Perhaps this practice helps sell more scheduling systems, but it often is a disservice to novice project managers.

So, what is the role of scheduling in the grand scheme of project management? It is primarily to time-phase the budget. This becomes clear in Chapters 3 through 6. In Chapter 7, we see that the start and end dates produced by an automated scheduling system for large projects, even resource leveled dates, are often not suitable for adoption as the project schedule dates. In Chapter 7 we assert that the project management staff needs to take several other things into consideration in adopting start and end dates for any given control package.

At this point we can only say that the reason this is so has to do with the fact that scheduling systems do not have the capability to discriminate such things as whether the task's client budget, control budget, or forecast resources should be used for resource leveling. Consequently, even modern scheduling systems often have to be used iteratively. It is important to understand that the success of a project is more dependent on the work sequencing than on the mechanical production of start and end dates by an automated scheduling tool.

The time-phased budget encapsulates the total project plan in a simple, easy-to-understand graph. The time-phased budget plays a fundamental role in all of project performance evaluation and productivity measurement. Another, somewhat less important, but useful, purpose for scheduling is to determine the critical path that we discuss in Chapter 7. Many project schedulers will no doubt disagree with this assessment, because they believe the most important project management function is to keep attention and effort focused on accomplishing those tasks on the critical path.

But on large projects there is usually not such a thing as a critical path. Depending on your viewpoint, there is either a "critical subnet" or a family of critical paths. In the mid-1960s, the author developed a (possibly the first) automated scheduling system that sorted all the different "critical paths" by criticality (total slack time) and plotted each family of a given criticality in a different color on a scrolling multipen plotter. Within each family there can be multiple paths with the same slack time.

On these large projects, the decision on which critical path to work on becomes blurred since the majority of the tasks are on some critical path. In such cases, the Schedule Performance Chart (introduced in Chapter 4) is often a better measure of schedule performance than is the critical path(s).

Scheduling often proves to be a low-level, time-consuming activity that requires the effort of a scheduling team, even with capable scheduling tools. Scheduling is an activity that can consume excessive resources when team members engage in it prior to doing the upfront *thinking* that is required for effective project planning. This is why our approach to project management is a top-down approach that begins with developing a WBS, rather than preparing a *task list*.

Figure 2-18 shows a schedule for the Foundation control package prepared using Microsoft Project. This includes all the tasks in the Siteprep, Forms, Rebar, and Concrete work packages. From this schedule, it can be seen that the start and end dates for these work packages can be determined from the start and end dates of the tasks they contain. Clearly, the start date for a work package is the earliest task start date for all the tasks contained in the package. Similarly, the work package finish date is the latest task finish date for all the tasks contained in the package. For the moment, assume that the start and end dates in Figure 2-18 are the start and end dates for our example project. Since they are difficult to determine precisely from Figure 2-18, these dates have been recorded explicitly in Figure 2-19.

Figure 2-18. Schedule for the Foundation control package.

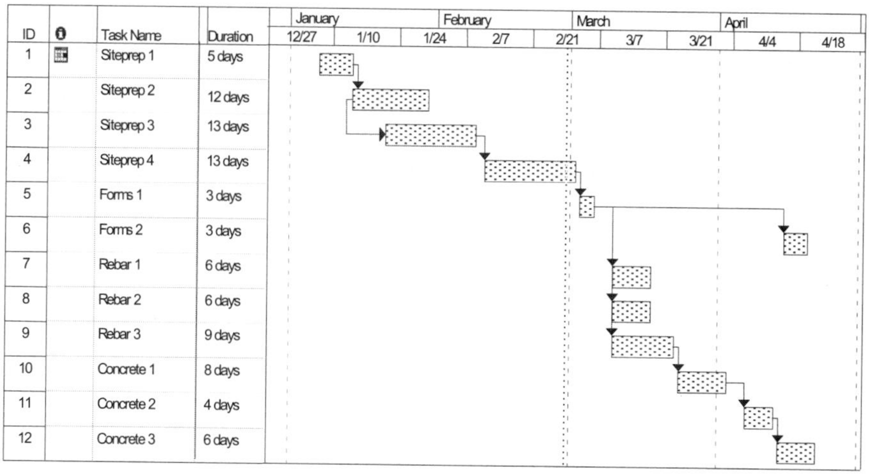

Figure 2-19. Start and end dates for Foundation control package.

Package ID	Task ID	Description	Original Start	Original End
Concrete	1	Pour Concrete	3/24/00	4/4/00
Concrete	2	Cure Concrete	4/7/00	4/11/00
Concrete	3	Finish	4/14/00	4/22/00
Forms	1	Forms	3/3/00	3/4/00
Forms	2	Forms	4/14/00	4/18/00
Rebar	1	Rebar	3/10/00	3/18/00
Rebar	2	Mesh	3/10/00	3/18/00
Rebar	3	Anchor Bolts	3/10/00	3/21/00
Siteprep	1	Clear & Grub	1/7/00	1/11/00
Siteprep	2	Earth Removal	1/14/00	1/31/00
Siteprep	3	Grading	1/21/00	2/8/00
Siteprep	4	Excavation	2/11/00	2/28/00

These start and end dates can now be manually entered into the example database. To enter these start and end dates, use the *Task Entry/Edit* tool that was previously discussed in Section 2.3.3 (see Figure 2-8). Enter the start and end dates shown in Figure 2-19 into the *Original Start* and *Original End* fields of the Task Entry/Edit tool for each task shown in Figure 2-19. Also, for now, you can enter these same start and end dates into the *Client Start* and *Client End* dates, into the *Control Start* and *Control End* dates, and into the *Forecast Start* and *Forecast End* dates.

In Chapter 3 we explain how to determine start and end dates for these other budgets more accurately. If you do not enter these dates for the client dates, the control dates, and the forecast dates, no harm will be done. If Modern Project gets to a point where it needs dates for these other budgets and the forecast and none have been entered, it automatically inserts these start and end dates into the Client, Control, and Forecast schedules, also, because at the beginning of a project there are no deviations from the project plan and all of these budgets and the forecast are the same.

It remains to explain the mechanics of time phasing the budget by the schedule. It is important to understand how it is done, even though Modern Project does it for you automatically. Time phasing is first computed at the work package level and then rolled up to obtain the time phasing at the higher control package levels. This rollup is more complex than the rollup for budget or schedule data individually. To time-phase a work package is to compute the pattern (graph) of the expenditure of resources (labor-hours) during the time period between the start date and the end date of the work package. This pattern is often referred to as a *spread curve*. There are several possible types of spread curves. Perhaps the simplest is to assume that the budget for each task in the work package is expended in one lump at the time of completion of the task. This assumption generates a *step function* spread curve, as shown in Figure 2-20 (a).

Another type of spread curve is based on the assumption that each task has a uniform (or constant) rate of expenditure during the time interval between its start date and its end date. This leads to what is called a *linear approximation function* spread curve, as shown in Figure 2-20 (b).

In the (infrequent) case where a single work package has a substantially larger budget than average and is not of short duration (such as an overhead work package), the "spreading" of the work package budget can be handled in a more sophisticated manner. Instead of developing the spread curve from the estimate for each task, as in cases 2–20(a) and 2–20(b), the spread curve can be based on historical information about the distribution of labor-hours (or costs) on similar work packages in the past. Such spread curves are often called *statistical distributions* or *historical distribution* spread curves. An example of a hypothetical historical distribution spread curve is shown in Figure 2-20(c).

Modern Project uses the linear approximation spread curve as shown in Figure 2-20(b). This is the time-phasing (spreading) method that is best for work packages that satisfy our assumptions about work packages. If one wants to spread a long duration work package via some historical distribution function, modeling the distribution function with tasks of unequal dura-

Figure 2-20. (a) Step function spread curve. (b) Linear approximation spread curve. (c) Statistical or historical distribution spread curve.

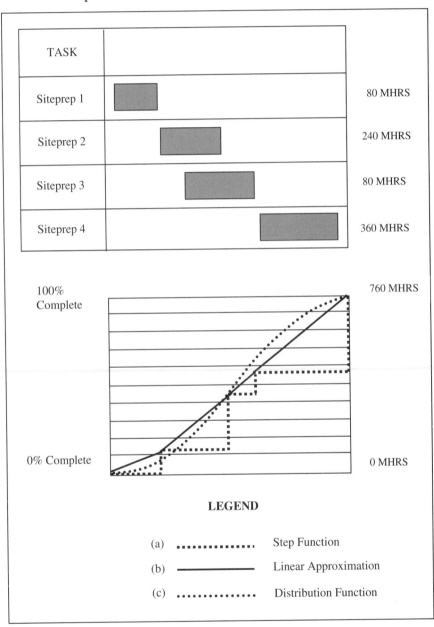

tion or quantification can do it. It will probably occur to the reader how to do such a thing but we will not take up space explaining it here.

Figure 2-21 illustrates how the time-phased budget for a summary level control package in the WBS is obtained. First, all the budgets that roll up into this control package are added to produce the budget for the control package. Next the start and the end dates for the control package are determined by taking the earliest start date and the latest finish date of the work packages that are contained in the control package. Finally, the budget contribution of each lower-level work package during each time period (reporting period) in the summary level control package's duration between its start and end dates are summed, yielding the summary level control package distribution.

2.7 The Baseline Chart

After the schedule dates have been entered into the database for the tasks, a *baseline chart* can be displayed that depicts the time phasing of the budget. Figure 2-22 shows the baseline chart for the example project so far. Figure 2-23 shows the baseline chart for the example project at a later point in time. We arrive at that point in Chapter 6, when the control budget has diverged significantly from the original budget. Figure 2-23 has been included here to emphasize that the baseline will evolve as the project progresses.

To display the baseline chart, click on the control button titled "Baseline Chart" on the Modern Project Main Menu.

Figure 2-21. Time-phasing a summary-level control package.

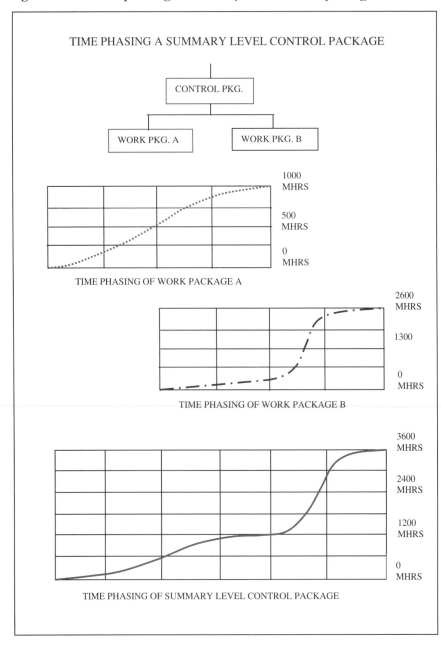

Figure 2-22. Example Baseline Chart (early data).

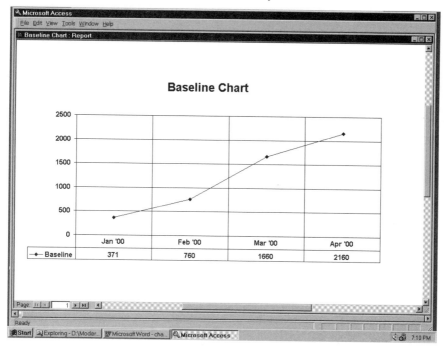

Figure 2-23. Example Baseline Chart (later data).

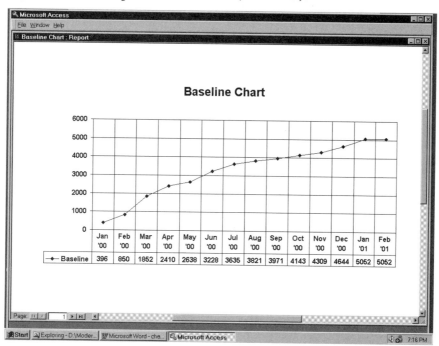

Chapter 3

Project Monitoring

In Chapter 2, we discussed project planning and the construction of a project plan. We also explained how this planning information could be entered into a database using the Modern Project desktop toolset supplied with this book. In this chapter we discuss what information needs to be collected as the project progresses. At this point it is worthwhile reviewing where it is we have been and where we are going to see how project monitoring fits into the project management process.

Recall that at the beginning of Chapter 2 we subdivided project management into *project planning* and *project execution*. We essentially covered project planning in Chapter 2. It will take us three more chapters to cover the core issues of project execution. For most readers who can envision themselves as project managers, whether or not they are one yet, the interesting part will not come until Chapters 4 and 5. This is where we consider how project managers use this information to make decisions, what kind of decisions are made, and what impact these decisions have on projects. But, before we can do this, we need to understand what information needs to be collected to allow us to make our decisions. Recall that project execution consists of the following five parts:

1. Cost accounting
2. Progress measurement
3. Variance tracking and change control

4. Performance evaluation
5. Productivity measurement

In this chapter we cover the first three of these functions. To conduct these functions, there are three classes of information that need to be collected on a regular basis. These are

1. Actual expenditure information
2. Progress information
3. Variance information

We explain these classes of information in this chapter and how they can be entered into the project database using the Modern Project tools. We then explain (in Chapters 4 and 5) how the Modern Project tools can be employed to get vital project performance and productivity measures and trends that will enable the successful control of the project.

3.1 Collecting Actual Expenditures

Project management is responsible for gathering actual expenditure data. Effective project control is based on documentation of all expenditures of resources (labor-hours, materials, equipment, and costs) by work package. All expenditure data are gathered and preserved as the project is executed, developing a record of expenditures that can be compared with the project baseline. In many project-oriented industry segments, this project management function is called *cost accounting*. It differs from general accounting in that the principal objective is to collect costs (expenditures) by WBS codes and other meaningful cost collection codes, rather than by general ledger codes.

In the example project discussed in Chapter 2, the reader will recall that the *cost codes* that were used within a work package were the general ledger codes themselves, but they can be any set of cost codes that is meaningful for a project organization. In many large corporations, the general ledger codes become quite complex in their reflection of the uses to which they are put for tax reporting and other regulatory compliance. This tends to make them unsuitable for cost accounting.

Cost accounting provides a basis for collecting actual expenditures for a number of other reasons, such as establishing historical records of the percentages of resources projects tend to expend on various classes of activities. Cost accounting is also used to monitor whether the rate of expenditure on a particular project is in accordance with the project baseline. For simplicity, we will continue assuming that the cost codes are the same as the general ledger codes in our example project, with the understanding that they could be some other set of cost accounting codes.

It may appear to some that it is unfortunate we are making such a simplifying assumption here when the real world often behaves differently. The reason for doing so is that cost accounting is a discipline in its own right, and it would take us too far afield to branch off into this discipline in a discussion of appropriate cost accounting codes. On the other hand, a large proportion of the readers of this book will no doubt have had some experience with general ledger codes in an introductory accounting class, and the assumption that the cost codes coincide with the general ledger codes is a realistic one for small companies.

It is the responsibility of project management to ensure the integrity and timeliness of the gathering, recording, and reporting of actual expenditures by work package. This includes recording any nonbudgeted expenditures as well. Project management accounts for these nonbudgeted expenditures through the project's change order procedures (discussed later in this chapter) in order to create an accurate picture of project expenditures.

When corrections of actual expenditures are required, project management should make these corrections *during the accounting period of their discovery.* This can be done with the

Modern Project tools, either by editing the original expenditure transactions or by entering offsetting transactions. It is often preferable to enter offsetting transactions in order to preserve historically the posting of perceived expenditures and the later corrections to these expenditures.

Also, project management is responsible for ensuring that all expenditures have been charged to the appropriate work package. This may seem obvious, but on large projects it is often difficult. Operational managers do not always have the same incentive to ensure correctness in the accounting of expenditures as the project management staff. It is time consuming and not something they always get credit for. Large-scale inaccuracies in accounting for actual expenditures can skew the performance and productivity evaluations so badly that a project can be in trouble and not know it for far too long.

Figure 3-1 shows the *Cost/Labor Transaction Entry/Edit* tool that is used for entering actual expenditure transactions. This tool can be executed by clicking on its button on the Modern Project Main Menu. The operation of this tool is similar to the operation of other data entry and edit tools already introduced. Notice that the form shown in Figure 3-1 has fields for both labor and cost. Not all cost transactions have associated labor-hour expenditures. If the cost transaction is for materials or

Figure 3-1. Cost/Labor Transaction Entry/Edit form.

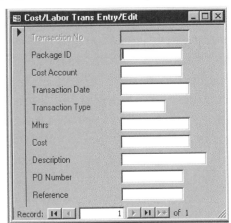

equipment expenditures, only the cost of the transaction is entered, and the labor-hour field is left blank.

The labor-hour expenditures are used in both the performance and the productivity assessments. There is a tendency by both laborers and their managers to charge work for a given work package to another work package if the charges to the given work package begin to exceed the budget for the package. The thinking here is that the deficit labor-hours can be made up on this other package to which they are charging, and project management will never be the wiser. While this sometimes occurs, often the deficit is just being rolled forward. It often occurs on large projects that project management is kept in the dark for months or even years about the productivity problems that exist on the project. For this reason, project management often relies on a system of independent audits of labor reporting to ensure that labor reporting is being conducted accurately.

For each cost or labor transaction to be entered into the database, the work package ID is entered first (into the *Package ID* field). Then the Cost Account to which the transaction applies is entered. This identifies the cost account in the work package to which this transaction applies. The first field of cost/labor transactions is an automatically assigned *transaction number*. You are not allowed to enter anything in the first field; the Modern Project system does this for you automatically.

The *Transaction Date*, which is the next field to be entered, usually refers to the date the cost was incurred, but it could refer to the date it was paid or to the date the expenditure was recorded (e.g., the date timesheets were recorded) for labor-hour expenditures. The policy for which dates to use for which types of Cost/Labor transactions is something that is set by project management and should be implemented uniformly, as Cost/Labor transactions are entered during the lifetime of the project.

The *Transaction Type* is an identifier that is used to identify transactions on the *Cost Transaction Listing* report, which is explained in the next section. Actual expenditure transactions (another commonly used name for Cost/Labor transactions) are usually labeled *labor transactions* or *journal vouchers* or *material invoices* or *equipment invoices* or some other identifying category of expenditure transaction. This labeling of actual expenditure transactions is often helpful at a later date in tracking down transaction errors.

If the transaction is a labor-hour expenditure transaction, the number of labor-hours expended for this transaction needs to be entered. Other cost expenditure transactions may not have labor-hour expenditures. There are also fields for entering a textual description of the transaction, a purchase order number if appropriate, and a *reference identifier*. The reference identifier is any identifier that will later help to identify the transaction, such as an invoice number. Figure 3-2 lists some actual expenditure transactions for you to enter for the example project.

3.2 Cost Reports

Figure 3-3 shows the *Cost Transaction Listing* report. It is simply a listing of all the actual expenditure transactions in the data-

Figure 3-2. Example expenditure transactions.

Trans No	Package ID	Cost Account	Trans Date	Trans Type	Mhrs	Cost	Description	PO Number	Ref
1	Siteprep	601	1/18/00	Labor	60	1200	Earth Removal		E1063
2	Siteprep	603	1/18/00	Labor	40	1200	Supervision-Earth Rm		E1063
3	Siteprep	605	1/18/00	SubLabor	20	560	SubLabor w/e 1/18/00	P12345 67	
4	Siteprep	651	1/18/00	Journal	0	600	Equipment Rental		E1063
5	Siteprep	652	1/18/00	Journal	0	120	Equip. consumables		E1063
6	Siteprep	601	2/1/00	Labor	80	1600	Earth Removal		
7	Siteprep	603	2/1/00	Labor	40	1200	Supervision-Earth Rm		
8	Siteprep	605	2/1/00	Labor	80	1760	SubLabor w/e 2/1/00		
9	Siteprep	601	2/15/00	Labor	80	1600	Grading		
10	Siteprep	603	2/15/00	Labor	40	1200	Supervision-Grading		
11	Siteprep	601	3/1/00	Labor	300	6000	Excavation		
12	Siteprep	603	3/1/00	Labor	120	3600	Supervision-Excavat.		
13	Concrete	601	4/3/00	Labor	100	2500	Concrete labor		
14	Concrete	603	4/10/00	Labor	100	3000	Concrete Labor		

Figure 3-3. Cost Transaction Listing.

Cost Transaction Listing

| Trans No | ---- Transaction Coding ---- | | | ---- Transaction Data ---- | | | ---- Expenditure ---- | | |
	Package ID	GL Account	Trans Date	Trans Type	Reference	PO Number	Description	Mhrs	Cost
1	Siteprep	601	1/18/00	Labor	E1063		Earth Removal	60	$1,200
2	Siteprep	603	1/18/00	Labor	E1063		Superv-Earth Rml	40	$1,200
3	Siteprep	605	1/18/00	SubLabor		P1234567	SubLabor w/e 1/18/00	20	$560
4	Siteprep	651	1/18/00	Journal	E1063		Equipment Rental		$600
5	Siteprep	652	1/18/00	Journal	E1063		Equip. consumables		$120
6	Siteprep	601	2/1/00	SubLabor			Earth Removal	80	$1,600
7	Siteprep	603	2/1/00	Labor			Supervision-Earth Rm	40	$1,200
8	Siteprep	605	2/1/00	SubLabor			SubLabor w/e 2/1/00	80	$1,760
9	Siteprep	601	2/15/00	Labor			Grading	80	$1,600
10	Siteprep	603	2/15/00	Labor			Supervision-Grading	40	$1,200
11	Siteprep	601	3/1/00	Labor			Excavation	300	$6,000
12	Siteprep	603	3/1/00	Labor			Supervision-Excavat.	120	$3,600
13	Concrete	601	4/3/00	Labor			Concrete labor	100	$2,500
14	Concrete	603	4/10/00	Labor			Concrete Labor	100	$3,000

Tuesday, January 25, 2000

base. It is used for correcting cost posting errors. This report can be obtained by clicking on its button on the Modern Project Main Menu. Figure 3-4 shows the *Cost Comparison Report*. It is used to get a picture of how the project is doing in terms of actual expenditure of resources. It is also useful for discussing the project with the client. It is organized around the WBS in that it lists the control packages in the order in which they appear in the WBS and gives the summary cost (expenditure) data for each control package. For work packages, it breaks out the costs by cost code within the work package. The Cost Comparison Report compares the *To Date Cost*, the *Total Cost*, and the *Forecast Budget* with the *Control Budget*.

The *To Date Cost* is the total amount that has been expended for a control package. The *Percent (%) Budget Expended* is the percentage of the control budget that has been spent. In addition to what has been spent is the open commitment (*Open Amount*) that has already been committed but not yet paid. The *Total Cost* is just the sum of what has been spent and what has been committed. We have not yet explained how the Forecast Budget is computed. This is done later in this chapter. The *Forecast Budget* (or simply the forecast) amount shown on the Cost Comparison Report is the amount we expect will be expended (for each control package) by the time the project completes.

At this point you may be wondering why this would be different from the control budget. The control budget is the budget that is used to control the project, but productivity variances on the control packages often cause the final costs to differ from the budgeted costs. Nevertheless, it is possible, using the techniques that are explained in this and later chapters, to know fairly accurately in advance what these final costs will be. And it is the computation of these costs that is printed in the Forecast Budget column of the Cost Comparison Report.

3.3 Progress Tracking

Progress tracking is fundamental to performance evaluation, variance analysis, and productivity measurement. The calcula-

Figure 3-4. Cost Comparison Report.

Cost Comparison Report

Hierarchy Position	Package ID / GL Account	Description	Control Budget	To Date Cost	% Budget Expended	Open Amount	Total Cost	Forecast Budget
0	Example Proj	5000 SF Building	$88,467	$23,140	26%	$0	$23,140	$88,467
1	Foundation	Construct Foundation	$88,467	$23,140	26%	$0	$23,140	$88,467
1.1	Siteprep	Site Preparation	$19,760	$20,640	104%	$0	$20,640	$19,760
	601	Direct Labor	$12,000	$10,400	87%	$0	$10,400	$12,000
	603	Supervision	$2,400	$7,200	300%	$0	$7,200	$2,400
	605	Sub-contract labor	$1,760	$2,320	132%	$0	$2,320	$1,760
	651	Equipment	$3,000	$600	20%	$0	$600	$3,000
	652	Equipment Consumables	$600	$120	20%	$0	$120	$600
1.2	Forms	Forms Installation & Removal	$9,700	$0	0%	$0	$0	$9,700
	601	Direct Labor	$6,800					$6,800
	603	Supervision	$1,800					$1,800
	632	Construction Materials	$1,100					$1,100
1.3	Rebar	Rebar, Mesh & Anchors	$26,627	$0	0%	$0	$0	$26,627
	632	Construction Materials	$627					$627
	601	Direct Labor	$17,600					$17,600
	603	Supervision	$3,600					$3,600
	631	Permanent Materials	$4,800					$4,800
1.4	Concrete	Concrete Pour, Cure & Finish	$32,380	$2,500	8%	$0	$2,500	$35,618
	602	Indirect Labor	$1,980					$1,980
	631	Permanent Materials	$18,000					$18,000

Tuesday, January 25, 2000

tions used to compute performance, variance, and productivity measures are all based on the *percent complete* (the final measure of progress) for each work package.

It is critical that progress data (for percent complete calculations) accurately reflect the physical progress on the work package and not some "subjective guess" the work package manager makes. It is the responsibility of project management to ensure that each work package is accurately *statused* (progress data accurately determined) each period. Consequently, various statusing techniques have been devised to ensure some degree of objectivity in determining progress. All of these methods attempt to reduce statusing to determining if some verifiable component of the work has been completed or not. Some of these statusing methods are:

· The Quantity method
· The Milestone method
· The Activity method
· The Indirect method

These statusing methods are all applied to the tasks within a work package to first compute a percent complete for each task. From the percents complete for all the tasks within a package, a *weighted percent complete* is calculated for the work package. This weighted percent complete is the percent complete for the work package.

The reason for this weighting is that the tasks within a work package do not necessarily have the same labor-hour budgets. Consequently, some tasks have more work content than others. This has to be taken into account when calculating the percent complete for the work package. The formula for computing the weighted percent complete for a work package is given later in this chapter. It is presented within the context of the following example of statusing using the quantity method.

The *quantity method* reduces statusing to counting. It is used when the output of a task consists of a number of identical (or very similar) products or operations, such as preparing 27 reports or pouring 86 columns of concrete or writing 2,000 lines of computer code. This is perhaps the most desirable statusing method because it is based on the simplest assumption—that it takes identical time to accomplish identical pieces of work. If the task consists of producing 100 items and 37 of them have been finished, the task is said to be 37% complete. Suppose now that the percents complete for each task in a work package have been computed using this quantity statusing method.

The next step is to combine these individual percent complete figures for each task to get a work package percent complete. This is done by using the following formula:

$$PC_{WP} = \Sigma_{t \in WP} (MB_t / MB_{WP}) \, PC_t$$

where

PC_{WP} = work package percent complete
PC_t = task percent complete
MB_t = task man-hour budget
MB_{WP} = work package man-hour budget

and where the summation is taken over all tasks in the work package. This formula uses the labor-hour budgets for each task divided by the labor-hour budget for the work package as the weighting factors in the summation.

The *milestone method* is often used to status work of subcontractors and, in fact, any work that does not lend itself well to the quantity statusing method. The milestone method is perhaps the least desirable statusing method because it is based on a subtle but often erroneous assumption, namely that it is possible to divide the work of a work package into a sequence of milestones and to determine the relative weight the completion of each milestone contributes to the status of the work package. Users of the milestone method often do not (or cannot) correlate the milestones to the tasks within a work package in a meaningful way. Often, the milestone estimates build a level of subjectivity into the statusing of the package, which is what the statusing method is trying to eliminate in the first place.

To see how this might work, assume that a work package is contracted out to a subcontractor and that an agreement (perhaps a contract) is reached with the subcontractor regarding how the percent complete (and, hence, the progress payments) for this work package is to be calculated. The project manager and the subcontractor agree that there will be four milestones. When the first one is reached, the work package will be considered to be 30% complete. When the second is reached, it will be considered 55% complete. When the third is reached, it will be considered 80% complete, and when all four milestones have been completed, the task will be 100% complete.

Next, suppose we want to status the tasks within the work package using the milestone method at a time when the first milestone has been completed. We want the computation to yield a work package percent complete of 30% because this was the agreed-upon value of the first milestone. We can achieve this by assigning a percent complete of 30% to each of the tasks in the work package. If we do this, the formula just presented for computing the weighted percent complete for the work package will yield a value of 30%, which is what we desire. So this is how we use the milestone method to status the tasks of a work package. The assumption here is that completion of the first milestone has the effect of causing each of the tasks in the work package to be 30% complete.

A more favorable way of applying the milestone method is in the specialized case where the work package can be quantified by these milestones. In other words, each milestone represents a task in the work package, and, therefore, labor-hour budgets exist for each milestone. This way of using milestones for statusing ensures that there is a meaningful relationship between the milestones and the tasks, that is, the milestones are the tasks. In this case, the proper weight for each milestone is the milestone man-hour budget divided by the work package man-hour budget. When used in this manner, the milestone method is called the *activity method*.

The *indirect statusing* method is normally used to status indirect labor or support activities. It is also referred to as *summary-level statusing*. It is actually the assignment of a percent complete to a work package on the basis of the percent complete of some other element in the WBS. The *indirect statusing method* is probably best explained by means of an example. Assume that the project control staff support effort for the software part of a large system development project is lumped into a single work package and that the effort is estimated based on the assumption that it will be a constant effort throughout the project. If the software part of the project is 46% complete (not counting the project control staff work), then we want this project control work package to also be 46% complete.

This situation is forced to happen by assigning the percent complete for the project control support staff work package to be the percent complete of a summary-level WBS element (control package) that is the parent of all software development work packages. If the percent complete for the project control support staff work package is to be the percent complete of this summary-level WBS element, then we must assign each task in the work package to have the same percent complete as this summary-level WBS element. This is the same situation that existed when we discussed the use of the milestone statusing method to status tasks.

The percent complete for summary-level WBS elements (control packages) has not yet been defined. It is simple, however, to extend the concept of percent complete to a control package by using the concept of weighted percent complete that has already been defined for work packages. Its formula for application at a control package level is given by:

$$PC_{CP} = \Sigma_{WP\, \varepsilon\, CP}(MB_{WP}/MB_{CP})PC_{WP}$$

where

PC_{CP} = control package percent complete
PC_{WP} = work package percent complete

MB_{WP} = work package labor-hour budget
MB_{CP} = control package labor-hour budget

and where the summation is taken over all work packages contained in the given WBS element (control package) in the hierarchical ordering.

Usually, the same status method cannot be used on all work packages. However, it is desirable that the majority of work packages on a project be statused the same way in order to promote a uniform philosophy of work (progress) measurement on the project. It is our belief that the majority of work packages on a project should be statused using the quantity method.

Modern Project can be used to support all of the statusing methods mentioned above. Let us see how this works. First, assume that a work package will be statused using the quantity statusing method. The *Progress Transactions Entry/Edit* tool (shown in Figure 3-5) gives the user three choices for entering statusing information for tasks. The most common method for entering progress information for this statusing method is to enter the number of units completed for a task in the *Qty to date* field. The Modern Project system converts this number into a

Figure 3-5. Progress Transactions Entry/Edit Tool.

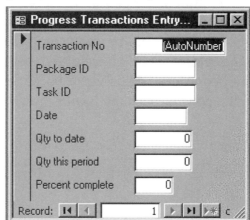

percent complete for the task by dividing it by the task's quantity budget.

If, instead, the *Qty to date* field is left blank and a number is entered into the *Qty this period* field, then Modern Project calculates the percent complete for the task a little differently. It first divides the number entered in the *Qty this period* field by the task's quantity budget. This determines the contribution to the percent complete achieved during this period. Next, it adds this contribution to the percent complete figure already in the database to get the percent complete for the task.

The third possibility is for the user to override the quantity method by entering a percent complete figure directly into the database for the task. In this case, Modern Project works backward to compute the number of units completed to produce the percent complete figure entered. It stores this number in the database, together with the percent complete figure entered. This third way of entering statusing information defeats the quantity statusing method for a task, but it is necessary in certain situations, as is explained later. If no progress has been made on a given task, then the quantity (completed) for the task should be zero.

Next, assume that a work package will be statused using the milestone method or the indirect statusing method. In either case, we already know the percent complete for the work package in advance. In the milestone method case, it is determined by how many of the milestones have already been completed and the agreement on how much each milestone is worth. With the indirect statusing method, the work package percent complete is the percent complete of the control package on which the work package is dependent. In either case, we simply enter this percent complete in the *Percent complete* field for each task in the work package.

When utilizing the indirect statusing method for a work package, the user can use one of the reporting tools that calculate status for summary level control packages (which is introduced in this chapter). The user can then determine the percent complete for the control package that the work package is linked to for statusing purposes. Then this percent complete is entered for each task in the work package to be statused.

The *Progress Transaction Entry/Edit* tool can be activated by clicking on the **Progress Transaction Entry/Edit** button on the Modern Project Main Menu. The way the data entry form works is as follows. The tool automatically (and sequentially) assigns a *transaction number*, just as in the case of the Cost/Labor Entry/Edit tool. The user does not need to be concerned with entering this information when entering a progress transaction. This transaction number is useful for identifying progress transactions at a later date.

The first information elements the user must supply are the package identifier and the task identifier. The next piece of information the user must supply is the date of the progress transaction. Finally, the user needs to enter one of the following pieces of information: *quantity to date, quantity this period*, or *percent complete*, depending on which status method is being used for this task.

If you are entering data for the example project into the example database using Modern Project, you should enter the data in Figure 3-6 now, using the Progress Transaction Entry/ Edit tool just described.

After you have entered these progress transactions, you need to update the example project database because the new status transactions affect several database tables other than the table in which the progress transactions are stored. You do this by clicking on the *Earned Value Update* control button on the Main Menu. You need to remember to do this every time you enter progress transactions. Earlier versions of Modern Project did not require the user to remember to do this because these updates were automatically performed at report time. However, this slows down report generation. The majority of users themselves prefer to control when the database is updated, since the entering of progress data usually only occurs once per reporting period while report generation often occurs several

Figure 3-6. Progress transaction data for example project.

Trans. No	Package ID	Task ID	Date	Qty to date	Qty this period	Percent complete
1	Siteprep	1	1/18/00	0	20000	0
2	Siteprep	2	1/18/00	90	0	0
3	Siteprep	2	2/1/00	240	0	0
4	Siteprep	3	2/15/00	12000	0	
5	Siteprep	3	3/1/00		0	100
6	Siteprep	4	3/15/00	260	0	0
7	Siteprep	4	3/29/00	300	0	
8	Concrete	1	4/3/00	0	0	50
9	Concrete	2	4/10/00	0	0	40
10	Concrete	3	4/22/00	0	0	30

times a day. Consequently, this mode of operation is significantly more efficient.

3.4 Progress and Status Reports

We can now produce the Progress Transaction Listing report and the Status Report. These reports can be obtained by clicking on the appropriate buttons on Modern Project's Main Menu. Figure 3-7 shows the Progress Transaction Listing and Figure 3-8 shows the Status Report. The Progress Transaction Listing is self-explanatory, but the importance of the Status Report warrants some discussion. The Status Report is actually one of the performance reports, because it includes the earned man-hours for each package and each task on the report. The concept of earned man-hours is explained in the next chapter.

What is important to notice now is that the Status Report calculates the percent complete for each control package listed on the report. Each of the percents complete for the packages is, as you will recall, a weighted percent complete. This is the report that calculates all the weighted percents complete for you at all summary levels of the WBS. In other words, this is

Figure 3-7. Progress Transaction Listing.

Progress Transaction Listing

Trans. No	Package ID	Task ID	Date	Qty to date	Qty this period	Percent complete
1	Siteprep	1	1/18/00	0	20000	0
2	Siteprep	2	1/18/00	90	0	0
3	Siteprep	2	2/1/00	240	0	0
4	Siteprep	3	2/15/00	12000	0	0
5	Siteprep	3	3/1/00	0	0	100
6	Siteprep	4	3/15/00	260	0	0
7	Siteprep	4	3/29/00	300	0	0
8	Concrete	1	4/3/00	0	0	50
9	Concrete	2	4/10/00	0	0	40
10	Concrete	3	4/22/00	0	0	30

Tuesday, January 25, 2000   *Page 1 of 1*

the report that tells you what the progress is for all the control packages. You entered progress information only for the tasks. This report calculates them for you at the package levels of the WBS.

Another interesting thing to notice is that the *Qty to Date* column of the report gives you an approximation of the actual quantities completed for each control package on the report. It does this by multiplying the percent complete for the package by the Control Quantity Budget for the package. These two progress figures, the percent complete and the quantity to date, give the project manager a sense of the real progress on each package.

3.5 Scientific Forecasting

Once work on a project is under way, the work may not progress as planned on each work package. In this section we assume that it has been determined that work is *not* progressing as planned on one or more work packages. There are three (and only three) reasons why work does not progress as planned:

Figure 3-8. Status Report.

Status Report

Hierarchy Position	Package / Task ID	Description	Quantities				Man-hours			
			Percent complete	Unit of Measure	Control Qty	Qty To Date	Control Mhrs	Earned Mhrs	Actual Mhrs	Forecast Mhrs
0	Example Proj	5000 SF Building	40	SF	5000	1990	2410	959	1060	2810
1	Foundation	Construct Foundation	40	CYC	319	127	2410	959	1060	2810
1.1	Siteprep	Site Preparation	86	SF	25000	21471	850	730	860	1250
	1	Clear & Grub	100	SF	20000	20000	80	80		80
	2	Earth Removal	50	CY	480	240	240	120		640
	3	Grading	100	SF	25000	25000	120	120		120
	4	Excavation	100	CY	300	300	410	410		410
1.2	Forms	Forms Installation &	0	SF	750	0	460	0	0	460
	1	Forms Installation		SF	825		276			276
	2	Forms Removal		SF	825		184			184
1.3	Rebar	Rebar, Mesh & Anchors	0	LBS	1000	0	528	0	0	528
	3	Anchor Bolts		LBS	110		176			176
	1	Rebar Installation		LBS	836		264			264
	2	Mesh Installation		LBS	154		88			88
1.4	Concrete	Concrete Pour, Cure &	40	CYC	319	128	572	229	200	572
	2	Cure Concrete	40	CYC	319	128	44	18		44
	3	Finish Concrete	30	SF	5588	1676	264	79		264
	1	Pour Concrete	50	CYC	319	160	264	132		264
2	Structure	Build Structure	0	SF	5000	0	0	0	0	0

Sunday, January 30, 2000

- Changes in the scope of the work
- Quantification deviations
- Productivity deviations

It may not be immediately apparent to the reader that these are the only three possibilities. However, a close inspection of the definitions of these terms that will now be given should convince the reader that there are no other possibilities. Changes in the scope of the work are redefinitions of the original requirements. They can be introduced by the client, by project management, or by those executing the work. Their basis can range from a change in policy or operating philosophy to the discovery of a better design alternative, to the change by the client of the original requirements. For instance, in the example project, the client could decide to change the requirement to a 6,000-square-foot building, instead of the original 5,000-square-foot building. Regardless of who originates a change in the scope of work, the change must be agreed to by the client and by project management. Such an agreement usually results in a change to the contract or agreement that governs the scope of the work. It is important that the reader understands that we are now talking about the agreed scope of work. This may be different from the real scope of work, as we now explain.

Changes in the scope of the work invariably involve changes in the quantification of some of the work packages. In fact, changes in the scope of the work often cause the addition of new work packages to the WBS. However, quantification deviations often arise that are independent of changes to the scope of the work.

The scope of the work may remain unchanged, and yet there may need to be changes to some of the quantifications. *Quantification deviations* are deviations that arise because of errors in the quantification process (i.e., they are estimating errors). For instance, on the example project, the Concrete work package has been quantified as 290 cubic yards of concrete. As the concrete workers begin putting up the forms into which they will pour the concrete, it may become apparent that quite a bit more concrete is going to be needed. This is an example of a quantification deviation. Instead of 290 cubic yards, 360 cubic yards may be required.

Productivity deviations arise from not accomplishing the work at the planned labor-hour per unit rate. The term *productivity deviation* includes all deviations that do not affect the quantification, such as deviations caused by late delivery by vendors or subcontractors and unforeseen scheduling conflicts. All of these can result in the productivity (output per labor-hour) being lower than planned. Consequently, all deviations that do not involve any quantification changes are considered to be productivity deviations.

If there are quantification deviations, then the real scope of work is different from the agreed scope of work. In practice, there is usually some time delay between the discovery of quantification deviations and their approval by the client and by project management as changes to the scope of the work. This is often caused by negotiations as to who is responsible for these errors and who will eventually pay for these errors. The outcome is determined by the type of contract or agreement the client and project management have entered into. Some quantity deviations are never approved by the client and as such do not become change orders.

Project management needs to distinguish among the causes of deviations from the plan for two reasons: first, management needs to understand why the work is not progressing as planned in order to know how to deal with the problem properly. Productivity and quantification deviations are dealt with in quite different ways. Applying pressure to increase productivity when the problem is errors in the quantification may introduce productivity problems where they previously did not exist.

Second, project management must distinguish among causes for deviations in order to *keep the baseline current*. This means providing an up-to-date account of the *real* scope of work and an audit trail of how the original baseline *evolved* into the current baseline. Earned value is a key measure of performance (discussed in Chapter 4), and it is always calculated from the current baseline (control budget), not the original budget. As we will see shortly, the control budget is formed from the original budget by taking all change orders and quantity deviations into consideration (but not productivity deviations). If the baseline is not kept current, the earned value computation will not be correct.

The capability to maintain multiple budgets in a formal (controlled) manner is an essential project management capability. The support that the Modern Project toolset provides for this capability is one of the features that distinguishes it from other desktop tools such as Microsoft Project. This capability is explained in what follows.

The term *variance* is used in this book to denote the *documentation of a deviation* from the plan or baseline. Note that this is not the conventional English usage of the word. It is a subtle but important distinction to use the word *deviation*, rather than variance, to denote a departure from the plan and to reserve the word *variance* to denote the documentation of the deviation. This terminology arose more than thirty years ago among those who first realized that a distinction in terms was necessary to differentiate between the concepts of variations that occur in the work plan and the documentation and tracking of these variations. At some point it was decided that the term *deviation* would be used to denote variations in the actual work, while the term *variance* would be used to denote the documentation of these variations. We use this terminology here because it is historically well established.

This terminology is extended to the phrase *variance tracking*, which means the formal process of documenting and reestimating the impact of deviations from the plan and, in some cases, obtaining project management or client approval for a change in the scope of the work. Three types of variances (documentation) correspond to the three types of deviations from the plan discussed earlier. They are:

· Change orders
· Quantification variances
· Productivity variances

Project managers often corrupt this terminology by referring to both deviations and the documentation of the deviations as variances. This leads to all kinds of confusion on projects, so in this book we are careful to distinguish between deviations and variances (the documentation of the deviations). Also, this usage of the term *variance* is not to be confused with the terms *cost variance* and *schedule variance*, which are used when dealing with the subject of Variance Analysis, presented in Chapter 4.

It is unfortunate that these seeming contradictions in terminology exist. It has a lot to do with the independent evolution in commercial and government project management styles and terminology, as is explained in Chapter 8. It also has to do with the fact that only a segment of the project management profession has recognized the significance of distinguishing among the causes of deviations from the plan and carefully documenting them in order to improve project management results. While this is a significant segment of the project management profession, it is by no means all of the project management profession.

A *change order* is a variance (documentation) that results from a client's agreeing to a change in the scope of the work. Change orders usually result in a change in the contractual agreement or addendum to it in some form. Consequently, the original contract plus all change orders represents the current contractual environment in which the work is being performed. For this reason, the original budget modified by all the new quantity and labor-hour estimates in all of the change orders has come to be known as the *client budget,* as is explained a little later in this chapter.

Variances other than change orders are designated *quantification* variances or *productivity* variances, depending upon whether they arose as a result of a quantification or productivity deviation. In practice, it is impractical to keep track of every observed quantification or productivity deviation, but significant deviations need to be documented by a variance. One relies on the so-called *Law of Compensating Error* to cancel out the effects of the smaller deviations.

Each variance must be assigned a variance number (identifier), and, in addition, change orders need to be assigned a change order number. No variance can be of more than one type (e.g., both a quantification and productivity variance). Observed deviations with both quantification and productivity components must be considered as separate deviations and documented by separate variances.

A variance can affect more than one task or cost element within a work package; it can also affect more than one work package. When this is the case, there needs to be a separate *line item* in the variance for each task and each cost element affected. Sometimes, new work packages need to be created for change orders or for quantification deviations. These work packages can have a zero original quantity or labor-hour budget (since they did not exist when the project originally started). They then obtain their budget only from the variances against them.

The *client budget* (sometimes called the *contract budget*) for a work package is the original budget together with all change orders that affect the package (change order line items that affect it). The client budget for the project is the sum of the client budgets for all the work packages that constitute the project.

The *control budget* (sometimes called the *working budget*) for a work package is the client budget together with all quantification variances affecting the work package. The control budget for the project is the sum of the control budgets for all work packages in the project. The control budget, is the budget that reflects the true scope of the work, since it has been adjusted to correct all significant quantification errors, and as such it is the budget that is used in performance measurement, as explained in Chapter 4.

Finally, the *forecast* for a work package is the control budget for the work package plus all productivity variances that affect the package. Similarly, the project forecast is the sum of the forecasts for all work packages that constitute the project. In summary, these budgets are defined by the following simple formulas:

- client budget = original budget + change orders
- control budget = client budget +
  quantification variances
- forecast = control budget + productivity variances

Figure 3-9 shows the comparison of the budgets and the forecast for a hypothetical project. Comparing the client budget to the original budget yields a summarization of the impact of

Figure 3-9. Comparison of original, client, control, and forecast budgets.

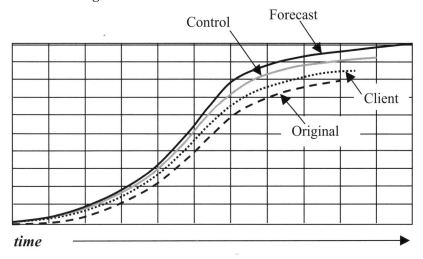

all change orders on the project budget. Comparing the control budget to the client budget gives a measure of how well the project was quantified. Poor productivity will show up in a comparison of the forecast to the control budget, but this comparison may also include the effect of forces beyond the control of project management.

Figures 3-10a, 3-10b, and 3-10c show the variances to be entered for the example project. Figure 3-10a shows the descriptions of the variances. Figure 3-10b shows the quantity and labor-hour line items for each of the variances and Figure 3-10c shows the cost line items for each of the variances. These three categories of information about a variance require three different data entry tools for their input as will be described in what follows.

Figure 3-10a. Variance descriptions for the example project.

Variance No	Variance Type	Approval Date	Change Order ID	Description
1	COR	1/11/00	A-001-00	Additional Grading & Excavation
2	QTY			Square Footage Quantity Variance
3	PRO			Earth Removal Productivity Variance

Figure 3-10b. Variance quantity and labor-hour line items.

Variance No	Package ID	Task ID	Unit of Measure	Qty	Mhrs
1	Siteprep	3	SF	5000	40
1	Siteprep	4	CY	40	50
2	Concrete	1	CY	29	24
2	Forms	1	SF	75	36
2	Rebar	1	LBS	76	24
2	Concrete	2	CY	29	4
2	Forms	2	SF	75	24
2	Rebar	2	LBS	14	8
2	Concrete	3	SF	508	24
2	Rebar	3	LBS	10	16
3	Siteprep	2	CY	0	400

Figure 3-10c. Variance cost line items.

Variance No	Package ID	Cost Account	Cost
1	Siteprep	601	$1,000.00
1	Siteprep	603	$1,200.00
1	Siteprep	651	$300.00
1	Siteprep	652	$60.00
2	Concrete	601	$920.00
2	Concrete	602	$180.00
2	Concrete	631	$1,800.00
2	Concrete	632	$90.00
2	Concrete	651	$248.00
2	Concrete	652	$16.00
2	Forms	601	$680.00
2	Forms	603	$180.00
2	Forms	632	$110.00
2	Rebar	601	$1,760.00
2	Rebar	603	$360.00
2	Rebar	631	$480.00
2	Rebar	632	$63.00
3	Siteprep	601	$7,200.00
3	Siteprep	603	$1,200.00

Notice from Figure 3-10a that there are only three different variances to enter in this example. One of them is a change order (denoted COR) in the *Variance Type* column, one of them is a quantity variance (denoted QTY), and one of them is a productivity variance (denoted PRO). So there is one variance of each type discussed earlier. But from Figures 3-10b and 3-10c it can be seen that there are several variance line items for each of these variances.

The data entry tool for entering variance descriptions is the *Variance Descriptions Entry/Edit* tool shown in Figure 3-11a. This tool is used to describe the variances to the Modern Project system. The other tools are used to enter the variance line items. If

Figure 3-11a. Variance Descriptions Entry/Edit form.

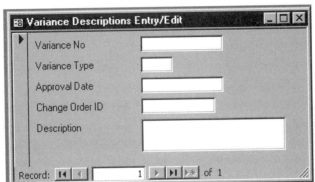

you are entering the example project data into Modern Project, you should use the Variance Desciptions Entry/Edit tool to enter the three variances shown in Figure 3-10a into the example project database now. To activate this tool, click on the **Variance Descriptions Entry/Edit** button on the Modern Project Main Menu.

The first variance to be entered (shown in Figure 3-10a) is a change order. Unlike the Cost/Labor and Progress Transaction data entry tools, the Variance Description data entry tool does not automatically assign numbers. The reason for this has to do with the design of the Modern Project system. For technical considerations having to do with ease of data entry and editing, it was decided to leave the assignment of variance numbers to the user. So enter the value "1" in the *Variance Number* field and "COR" in the *Variance Type* field. The "COR" type indicates that Variance 1 is a change order.

Change orders usually have approval dates associated with them. The approval date in this case corresponds to the date when the client approves the variance as a change order. This change order has an approval date of 1/11/00, so enter that date in the *Approval Date* field. In addition, change orders usually have a *change order identifier*. This is usually the identifier the client uses to track them, but this field could be used for other purposes or not at all. In the example, the change order

identifier is A-001–00. You should enter the change order identifier and the change order description in their corresponding
fields now.

Variances 2 and 3 in Figure 3-10a are not change orders.
Variance 2 is a quantification variance, and Variance 3 is a productivity variance. Since Variances 2 and 3 are not change orders, they do not have approval dates or change order
identifiers associated with them. You should enter these remaining two variances now.

To enter the variance quantity and labor-hour line items
into the system you need the *Variance Transactions (Qty/Mhrs)
Entry/Edit* tool. To activate this tool, click on the **Qty/Mhr Variance Entry** button on the Modern Project Main Menu. When
you select this tool you will get an entry/edit form like the one
shown in Figure 3-11b. Figure 3-11b shows that in order to
enter quantity and labor-hour line items for the individual variances, you must first enter the *Variance Number* and the *Package*
and *Task Identifiers*. This specifies which task in which work
package the variance line item being entered refers to.

The variance quantity and labor-hour line items to be entered for the three variances you previously entered into the
example project database are shown in Figure 3-10b. Variance 1
has two quantity and labor-hour line items associated with it.
They correspond to tasks 3 and 4 of the Siteprep work package.

Figure 3-11b. Variance Transactions (Qty/Mhrs) Entry/Edit form.

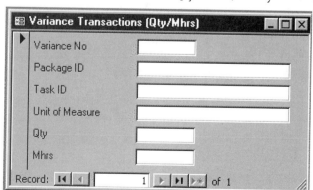

To enter the first line item, enter "1" in the *Variance Number* field, "Siteprep" in the *Package ID* field, and "3" in the *Task ID* field. This tells the variance quantity and man-hours entry tool which variance and which task this line item refers to. The rest of the fields on the form are for entering the quantity and man-hour data for this line item. Now that you know how to enter a variance quantity and labor-hour line item into the example project database, you should enter all of those shown in Figure 3-10b.

Figure 3-11c shows the form that is presented to the user by the *Variance Transactions (Costs) Entry/Edit* tool. It is used to enter the cost line items for variances. This tool is activated by clicking on the **Cost Variance Entry/Edit** button on the Modern Project Main Menu. The cost line items associated with the three variances you have already entered into the system are shown in Figure 3-10c. To enter a variance cost line item, you must first enter the *Variance Number,* the *Work Package ID* and the *Cost Account* it is associated with. This tells the cost variance entry and edit tool which variance and which cost accounts within which work package to associate this line item with.

Variance 1 has four cost line items associated with it. They are all associated with the Siteprep work package. Each variance cost line item corresponds to a different cost account. The first cost line item for Variance 1 corresponds to the 601 cost account, and the cost is $1,000. Consequently, you should enter "1" in the *Variance Number* field, "Siteprep" in the *Package ID*

Figure 3-11c. Variance Transactions (Costs) Entry/Edit form.

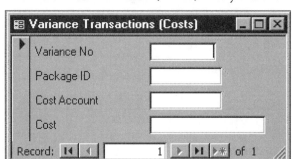

field, "601" in the *Cost Account* field, and $1,000.00 in the *Cost* field. Now enter the rest of the variance cost line items shown in Figure 3-10c.

Other changes associated with these variances also need to be made to the example project database. The first are changes to the schedule dates of the affected tasks. The second are changes to the quantifications of summary level control packages. Often a variance will cause a change to all the schedule dates of tasks associated with the line items of quantity and man-hour variances; a change in the scope, quantity, or productivity rate usually affects how long it will take to complete work on the task.

To change these start and end dates, you must enter new dates for the task, using the *Task Entry/Edit* tool discussed in Chapter 2. However, it is wise not to change the original start and end dates because once they are changed, they are lost. Then you will not be able to see what the original schedule was unless you saved the original reports. A better way is to enter new *Client start* and *Client end* dates for tasks with change orders, *Control start* and *Control end* dates for tasks with change orders or quantity variances, and *Forecast start* and *Forecast end* dates for tasks with any type of variance.

These schedule changes can be determined manually or by rerunning the scheduling system. However, trying to determine these new dates with an automated scheduling system is often tricky, as is explained in Chapter 7. First, if additional tasks have been created, these must be entered into the scheduling system. Since you probably will not want to lose your original schedule in the scheduling system, you will probably want to create a *new Control Schedule* that includes these new tasks caused by the change orders and quantity variances.

We defer changing the schedule dates in the example project database until Chapter 7, where we discuss automated scheduling in detail and introduce an automated interface between the Microsoft Project scheduling tool and the Modern Project project management toolset.

Usually project managers keep a copy of the original schedule for historical purposes but use the scheduling system to maintain the dates for the control budget. This is the budget that is used for managing the project and for computing performance and productivity data. Knowing the dates that correspond to the control budget usually allows one to calculate manually an estimate of what the client dates and forecast dates should be. Such a manual calculation is usually accurate enough for the purpose to which these dates are put. The exception might be if the client insists on performance and productivity reports based on the client schedule. In this case it might be necessary to maintain two schedules with your scheduling system. It should be noted that the version of the Modern Project system supplied with this book does not provide the capability to directly generate these reports based on the client schedule. To do this requires a method described in the following paragraph.

If a separate schedule is to be maintained for the client in accordance with the client budget, it will be necessary for you to do more than just maintain two separate schedules. To get reports for the client based on the client budget, the system will have to think that the client budget is the control budget. To do this, you will have to copy the example database (call it the *alternate* database) and remove all the quantification and productivity variances from the alternate database (using the variance entry/edit tools). Next you will also have to remove all the control start and end dates and all of the forecast start and end dates from the alternate database (using the task entry/edit tool).

After doing all this, the alternate database will have a control budget that is the same as the client budget in the example project database. Then, if you produce reports using the alternate database, the performance and productivity calculations will be made using the client budget and schedule. This is not a satisfactory method to accomplish this on a large project. But few projects will require this capability and the intent was to keep this version of the toolset simple.

Since many of the work packages may have already been complete by the time a variance is entered, it is necessary to constrain the scheduling system to use the start and end dates that actually occurred. Most scheduling systems have a capability for entering actual start and completion dates and for requiring the scheduling system to use these when they are present. This can still be a tricky undertaking. For this reason, project teams often find it easier and more accurate to manually schedule the client and forecast schedules.

The next thing project management must update when variances are entered is the summary level control package quantifications. These are updated using the WBS Entry/Edit tool. Since the units of measure at summary-level control packages can be independent of the units of measure in the lower-level control packages they contain, the determination of which control package quantifications to change and what the changes should be is often a subject of much consideration. Figure 3-12 shows the WBS Listing with the new quantifications after the variances for the example project were entered. You should update the summary level quantities in the example project database using the WBS Entry/Edit tool accordingly.

We have assumed that Variance 1, which is a change order, occurred because the client decided to have 25,000 square feet of land cleared rather than the original 20,000 recorded in the Original Budget for the Siteprep work package. Consequently, the quantification of the Siteprep work package for the Client Budget is now 25,000, whereas for the Original Budget it still is 20,000. For Variance 2, the amount of concrete to be poured increased by 29 cubic yards, or 10%. Since the original quantification for the Concrete work package was 290, and there are no change orders that affect the Concrete work package, the Client Budget quantity remains 290, but the Control Budget quantity is now 319. Variance 3 is a productivity variance, so it does not cause any quantity changes.

The question now is how to change the quantifications of the summary-level control packages that contain the Concrete

Figure 3-12. WBS Listing.

WBS Listing

WBS Position	*Package ID*	*Description*				
	Active Indicator	Unit of Measure	Original Qty	Client Qty	Control Qty	Forecast Qty
0	*Example Proj*	*5000 SF Building*				
		SF	5000	5000	5000	5000
1	*Foundation*	*Construct Foundation*				
		CY Concrete	290	290	319	319
1.1	*Siteprep*	*Site Preparation*				
		SF Land	20000	25000	25000	25000
1.2	*Forms*	*Forms Installation & Removal*				
		SF Forms	750	750	750	750
1.3	*Rebar*	*Rebar, Mesh & Anchors*				
		LBS	1000	1000	1000	1000
1.4	*Concrete*	*Concrete Pour, Cure & Finish*				
		CY Concrete	290	290	319	319
2	*Structure*	*Build Structure*				
		SF	5000	5000	5000	5000
2.1	*Frame*	*Framing & Misc. Carpentry*				
		LF Lumber	20000	20000	20000	20000
2.2	*Sheetrock*	*Sheetrock Tape, Bed & Float*				
		SF Sheetrock	10000	10000	10000	10000
2.3	*Roofing*	*Roofing*				
		SF Roofing	6000	6000	6000	6000
2.4	*Painting*	*Painting*				
		SF Surface	10000	10000	10000	10000
3	*Systems*	*Systems*				
		EA	3	3	3	3
3.1	*Plumbing*	*Plumbing*				
		EA	10	10	10	10
3.2	*Electrical*	*Electrical*				

Thursday, September 16, 1999 *Page 1 of 2*

and Siteprep work packages. Since the Foundation control package, that is, the parent package for both the Concrete and Siteprep work packages, is quantified with a unit of measure of cubic yards of concrete, it makes sense to change the quantification of the Foundation control package to 319, also. But what about the top control package for the example project? In this case we assume that, even though all of these other quantifications have changed, the project itself is still best quantified as 5,000 square feet.

It is often the case with changes in the scope of the work that the change itself is introduced at a summary level, and this drives what needs to be changed at lower levels. This is not the case with the variances we introduced for the example project, but it is nonetheless a common occurrence. Changes in the scope of the work at summary levels often cause the addition of new control packages and work packages. This can complicate the budgeting and scheduling of the project if these summary level changes are extensive.

Variances provide an audit trail that shows how the client budget, target budget, and forecast evolved from the original budget. This audit trail can be displayed or printed out in two different ways. First, the *Qty/Mhr Variance by Variance Number* report (shown in Figure 3-13) can be used to list all the variances sorted by Variance Number. Second, the *Qty/Mhr Variance by Work Package Number* report (shown in Figure 3-14) can be used to list all the variances sorted by work package identifier.

It is essential that the project manager ensure that an appropriate level of effort is expended on maintaining a meaningful variance audit trail. Maintaining such a trail is essential for obtaining meaningful performance and productivity measurement data. It is a function of project management that is often ignored, either because it is misunderstood or because of the amount of work it entails. On large projects with many changes, it often requires a level of replanning effort that approaches the level of effort required to produce the original plan.

Figure 3-13. Qty/Mhr Variances by Variance Number.

Qty/Mhr Variances by Variance Number

Variance Number	Variance Type	Package ID	Task ID	Unit of Measure	Qty	Mhrs
1	COR	Siteprep	3	SF	5000	40
1	COR	Siteprep	4	CY	40	50
2	QTY	Concrete	1	CY	29	24
2	QTY	Concrete	2	CY	29	4
2	QTY	Concrete	3	SF	508	24
2	QTY	Forms	1	SF	75	36
2	QTY	Forms	2	SF	75	24
2	QTY	Rebar	1	LBS	76	24
2	QTY	Rebar	2	LBS	14	8
2	QTY	Rebar	3	LBS	10	16
3	PRO	Siteprep	2	CY Earth	0	400

Friday, September 10, 1999   *Page 1 of 1*

Usually, even on projects with substantial changes, the changes do not come all at once. Quantification and productivity variance usually show up continuously as the work of the project unfolds. Consequently, replanning should be assumed to be a continuous process, from developing the original plan until late in the project life cycle. It is one of the project manager's most important duties to ensure that this replanning and variance documentation job is done effectively.

In conclusion of this section on variance transactions, it is necessary to point out that anytime variance transactions are entered into the example project database, you need to remember to update the database for the same reason you need to update the database after you enter progress transactions as explained in a previous section. You do this by clicking on the **Variance Update** control button on the Main Menu.

Figure 3-14. Qty/Mhr Variances by Work Package Number.

Qty/Mhr Variances by Work Package

Package ID	*Task ID*	*Variance Number*	*Variance Type*	*Unit of Measure*	*Qty*	*Mhrs*
Concrete	1	2	QTY	CY	29	24
Concrete	2	2	QTY	CY	29	4
Concrete	3	2	QTY	SF	508	24
Forms	1	2	QTY	SF	75	36
Forms	2	2	QTY	SF	75	24
Rebar	1	2	QTY	LBS	76	24
Rebar	2	2	QTY	LBS	14	8
Rebar	3	2	QTY	LBS	10	16
Siteprep	2	3	PRO	CY	0	400
Siteprep	3	1	COR	SF	5000	40
Siteprep	4	1	COR	CY	40	50

Friday, September 10, 1999 ***Page 1 of 1***

Chapter 4

Project Performance Evaluation

B efore we begin the discussion of the main topic of this chapter, it will serve us well to again recall the subdivision of project management into project planning and project execution introduced in Chapter 2. Project planning was covered in Chapter 2, and we began discussing project execution in Chapter 3. Recall that project execution was subdivided into five activities:

1. Cost accounting
2. Progress measurement
3. Variance tracking and change control
4. Performance evaluation
5. Productivity measurement

We covered the first three of these in Chapter 3. We will need two more chapters to cover the last two activities of project execution. These are activities that occupy much of a project manager's time. Project planning, while guided by the project manager, is largely performed by others on large projects. While the project manager and his immediate staff work closely with those who frame the project specification, on large projects estimators and schedulers, working under the direction of the project manager, actually develop the plan.

During project execution, cost accountants working under the direction of the project manager perform the cost accounting and often the progress measurement functions. While cost accountants often discover situations that lead to changes in the contract or the quantification of work, the same personnel that developed the project plan in the first place primarily do variance tracking and change control. The project manager guides the variance tracking and change control and approves all changes. The project manager also negotiates change orders with the client. This negotiation process is usually done with a view toward covering as many of these changes as possible with change orders.

In this chapter and the next, where we discuss performance evaluation and productivity measurement, we focus on the information project managers need to make decisions, what kinds of decisions they make, and what impact these decisions have on projects.

4.1 How Is Performance Evaluated?

Performance Evaluation is that element of project control that compares actual progress and expenditures to the project plan and identifies deviations from the plan. This identification of deviations from the plan is done in a way that isolates the problems so that solutions can be determined. Actual expenditures and the baseline (project plan) are both expressed in labor-hours spread over time, as shown in Figure 4-1. But progress is measured in percent complete, as discussed in the previous chapter. In order to measure progress in the same units as the budget (baseline) and expenditures so that comparisons can be made, one uses the concept of *earned value* (earned labor-hours). Earned value (EV_{WP}) for a work package (WP) is defined as:

$$EV_{WP} = MB_{WP} * PC_{WP}$$

where MB_{WP} denotes the work package man-hour budget and PC_{WP} denotes the work package percent complete. Conceptually, earned value represents the (man-hour) value of work accomplished relative to the (man-hour) budget. To compute earned value for a control package, one simply sums the earned value for all work packages under the given control package.

Earned value is a concept that has been in use since the 1960s by project managers and has proven to be one of the two most effective measures available to project management. The other is the measure of productivity, which is discussed in Chapter 5. The concept of earned value is perhaps the most central concept for project management because it also lies at the foundation of Variance Analysis (discussed later in this chapter) and of Productivity Measurement (discussed in Chapter 5).

A plot of earned man-hours and actual man-hours expended, compared to the baseline (plan) for a hypothetical project, is shown in Figure 4-1. In this example the baseline curve is labeled "B," the actual man-hour expenditure curve is labeled "A," and the earned man-hour curve is labeled "E." At the point in time t, the points $A(t)$, $B(t)$, and $E(t)$ on these curves represent the *baseline budget to-date*, the *actual man-hour expenditure to-date*, and the *earned man-hours to-date*, respectively.

Figure 4-1. Actual vs. Earned labor-hours plotted against the Baseline.

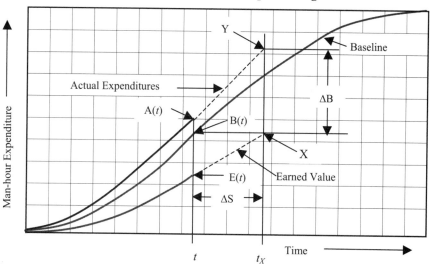

The amount $E(t) - A(t)$ is defined to be the *cost variance* for the project at time t, and the amount $E(t) - B(t)$ is defined to be the *schedule variance* at time t. Notice that both concepts of cost variance and schedule variance are measured in man-hours. It may seem strange when encountering these ideas for the first time that the schedule variance is measured in man-hours instead of time. As you read on, it should become clear why man-hours are a meaningful measure for the schedule variance.

A negative cost variance at time t implies that there is a cost overrun at t, and a negative schedule variance at time t signifies the project is behind schedule at t. Cost and schedule variances are discussed in detail in the next section, which deals with Variance Analysis. Cost and schedule variances are not to be confused with the usage of the term *variance* as introduced in Chapter 3. It is an unfortunate conflict of terminology that is often confusing to the novice, but it is a terminology that has been around for a long time, so we will not try to change it. Unfortunately, the amount $E(t) - A(t)$ is also referred to as the *productivity deviation* at time t. Fortunately, however, when it is referred to as the productivity deviation, it is in a different context than when referred to as the cost variance, so it should cause us no problems.

In Figure 4-1, the earned value graph E and the actual expenditure graph A are not tracking the baseline curve very closely. The fact that the E curve is "trailing" the B curve means the project is behind schedule. The reason for this is that at any time t, $B(t)$ man-hours' worth of work should have been accomplished, but only $E(t)$ man-hours' worth of work was actually accomplished. The fact that the E curve is trailing the A curve means that productivity on the project is less than planned, because at any time t, it took $A(t)$ man-hours to accomplish only $E(t)$ man-hours' worth of work.

When a project is not progressing as planned, a common question is: "How far behind schedule is it?" This is different from the question "What is the schedule variance?" because the schedule variance is measured in labor-hours, not time. This question can be answered (approximately) by comparing the earned value curve to the baseline curve. For example, at time t, $B(t)$ represents how much value should have been earned at time t. Drawing a horizontal line through $B(t)$ and extending the earned value curve E (linearly) until it intersects the horizontal line through $B(t)$ gives a point "X" and a corresponding time t_X at which $B(t)$ value will be earned (if progress continues at its present rate). In other words, it will take until time t_X to earn as much value (as many man-hours) as should have been earned at time t. The *schedule deviation* ΔS is given by:

$$\Delta S = t_X - t$$

This is the appropriate answer to the question. Another question is: "How much over (under) budget is the project?" One answer to this question is the cost variance defined earlier.

But another, perhaps better answer is as follows. The *overrun (underrun)* at time t is defined as $A(t) - E(t)$. It is just the negative cost variance. In Figure 4-1 we can see that $B(t)$ value (labor-hours) will not be earned until time t_X. If the actual curve is also extended (linearly) to t_X, we get a point $Y = A(t_X)$. Now Y labor-hours will have been expended by time t_X if expenditures occur at the present rate. Consequently, the *budget deviation* at t is sometimes defined as:

$$\Delta B = X - Y = B(t) - A(t_X).$$

In other words, the budget deviation is the overrun corresponding to the time t_X at which time $B(t)$ value will have been earned providing the current trend does not change.

The information obtainable from these curves lends itself well to the so-called management-by-exception philosophy. If the actual expenditure and earned value curves are tracking the baseline curve closely, the indication is that the project is progressing as planned. If they are not, corrective action may need to be taken. To determine where corrective action is needed, one relies on variance analyses, described in Section 4.3.

The summary-level control packages where the actual expenditure and earned value curves are tracking the baseline closely can be considered to be "on schedule" and "on budget." It is possible to plot these curves for each control package in the WBS from the data that the Modern Project system keeps in its database. Some projects try to do this for the higher-level control packages. But, rather than analyze lots of charts, it is usually a lot simpler to determine the problem control packages using variance analysis. This is done by looking at a report that lists all the cost and schedule variances hierarchically in accordance with the WBS.

Project management then takes action on the *exception* control packages (the ones with excessive cost or schedule variances) and assumes that all the others are under control. By using this management-by-exception approach, the project manager can focus on the important problem areas and not be inundated with minor problems.

To determine the exception control packages, project management uses the *Cost and Schedule Variance Report* discussed in Section 4.3.3. This report reveals which work packages have excessive cost and schedule variances and sums these work package variances to produce the corresponding variances for all the control packages in the WBS hierarchy.

4.2 Performance Evaluation Reports

There are several performance reports that project management needs and that Modern Project can produce. They include the following:

a. Earned Value Report (Figures 4-2 and 4-3)
b. Cost and Schedule Variance Report (Figure 4-4)

c. Schedule Performance Trend Chart (Figure 4-7)

d. Productivity Report (Chapter 5)

We discuss the *Earned Value Report* in this section. The *Cost and Schedule Variance Report* and the *Schedule Performance Trend Chart* are discussed in the sections of this chapter where they arise in the discussion. Productivity measurement and the *Productivity Report* are a big topic that we will save for Chapter 5.

The Earned Value Report for the example project at a later date is shown in Figure 4-2. We exhibit it now so the reader can see what a representative earned value report looks like. The Earned Value Report for the example project based on the data we have entered so far is shown in Figure 4-3. The Earned Value Report is the most fundamental technical tool the project manager has for evaluating performance on the project. It can be produced by clicking on the **Earned Value Chart** button on the Main Menu.

We have already discussed the mechanics of producing the Earned Value Report, and from that discussion it is clear that

Figure 4-2. Earned Value Report (later data) for example project.

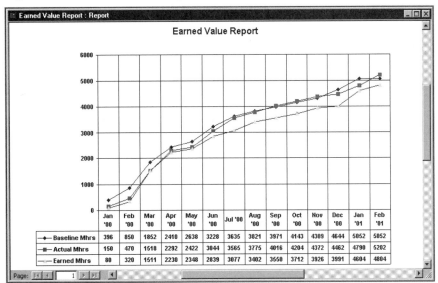

	Jan '00	Feb '00	Mar '00	Apr '00	May '00	Jun '00	Jul '00	Aug '00	Sep '00	Oct '00	Nov '00	Dec '00	Jan '01	Feb '01
Baseline Mhrs	396	850	1852	2410	2638	3228	3635	3821	3971	4143	4309	4644	5052	5052
Actual Mhrs	150	470	1518	2292	2422	3044	3565	3775	4016	4204	4372	4462	4790	5202
Earned Mhrs	80	320	1511	2230	2348	2839	3077	3402	3550	3712	3926	3991	4604	4804

Figure 4-3. Earned Value Report (earlier data) for example project.

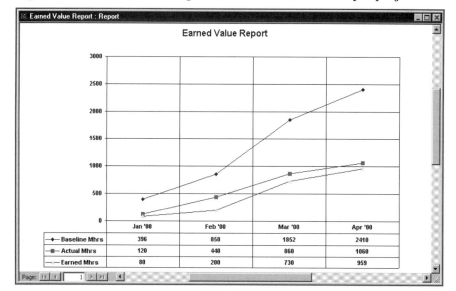

this report would be difficult to produce manually for a large project. Fortunately, project management systems exist that produce these kinds of reports automatically, just as we have scheduling systems that produce scheduling charts automatically.

What we need to discuss now is how the project manager uses the Earned Value Report in conjunction with the Cost and Schedule Variance Report. While it is possible to make updates to the actual expenditure, progress, and variance transactions at any time using the Modern Project transaction entry/edit tools, thereby affording the ability to continually update the Earned Value Report, it does not usually happen this way on a real project. The various project monitoring transactions are usually entered into the system on a periodic basis that agrees with the project reporting cycle. Cost accountants work from time-sheet summaries and other data sources that tend to be periodic in nature. So the project manager customarily gets an update of the Earned Value Report weekly or monthly.

In the fortunate situation where the earned and actual curves are tracking the baseline curve closely, there is nothing for the project manager to do in the way of taking corrective action. The project manager's time can then be spent on the host of other project management responsibilities, such as team building, optimizing project logistics, or optimizing the project schedule.

In the case where either the actual expenditure curve or the earned value curve is not tracking the baseline curve closely enough, the project manager needs to evaluate what is causing this situation. The Cost and Schedule Variance Report is used to isolate the control packages that are causing this situation to occur. This process is explained in more detail in the next section.

An important consideration for the project manager is the dissemination of this project performance data in the Earned Value Report and in the Cost and Schedule Variance Report. Many project management teams keep a close hold on project performance information, especially if it is negative. They fear possible repercussions from their management or from the client. But the author has found that wide dissemination of the project performance reports often contributes to the success of a project. If everyone on the project has a copy of the Earned Value Report and the Cost and Schedule Variance Report, everyone can see how everyone else is doing. With everyone's performance evaluation out in the open, there is a tendency for everyone to compete to have the best performance.

Also, with the performance evaluation information out in the open, large performance fluctuations do not come as a surprise to higher levels of management because they can see the trends begin to unfold. In fact, if upper management is kept aware of the trend on projects, it may be able to direct additional key resources to the project to turn unfavorable trends around before they become unmanageable. In short, the competent project manager usually has nothing to fear and a lot to gain by wide dissemination of the project performance evaluation reports.

Lower-level managers who are responsible for the execution of control packages need to know the cost and schedule variances for the control packages for which they are responsible. So, whether or not the performance evaluation reports are distributed widely on the project, the control package managers must at least be aware of them. Another approach to handling the distribution of performance evaluation information is as follows. The project manager discusses the performance of each control package with the control package manager and allows the control package managers to share the information about their own performance to lower-level managers below them and so on down the organizational hierarchy. This way, everyone knows what his or her own performance evaluation is, even if performance information about the overall project is not disseminated widely throughout the project. Moreover, under this scheme the higher up one is in the project's management hierarchy, the more one knows about the overall performance evaluation data on the project.

4.3 Variance Analysis

Variance Analysis is the term given to the project management activity that might be better titled "problem identification." Two concepts that are fundamental to problem identification are the *cost variance* and the *schedule variance*; hence the title "Variance Analysis." Recall that the cost variance at time t for the total project is $E(t) - A(t)$ in Figure 4-1 and the schedule variance at time t is defined to be $E(t) - B(t)$. If a control package manager knows the cost variance and the schedule variance for his or her control package, then the control package manager knows whether or not the package is progressing as planned.

4.3.1 Cost Variances

The cost variance for a work package is defined as the earned man-hours for the package minus the actual man-hour expenditure for the package. The cost variance can be expressed in either dollars or labor-hours, but in this book we consider only cost variances expressed in labor-hours. Since the earned man-hours and the actual man-hour expenditure (actual man-hours) for a control package can be obtained by summing all the earned and actual man-hours of the work packages contained in the given control package, it follows that this is also true for the cost variance.

In other words, the cost variance for a summary-level control package is the sum of all the cost variances of the work packages that are contained in the given control package. Consequently, it is possible to have cost variances from different work packages that effectively *cancel each other out* at a summary-level control package in which they are all contained. In other words, it is possible that the overall cost performance goals of a project are being met even though they are not being met at the work package level.

The tendency of variances to cancel each other is referred to as the *Law of Compensating Error* in the project management world. Successful managers of large projects tend to rely on the Law of Compensating Error to help them meet their performance goals, because on large projects, there is not enough time to analyze every deviation from the plan. Managers of large projects normally adopt a *management-by-exception* philosophy. They look at performance measures (such as cost and schedule variances) at summary levels, and, if they are acceptable at the summary level, they often do not attempt to analyze the problem further.

It is only in the case where performance at the summary level is not acceptable that further analysis is necessary, and this is one of the advantages of the cost variance: it can be examined at any level of the WBS hierarchy. Normally, the cost variance at the top level is observed by comparing the earned man-hours and actual man-hour expenditure on an earned value plot, as shown in Figure 4-2. Project management relies heavily on these plots because they show a good deal more about performance of the project than just the cost variance. Then, if it is determined that there is an unacceptable total cost variance at the top level of the project WBS, more information is needed to isolate the problem(s).

What is needed at this point is a listing of all the cost variances of all the control packages. Such is the *Cost and Schedule Variance Report*, discussed in Section 4.3.3. But, before we discuss this report, a discussion of the schedule variance is in order.

4.3.2 Schedule Variances

The schedule variance is defined, for each control package in the WBS, as the earned man-hours minus the budgeted man-hours to-date. For the total project this is $E(t) - B(t)$, as shown in Figure 4-1. In Figure 4-1, the project schedule variance at time t is negative. This negative amount indicates how many man-hours it will take (at the planned productivity rate) to earn enough man-hours to catch up to where the project should be at the current time.

Figure 4-1 also shows a schedule deviation ΔS expressed in time, rather than in man-hours. We can translate between the man-hours version of the schedule variance and the time version of the schedule deviation by means of the *slope* of the earned man-hours curve for *any* control package. The slope of the earned man-hours curve for any control package is simply the schedule variance of the control package divided by its schedule deviation. The geometrical meaning of the slope is as follows. In Figure 4-1 the slope of this earned man-hours curve E at time t (for the total project control package) is simply the tangent of the angle φ that a straight line tangent to the curve E at the point $E(t)$ makes with the x-axis (time axis). Whether or not you understand what the angle φ or the tangent of φ (*tan* φ) means, it suffices to understand the following formulas:

SV = ΔS * *tan* φ   (SV means schedule variance of control package)

$$\Delta S = SV/tan \; \phi$$
$$tan \; \phi = SV/\Delta S$$

So, if we know any two of these three terms (SV, ΔS, *tan* ϕ), we can compute the third term. For instance, in Figure 4-1 we know SV and ΔS for the total project, so we can calculate the tangent to the E curve at the time *t* by dividing SV by ΔS.

The schedule variance is somewhat more complex than the cost variance. All that was said about the cost variance—the tendency of variances to cancel one another, the Law of Compensating Error, and the analysis of variances at greater levels of detail when a variance proves to be unacceptable at some summary level control package—applies equally well to schedule variances.

But there is another aspect of the schedule variance that needs to be discussed. An acceptable schedule variance at the total project level or at some summary level control package means only that "overall" the work considered at this level is being accomplished at or better than the planned rate. It does not mean that tasks on the *critical path* (critical subnet) of the schedule are being accomplished on schedule. We have not yet discussed the meaning of the term "critical path" or its significance. This is covered in Chapter 7. But at this point we can point out that the tasks on the critical path play a role in determining whether or not the project will complete on schedule.

Conversely, accomplishing the tasks on the critical path on schedule does not imply that the total work content will ultimately be accomplished as planned. Both the schedule variances and the accomplishment of tasks on the critical path are important measures of project performance with respect to the schedule. The schedule variance is a more global measure of schedule performance, whereas the critical path is a more local measure of schedule performance at any level in the WBS. The critical path can almost always be changed by resequencing the work, whereas the schedule variance is often the measure of a fundamental resource or productivity problem.

4.3.3 Variance Reporting

In this section we discuss the *Cost and Schedule Variance Report* and two other reports (charts) that are closely related. These are the *Cost Performance Trend Chart* and the *Schedule Performance Trend Chart*. These charts are not, strictly speaking, variance reports but are based on related concepts, namely the *cost performance ratio* and the *schedule performance ratio*. These concepts are closely related to the concepts of cost variance and schedule variance. We discuss these concepts later in this section.

The Cost and Schedule Variance Report is shown in Figure 4-4. It can be produced by clicking on the **Cost/Schedule Variance Report** button on the Main Menu. This report shows the cost variance and the schedule variance for each control package in the WBS hierarchy. This is the performance report that is of particular interest to the control package managers on large projects. In the old days (when project management systems ran on mainframe computers and project control reports were printed on line printers), the Cost and Schedule Variance Reports usually had page breaks after each control package. This way, the reports could be easily separated so that each control package manager could get the part of the report that corresponded to his or her individual responsibility.

Modern Project does not provide this capability, since in this age of personal computers and workstations it is possible to share copies of Modern Project databases (e.g., via diskettes, via e-mail attachments, or directly over a network). In this way individual project team members are able to scan these reports on-line rather than print them out, or they can selectively print only the pages they need.

As previously mentioned, the Cost and Schedule Variance Report is tailored for management-by-exception. Each control package manager can use it to see how his or her control packages are performing. If their performance is acceptable, the manager can elect to look no further; if not, the manager can observe the cost and schedule variances at the next lower level

Figure 4-4. Cost and schedule variance report for example project.

Cost and Schedule Variance Report

Hierarchy Position	Package ID	Cost Variance	Schedule Variance
0	Example Proj	19	-1331
1	Foundation	19	-1331
1.1	Siteprep	-10	0
1.2	Forms	0	-460
1.3	Rebar	0	-528
1.4	Concrete	29	-343
2	Structure	0	0
2.1	Frame	0	0
2.2	Sheetrock	0	0
2.3	Roofing	0	0
2.4	Painting	0	0
3	Systems	0	0
3.1	Plumbing	0	0
3.2	Electrical	0	0
3.3	HVAC	0	0

Sunday, September 19, 1999   *Page 1 of 1*

in the WBS hierarchy in search of the offending control package(s). This process can be repeated recursively until all the offending work packages are isolated. With the help of this information, the control package manager can begin the process of planning how to recover from this situation.

4.3.4 The Cost Performance Ratio

In addition to the Earned Value Chart and the Cost and Schedule Variance Report, project management also uses the *Cost Per-*

formance Trend Chart and the *Schedule Performance Trend Chart* to measure cost and schedule performance. These two reports are based on the concepts of the *cost performance ratio* and the *schedule performance ratio.*

While the cost variance for the project at time *t* is defined to be the difference between the earned man-hours and the actual man-hours expended, the Cost Performance Ratio (CPR) is defined to be the ratio of the earned man-hours to the actual man-hours expended at time *t*:

$$CPR(t) = E(t)/A(t)$$

where *CPR(t)* is the cost performance ratio for the project at time *t*, *E(t)* is the earned man-hours at time *t* and *A(t)* is the actual man-hours expended at time *t*, as depicted in Figure 4-1.

Figure 4-5 shows the Cost Performance Trend Chart for the example project. It consists of two curves, the *total* or *cumulative* cost performance ratio curve for the total project and the *period*

Figure 4-5. Cost Performance Trend Chart (early data) for example project.

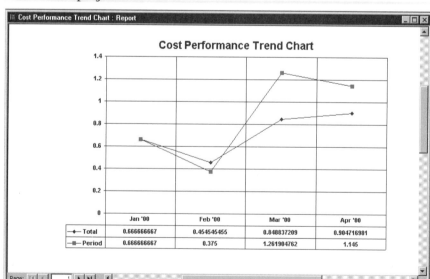

cost performance ratio curve for the project. The curve with the diamond-shaped markings is the *cumulative* cost performance ratio curve, and the curve with the square marks is the *period* cost performance ratio curve for the project. Both of these curves are plotted with respect to time *t*. This chart can be produced by clicking on the **Cost Performance Chart** button on the Main Menu.

At any time *t* the cumulative cost performance ratio is just *CPR(t)*. The so-called period cost performance trend curve is the cost performance ratio for each period (e.g., each week or month). If *t* represents time at the end of some month *m* and *t*-1 represents time at the end of the previous month, then the period cost performance ratio at time *t*, denoted *PCPR(t)*, is defined by:

$$PCPR(t) = \frac{[E(t) - E(t\text{-}1)]}{[A(t) - A(t\text{-}1)]}$$

It is common for the period cost performance ratio curve to be somewhat erratic, especially at the beginning of a project when the staffing of the project is ramping up and project team members are learning how to work with each other. To get an idea of what a typical Cost Performance Trend Chart looks like, we have also included, in Figure 4-6, a version of this chart for the example project at a later period of time.

Even if the period cost performance ratio curve remains erratic over time, on a well-managed project the cumulative cost performance ratio curve should approach the value 1 asymptotically, because in the long run, the actual man-hour expenditure should be approximately the same as the earned man-hours. It should be clear to the reader that a cost performance ratio that is greater than 1 is "good," while a cost performance ratio less than 1 is considered "bad." Consequently, project management looks to the Cost Performance Trend Chart and to the Schedule Performance Trend Chart to see if these ratios are tending toward the value of 1.

Figure 4-6. Cost Performance Trend Chart (later data) for example
              project.

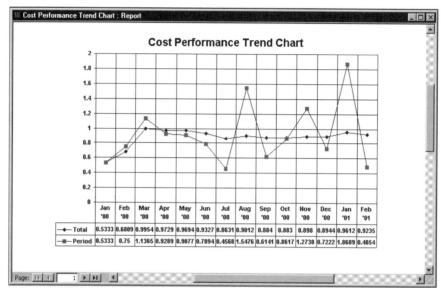

4.3.5 The Schedule Performance Ratio

Similarly, the Schedule Performance Ratio (SPR) for the project
at time t is defined to be the ratio of the earned man-hours to
the budgeted man-hours to-date at time t:

$$SPR(t) \;=\; E(t)/B(t)$$

where SPR(t) is the schedule performance ratio for the project
at time t, $E(t)$ is the earned man-hours at time t, and $B(t)$ is the
earned man-hours at time t.

   The Schedule Performance Trend Chart for the example
project is shown in Figure 4-7. It can be produced by clicking
on the **Schedule Performance Chart** button on the Main Menu.
As with the cumulative cost performance trend ratio, the cumulative schedule performance trend ratio for the total project is
just SPR(t) for each time t, so the cumulative schedule performance trend curve is just the graph of the function SPR(t).

Figure 4-7. Schedule Performance Trend Chart for example project.

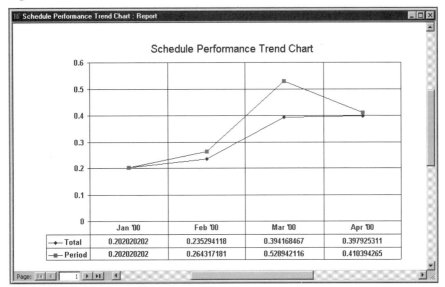

Schedule Performance Trend Chart : Report

Schedule Performance Trend Chart

	Jan '00	Feb '00	Mar '00	Apr '00
Total	0.202020202	0.235294118	0.394168467	0.397925311
Period	0.202020202	0.264317181	0.528942116	0.410394265

Similarly, the so-called period schedule performance ratio at some time *t* that represents the end of some month *m* is defined to be:

$$PSPR(t) = \frac{[E(t) - E(t - 1)]}{[B(t) - B(t - 1)]}$$

where $t - 1$ represents the end of the previous month. Everything that was said about the cost performance ratio is applicable to the schedule performance ratio. However, just because the schedule performance ratio curve is tending toward the value 1, we cannot conclude that tasks that are on the critical path of the schedule are all being executed on schedule. Conversely, the accomplishment of the tasks on the critical path on schedule does not necessarily mean the schedule performance ratio curve will eventually tend to 1. Either of these measures of schedule performance could signal schedule problems in the future.

Chapter 5

Productivity Measurement

In Chapter 4, we discussed the earned value approach to project performance evaluation and the variance analysis approach to performance problem isolation. Project managers have used the earned value approach to performance evaluation since the 1960s. But the importance of productivity measurement was not recognized this early. One of the earliest papers to clarify the importance of productivity measurement was the author's 1984 paper "Managing Software Development Projects for Maximum Productivity," which appeared in the *IEEE Transactions on Software Engineering* (Vol. SE-10, January, pp. 27–35). This paper was based on ideas that grew out of discussions with T. Lance Barlow and W. Douglas Tiner during the 1970s.

At that time monitoring the cost performance ratio and the schedule performance ratio, discussed in Chapter 4, was not widely practiced even though these concepts had been introduced in the project management literature earlier than this. At Brown and Root, where the author was working at that time, a few projects were tracking the cost performance ratio and the schedule performance ratio. Also at that time, the relationship between the cost performance ratio and productivity was not clearly understood. By the mid-1970s, some projects were using the rudimentary productivity measurement method of comparing achieved *unit rates* for tasks with the *budgeted unit rates*, as is explained in the next section. But, since this measure involved quantification, it was not clear how this technique could be generalized to summary-level control packages in the WBS, since the unit of measure for a control package is independent of the units of measure for the tasks it contains.

Also at that time, it was not understood that budget variances, as defined in Chapter 3, should be separated into quantification variances and productivity variances. This caused the earned value calculations to be performed in a nonuniform manner over the project lifetime, because the budget that project management was using for project control was continually being corrupted by the addition of productivity variance components. This tended to make the earned value look better as the productivity got worse. Nor was it understood that productivity measurement should be undertaken systematically for the purpose of discovering the cause of productivity deviations.

Since that time, the author has made progress in clarifying these concepts both in papers and in project management computer systems for personal computers. The first of these project management systems was copyrighted in 1983 but not distributed widely. It had much of the functionality of the Modern Project toolset provided with this book. But the limitations of 1983-vintage personal computer technology made it somewhat harder to use than Modern Project. This early version was enhanced in the mid-1980s and used in the management of the Space Station Data Management System (DMS) testbed program. Recently it has been totally rewritten, and this new version is Modern Project.

5.1 Unit Rates

In the early days of the modern project management era, the idea of comparing actual unit rates to budgeted unit rates was already in use, although it was not practiced widely. For instance, at Brown and Root in the mid-1970s, we found that only a handful of the scores of projects managed used this technique at that time. To understand this technique, it is necessary to understand what is meant by unit rates. The dictionary definition of productivity is "output per man-hour." Since tasks have both a quantity budget and a man-hour budget, we can divide the quantity budget by the man-hour budget to get a (budgeted) "quantity per man-hour" ratio, which is the planned productivity for the task.

Notice that this definition of planned productivity for the task involves the quantification of the task in a particular unit of measure. Since there may be several tasks with different units of measure in a work package, it is not immediately clear how we could give a corresponding definition of productivity for the work package that could be calculated from the productivity ratios of the individual tasks contained in the work package. This is because, in general, the unit of measure for the work package is different from at least one of the units of measure of the tasks that constitute the work package.

For some reason, rather than defining a productivity measure by dividing the quantity budget by the man-hour budget, early practitioners of the unit rate method divided the task man-hour budgets by the quantity budgets to get a *unit rate* measure instead. This unit rate measure is a "man-hour per quantity" ratio, instead of a quantity per man-hour ratio. It is referred to as the (budgeted) *unit rate* for the task. It is the planned number of man-hours necessary to complete a single unit of work in the task's unit of measure. Consequently, the unit rate for a task is simply the inverse of the planned productivity for the task.

Why early productivity measurement evolved in this backward manner is not clear. The author is familiar with papers from the 1970s time frame that explain this unit rate method, but when it first began and how it evolved to the state in which it existed in the 1970s is not known to the author. In what follows we will refer to this unit rate as the *budgeted unit rate* in order to distinguish it from the *actual unit rate* that we will now define.

The actual unit rate for a task is defined to be the ratio obtained by dividing the actual man-hours expended by the number of units completed in the task's unit of measure. If the task is being statused by the quantity method (explained in Chapter 3), then the number of units completed is what is being reported periodically in order to compute the task's percent complete. If the task is being statused by some other method, the task's percent complete is being entered directly into the Progress Transaction Entry/Edit tool, as discussed in Chapter 3. Consequently, the system can compute a "number of units completed" figure, say n, by multiplying the task's quantity budget by the task's percent complete. To summarize, the actual unit rate AUR_t for a task t is computed using the following formula:

$$AUR_t = AM_t/[QB_t * PC_t]$$

where AM_t is the actual man-hours expended for the task t, QB_t is the quantity budget for t, and PC_t is the percent complete for t. The actual unit rate for a task is then a measure of the actual productivity for a task in the same sense that the budgeted unit rate is a measure of the planned productivity for the task. Namely, it is the inverse of actual productivity.

It is natural to think of comparing the actual unit rates to the budgeted unit rates to see if the budgeted unit rates are actually being achieved. Since the planned unit rate is the inverse of the planned productivity, we should interpret the actual unit rate as the inverse of the actual productivity. Consequently, comparing the actual unit rate with the budgeted unit rate is the inverse of comparing the actual productivity to the budgeted productivity. Therefore, if we compare the budgeted unit rate to the actual unit rate instead, we are then comparing the actual productivity to the planned productivity.

For this reason, the author defined the *productivity ratio PR$_t$* for a task *t* as follows:

$$PR_t = BUR_t / AUR_t$$

It will be seen in the next section that working with the productivity ratio has more favorable properties than working with unit rates, and that the productivity ratio can also be calculated in such a way that we can generalize the concept so that it applies to control packages as well.

To conclude this section on unit rates, there are still a couple of points that need to be mentioned. First, the budgeted unit rates are always calculated from the control budget for the same reasons that the earned values are always calculated from the control budget. Moreover, if the budget we used to compute the unit rates included productivity variances, then the man-hour budgets would contain man-hours generated from performing the work at a different productivity rate than was planned. This would make the budgeted unit rates tend toward the actual unit rates, giving the impression that the planned unit rates were being achieved, when in fact they were not. This is another reason why it is important to segregate quantity variances from productivity variances and have separate budgets that incorporate these different variance components.

This leads us to the next point about unit rates. In addition to the budgeted unit rate and the actual unit rate, it is possible to introduce the concept of the forecast unit rate. This concept was introduced in my 1984 IEEE paper. The forecast unit rate *FUR$_t$* for a task *t* is defined as follows:

$$FUR_t = FMB_t / FQB_t$$

where *FMB$_t$* denotes the forecast man-hour budget for the task *t* and *FQB$_t$* denotes the forecast quantity budget. The forecast unit rate for a task *t* represents a projection of what the actual rate will be at completion of the task. Consequently, one would expect to see the actual unit rates less than or equal to the fore-cast unit rates. If, for a particular task this is not the case, there must either exist some explanation why project management believes the actual unit rate at completion will not exceed the forecast unit rate, or else this task is a candidate for having a new productivity variance issued against it.

5.2 The Productivity Ratio

An important fact about the productivity ratio PR_t for a task t is that it can be defined equivalently as:

$$PR_t = EM_t/AM_t$$

where EM_t denotes the earned man-hours for the task t and AM_t denotes the actual man-hours expended for t. This can be seen from the following calculation:

$$PR_t = \frac{BUR_t}{AUR_t} = \frac{MB_t/QB_t}{AM_t/[QB_t * PC_t]} = \frac{MB_t * PC_t}{AM_t} = \frac{EM_t}{AM_t}$$

This calculation is based on factoring out the quantity budget QB_t for the task t in both the numerator and denominator of the term PR_t. Factoring out the quantity budget QB_t is an important reformulation of the productivity ratio because it makes it inde-pendent of the task's quantification and defines it strictly in terms of man-hours. This is the needed generalization to apply the concept to the work packages and control packages of the WBS. Moreover, it allows us to compute the productivity ratio for a work package or control package from the information contained in the lower level components that comprise the package. Therefore, we define the productivity ratio PR_P for any package P in the WBS as:

$$PR_P = EM_P/AM_P$$

where EM_P denotes the earned man-hours for the package P and AM_P denotes the actual man-hours expenditure for P.

We have already encountered the ratio EM_P/AM_P for a package P in Chapter 4 in the case where the package was the top-level package for the project. In that case it was called the *cost performance ratio* for the project. So the productivity ratio for a total project is simply the cost performance ratio for the project. Now, however, we have a way to measure productivity for each package in the WBS.

5.3 The Productivity Report

A copy of the *Productivity Report* for the example project is shown in Figure 5-1. The Productivity Report plays the same role for the Cost Performance Trend Chart as the Cost and Schedule Variance Report does for the Earned Value Chart. If the Earned Value Chart reveals an unfavorable trend, project management needs a way of isolating the work packages that are causing this unfavorable trend. For this purpose, project management uses the Cost and Schedule Variance Report to locate the work packages with unfavorable cost or schedule variances.

Similarly, if the Cost Performance Trend Chart reveals an unfavorable trend, project management needs a way to isolate the offending work packages. For this purpose project management can use the Productivity Report. It should be apparent from the definition of the productivity ratio (earned man-hours divided by actual man-hours expended) that the productivity ratio for any package in the WBS can be calculated from the earned and actual man-hours from the packages or tasks that it contains.

Consequently, the Productivity Report lends itself to the management-by-exception philosophy, since, if the productivity ratio is favorable for any control package in the WBS, the package manager can choose to ignore all productivity infor-

Figure 5-1. Example Productivity Report for example project.

Productivity Report

Hierarchy Position	*Package ID*	*Productivity*
0	Example Proj	90%
1	Foundation	90%
1.1	Siteprep	85%
1.2	Forms	0%
1.3	Rebar	0%
1.4	Concrete	115%
2	Structure	0%
2.1	Frame	0%
2.2	Sheetrock	0%
2.3	Roofing	0%
2.4	Painting	0%
3	Systems	0%
3.1	Plumbing	0%
3.2	Electrical	0%
3.3	HVAC	0%

Tuesday, January 27, 2000   *Page 1 of 1*

mation at lower levels. The argument for this is based on the Law of Compensating Errors discussed in Chapter 4. That the Law of Compensating Errors applies to the productivity ratios follows from knowing that the information used to calculate the task productivity ratios is the same information that is used to calculate the productivity ratio for the packages that contain them.

5.4 The Importance of Productivity Measurement

More than anything else on a project, productivity is the thing a project manager can manage once the actual work of the project has begun. In a sense, the project manager cannot manage quantification deviations or changes in the scope of the work. Quantification deviations are ultimately caused by estimating errors by those who have estimated the work. They are already there waiting to be discovered. Also, changes in the scope of the work either are introduced by the client or are discoveries that significant design or specification options were either overlooked or have become available through new technologies or methods. The project manager can do little about any of these types of deviations on a day-to-day basis.

But productivity is something that is happening day by day. Moreover, project expenditures on labor are usually the dominant cost component on a project. It is through enhancing productivity that a project manager can increase project performance and build a cushion against unperceived difficulties down the road. While the project manager often oversees the development of the project plan, it is frequently the case that a business development department within a company develops the project plan and the project manager is not selected until after the contract is successfully negotiated. In such cases the project manager has little to no control over the original estimates of time and resources. Also, the project manager often has little influence over the final negotiated rates for materials and equipment. These expenditures are often determined by purchasing departments or internal equipment management departments.

The experienced project manager knows that the primary resource over which he or she has control is the labor resource. It is the productivity ratio that measures how well this resource is being put to use. While productivity can be influenced by factors outside the project manager's control, such as inclement weather and slow materials and equipment arrivals, it is often the case that productivity is largely influenced by the motivation of the workforce.

On large projects that span long periods of time, the project manager has an extended opportunity to motivate the workforce and to enhance productivity. On high-technology projects, productivity can often be enhanced by judicious expenditures on automation support and training. Even on low-technology projects in the construction industry, it has been found that workers respond positively to the perception that they are learning something new on the job. On large projects, workers' salaries go on for long periods of time. The cost of short courses to improve worker skills at company expense (perhaps after working hours) can often be offset by improved productivity. In short, the project manager needs to study the possibilities for improving productivity for the specific situation at hand. The productivity ratio is only the measure. It can tell if the actual productivity exceeds or trails the planned productivity. How to improve productivity depends on the creativity of the project manager.

Chapter 6

Alternate Views

It was mentioned in Chapter 2 that there are subdivisions of the work for a project other than the WBS that are of interest. In Chapter 2, Organizational Breakdown Structures (OBS) and Product Breakdown Structures (PBS) were mentioned as examples. These alternate breakdown structures are essentially different *views* of the project from different perspectives. While the WBS view of the project, which views the project from the perspective of how the work will be accomplished, is essential for performance evaluation, there are other views of the project that are also useful.

It is therefore desirable for project personnel to get reports from their project management system that are organized around these alternate views of the project. Modern Project, the project management toolset supplied with this book, has been design to do this. The design philosophy for this capability was to make available to the project personnel an unlimited capability to organize their project reports.

In order to allow unlimited capability for organizing project data and at the same time keep the Modern Project toolset simple, it was decided to base all hierarchically organized reports on general algorithms that are independent of which hierarchy is being used at the moment. The idea is to have a single database and to switch in alternate hierarchies as needed for generating reports rather than preplan what hierarchical relationships are needed and then build them into the database.

Also, to keep the Modern Project toolset simple, it was decided to use the Microsoft Access export facility for moving hierarchy tables in and out of the database. This requires the user to maintain another database that houses the alternate hierarchy tables. Then, when you want to generate reports organized around an alternate hierarchy, you just export that hierarchy table into your database and rename it WBS. The Modern Project reporting algorithms know to always base their reports on a hierarchy that is located in a database table named WBS. Therefore, whichever alternate hierarchy happens to be residing in the WBS table at any given time is how the requested reports are organized.

The rest of this chapter is devoted to constructing an alternate hierarchy, building a separate database for housing both the example project WBS and this other hierarchy, and demonstrating how to generate reports based on either of these hierarchies. Before we introduce an alternate hierarchy, we first complete the task list for all the work packages in the WBS hierarchy that we already have in order to make it a more interesting example.

6.1 Expanding the Task List

You will recall from Chapter 2 that, while the WBS hierarchy that was entered into the example project database was complete, not all the tasks for all the work packages in that hierarchy were entered. This was intended to keep the data input simple at that time so that we could get on with the other topics of project management. Now that we have finished the core chapters on what project management is and how the Modern Project toolset supports it, we have the leisure to go back and tie up some of the loose ends.

It is difficult to get a realistic idea of what project reporting consists of on a real-world project with such a small example. It may also be difficult to visualize the difference in views, since the different views are seen in the reports (the views essentially reorganize the reports).

We now complete the model project by entering more data. The additional data will specify the additional tasks required to complete the project as well as the associated cost, status, and variance data. This expansion in the size of the example project data will give us a better realization of project reporting and also allow us to better visualize the different views in the project reports.

In order to save you the effort of entering all this new data, another example database has been included on the electronic medium provided with this book that has this new data in it. This database is titled *exampleChapt6.mde* since it is a copy of how the example project database should look at the end of Chapter 6. You will want to start using this database from now on. Figure 6-1 shows the additional tasks added to the example database. You will notice from Figure 6-1 that schedule dates are also specified for each new task.

You may be wondering where these quantity and man-hour budgets and schedule dates came from, since we have not yet discussed quantification, sequencing, estimating, and scheduling of these new tasks. For the time being, you should just assume that all these activities were done and that Figure 6-1 represents the result of these activities. In Section 6.3 we discuss the estimating assumptions for these new tasks. In Chapter 7 we discuss how the new schedule was arrived at, including how to prepare work-sequencing charts and project schedules using Microsoft Project.

Now that we have completed the task list, we have man-hour budgets for work packages that extend further out in time. Consequently, we should obtain an updated copy of the project baseline. Recall that the baseline chart can be displayed by clicking on the **Baseline Chart** button on the Main Menu for the Modern Project system. When you do this you should get a display that looks like Figure 6-2.

Figure 6-1. Additional tasks added to the example project database.

Package ID	Task ID	Description	UOM	Orig. Qty	Orig. Mhrs	Orig. Start	Orig. End
Electrical	1	Main Breaker Boxes	EA	2	40	8/15/00	8/21/00
Electrical	2	Install Outlets	EA	112	80	8/23/00	9/7/00
Electrical	3	Install Light Fixtures	EA	47	120	9/11/00	9/29/00
Electrical	4	Interior Wiring	LF	2140	120	10/2/00	10/20/00
Electrical	5	Install Appliances	EA	12	42	10/24/00	10/27/00
Frame	1	Cap Foundation	SF	5000	80	5/15/00	5/19/00
Frame	2	Erect Stud Walls	LF	1000	120	5/22/00	6/2/00
Frame	3	Erect Roof	SF	6000	80	6/5/00	6/14/00
Frame	4	Exterior Walls and Siding	SF	10000	160	6/15/00	6/26/00
Frame	5	Install Moldings	LF	680	120	1/15/01	1/24/01
Frame	6	Install Cabinets	EA	12	240	12/14/00	1/10/01
HVAC	1	Air Handling Units	EA	3	78	6/30/00	7/10/00
HVAC	2	Ducts and Vents	LF	880	120	7/12/00	7/27/00
HVAC	3	Install Plenums	EA	6	90	7/13/00	8/10/00
HVAC	4	Heat Exchangers	EA	6	68	8/14/00	8/23/00
HVAC	5	Connect HVAC	EA	3	44	10/31/00	11/8/00
Painting	1	Paint Exterior	SF	10000	80	6/27/00	7/5/00
Painting	2	Paint Interior Walls	SF	12000	120	12/14/00	1/3/01
Painting	3	Paint Moldings	LF	680	40	1/17/01	1/24/01
Painting	4	Paint Cabinets	EA	12	160	1/5/01	2/1/01
Plumbing	1	Subfoundation Pipes	LF	590	38	5/19/00	5/24/00
Plumbing	2	Drains, Ducts and Pipes	LF	1875	120	6/5/00	6/20/00
Plumbing	3	Basins, Toilets and Tubs	EA	32	120	6/22/00	7/7/00
Plumbing	4	Install Fixtures	EA	71	80	7/10/00	7/19/00
Roofing	1	Install Flashing	EA	10	32	6/15/00	6/19/00
Roofing	2	Black In	SF	6000	15	6/20/00	6/22/00
Roofing	3	Install Roofing	SF	6000	40	6/23/00	6/28/00
Sheetrock	1	Insulate	SF	10000	50	11/10/00	11/16/00
Sheetrock	2	Install Sheetrock	SF	10000	65	11/20/00	11/27/00
Sheetrock	3	Bed and Float	SF	10000	80	11/29/00	12/12/00

6.2 The Expanded Cost Accounts

After the Task List was completed, we expanded the cost accounts for the work packages that were not completed earlier. Figure 6-3 shows the additional cost accounts that were added to the example database. Given the quantifications and man-hours for the tasks shown in Figure 6-1, the estimated costs for

Figure 6-2. Baseline Chart including new tasks.

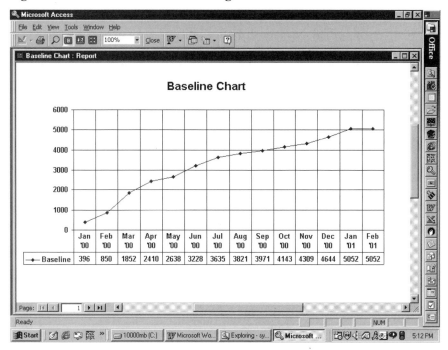

the various cost accounts within the work packages were arrived at via the following procedure.

For each work package, the man-hours for all the tasks
within it were summed to obtain the total man-hours for the
package. From this total, estimates of how many man-hours are
direct labor, as opposed to supervision labor, subcontract labor,
and so on, were determined. To these different man-hour category totals were applied the different labor rates and mark-ups
for overhead, profit, and other factors. Estimates were then
made for materials and equipment accounts. A summary of this
process and the resulting estimating assumptions is shown in
Figure 6-4.

With the new cost budgets shown in Figure 6-3, expanded
cost budget reports can be obtained. For instance, you can select

(text continues on page 142)

Figure 6-3. Additional cost accounts for example project.

Package ID	Cost Account	Original Budget
Electrical	601	$9,000
Electrical	602	$2,926
Electrical	603	$1,050
Electrical	631	$17,300
Electrical	632	$1,250
Frame	601	$26,220
Frame	603	$5,120
Frame	605	$8,100
Frame	631	$32,000
Frame	632	$3,750
Frame	651	$1,370
Frame	652	$980
HVAC	601	$20,400
HVAC	603	$4,200
HVAC	605	$3,800
HVAC	651	$28,500
HVAC	652	$3,100
Painting	601	$10,080
Painting	602	$3,360
Painting	603	$1,840
Painting	632	$4,700
Painting	651	$1,210
Painting	652	$760
Plumbing	601	$21,700
Plumbing	603	$3,936
Plumbing	632	$1,960
Plumbing	651	$2,150
Plumbing	652	$1,432
Roofing	601	$1,675
Roofing	603	$600
Roofing	631	$4,800
Roofing	632	$660
Sheetrock	601	$5,760
Sheetrock	603	$1,610
Sheetrock	631	$4,620
Sheetrock	632	$1,160

Figure 6-4. Estimating assumptions for new tasks.

Package ID	Cost Account	Mhrs	Rate	Markup	Cost
Concrete	601	400	$17.00	100	$13,600.00
Concrete	602	80	$19.00	100	$3,040.00
Concrete	603	40	$23.00	100	$1,840.00
Concrete	631	0	$0.00	0	$18,000.00
Concrete	632	0	$0.00	0	$900.00
Concrete	651	0	$0.00	0	$2,480.00
Electrical	601	300	$30.00	100	$18,000.00
Electrical	602	77	$38.00	100	$5,852.00
Electrical	603	25	$42.00	100	$2,100.00
Electrical	631	0	$0.00	0	$17,300.00
Electrical	632	0	$0.00	0	$1,250.00
Forms	601	350	$15.00	100	$10,500.00
Forms	603	50	$19.00	100	$1,900.00
Forms	632	0	$0.00	0	$1,100.00
Frame	601	670	$23.00	100	$30,820.00
Frame	603	80	$32.00	100	$5,120.00
Frame	605	150	$27.00	100	$8,100.00
Frame	631	0	$0.00	0	$32,000.00
Frame	632	0	$0.00	0	$3,750.00
Frame	651	0	$0.00	0	$1,370.00
Frame	652	0	$0.00	0	$980.00
HVAC	601	300	$34.00	100	$20,400.00
HVAC	603	50	$42.00	100	$4,200.00
HVAC	605	50	$38.00	100	$3,800.00
HVAC	651	0	$0.00	0	$28,500.00
HVAC	652	0	$0.00	0	$3,100.00
Painting	601	280	$18.00	100	$10,080.00
Painting	602	80	$21.00	100	$3,360.00
Painting	603	40	$23.00	100	$1,840.00
Painting	632	0	$0.00	0	$4,700.00
Painting	651	0	$0.00	0	$2,840.00
Painting	652	0	$0.00	0	$1,210.00
Plumbing	601	310	$35.00	100	$21,700.00
Plumbing	603	48	$41.00	100	$3,936.00
Plumbing	631	0	$0.00	0	$21,900.00
Plumbing	632	0	$0.00	0	$1,960.00
Plumbing	651	0	$0.00	0	$2,150.00
Plumbing	652	0	$0.00	0	$1,432.00
Rebar	601	400	$23.00	100	$18,400.00
Rebar	603	80	$24.75	100	$3,960.00
Rebar	631	0	$0.00	100	$4,870.00
Rebar	632	0	$0.00	100	$1,121.00
Roofing	601	67	$12.50	100	$1,675.00
Roofing	603	20	$15.00	100	$600.00
Roofing	631	0	$0.00	0	$4,800.00
Roofing	632	0	$0.00	0	$660.00
Sheetrock	601	160	$18.00	100	$5,760.00
Sheetrock	603	35	$23.00	100	$1,610.00
Sheetrock	631	0	$0.00	0	$4,620.00
Sheetrock	632	0	$0.00	0	$1,160.00

the Budgeted Cost Listing from the Main Menu of the Modern Project toolset. However, we postpone discussing expanded cost reports for now so we can get on with discussing the expanded project performance charts we can obtain with the new transaction data that we also entered into the example database.

The expanded project performance charts we produce will give the first glimpse of what trend charts on real projects look like. The transactions that were entered during the course of the first five chapters of this book were intentionally kept to the bare minimum so the reader could concentrate on learning the concepts, rather than data entry. Consequently, they are not very representative of real project performance charting after a project is well under way.

6.3 The Expanded Transaction Lists

Now that we have these expanded original quantity and labor-hour budgets, we should assume that we are at a later stage of the example project's life to make things more interesting. This assumption leads to the observation that there will therefore be additional cost, progress, and perhaps variance transactions that have occurred. This section of the chapter is devoted to explaining the new transactions that were entered into the example database (they are already in the *exampleChapt6.mde* database).

6.3.1 New Cost Transactions

At the end of Chapter 5 there were only 14 actual expenditure transactions in the example database. These were the cost transactions shown in Figure 3-2 that were entered during the reading of Chapter 3. The additional cost transactions included in the *exampleChapt6.mde* database are shown in Figure 6-5. With these new cost transactions, it is now possible to produce ex-

Figure 6-5. Additional cost transactions for example project.

Trans No	Package ID	Cost Account	Trans Date	Trans Type	Mhrs	Cost	Description
15	Concrete	601	4/12/00	Labor	130	4875	Pour & Cure Labor
16	Concrete	603	4/16/00	Labor	46	2208	Pour & Cure Supervis
17	Concrete	603	4/16/00	Reversal	-100	-3000	Concrete Labor
18	Concrete	602	4/25/00	Labor	78	2964	Finish Concr. Labor
19	Concrete	601	4/25/00	Labor	160	5440	Finish Concr. Labor
20	Concrete	631	4/25/00	Material	0	18780	Concrete purchase
21	Concrete	632	4/25/00	Material	0	631	Concrete consumables
22	Concrete	651	4/30/00	Equip.	0	2813	Portable mixers
23	Electrical	601	9/15/00	Labor	160	9760	Dir. Elect. Labor
24	Electrical	602	9/15/00	Labor	81	6237	Indir. Elect. Labor
25	Electrical	601	10/31/00	Labor	160	9280	Dir. Elect. Labor
26	Electrical	603	10/29/00	Labor	28	2408	Elect. Supervision
27	Electrical	631	11/2/00	Material	0	17280	Perm. Elect. Matrl.
28	Electrical	632	11/3/00	Material	0	1881	Elect. Consumables
29	Forms	601	3/31/00	Labor	180	5220	Dir. Forms Labor
30	Forms	601	4/22/00	Labor	180	5220	Dir. Forms Labor
31	Forms	603	4/15/00	Labor	40	1460	Forms Supervision
32	Forms	632	4/25/00	Material	0	1560	Perm. Forms Matrl.
33	Frame	601	5/20/00	Labor	80	4000	Dir. Framing Labor
34	Frame	603	5/24/00	Labor	10	620	Framing Supervision
35	Frame	601	6/5/00	Labor	128	3136	Dir. Framing Labor
36	Frame	603	6/5/00	Labor	10	640	Framing Supervision
37	Frame	601	6/21/00	Labor	84	4200	Dir. Framing Labor
38	Frame	603	6/21/00	Labor	10	660	Framing Supervision
39	Frame	601	6/30/00	Labor	172	8944	Dir. Framing Labor
40	Frame	603	6/30/00	Labor	10	660	Framing Supervision
41	Frame	601	1/30/01	Labor	188	4606	Dir. Framing Labor
42	Frame	603	2/7/01	Labor	40	2560	Framing Supervision
43	Frame	605	2/12/01	Labor	164	4838	Subcontr. Framing
44	Frame	631	4/15/00	Material	0	1800	Framing Lumber
45	Frame	632	4/15/00	Material	0	700	Framing Supplies
46	Frame	651	4/15/00	Equip	0	400	Framing Equipment
47	Frame	652	4/18/00	Equip	0	250	Equipment Supplies
48	Frame	631	5/15/00	Material	0	4000	Framing Materials
49	Frame	632	5/15/00	Material	0	800	Framing Supplies
50	Frame	651	5/18/00	Equip	0	300	Equipment Supplies
51	Frame	652	5/19/00	Equip	0	150	Equipment Supplies
52	Frame	631	6/12/00	Material	0	12200	Framing Material
53	Frame	632	6/15/00	Equip	0	400	Framing Supplies
54	Frame	651	6/21/00	Equip	0	150	Framing Equipment
55	Frame	652	6/14/00	Equip	0	100	Equipment Supplies
56	Frame	631	7/5/00	Material	0	24400	Framing Materials
57	Frame	632	7/15/00	Material	0	800	Framing Supplies
58	Frame	632	7/7/00	Material	0	750	Framing Supplies
59	Frame	651	7/14/00	Equip	0	150	Framing Equipment
60	Frame	652	7/21/00	Equip	0	180	Equipment Supplies
61	Frame	631	12/27/00	Material	0	8100	Framing Material
62	Frame	632	1/15/01	Material	0	2800	Framing Supplies
63	Frame	651	1/31/01	Equip	0	480	Framing Equipment
64	Frame	652	2/21/01	Equip	0	420	Equipment Supplies
65	HVAC	601	7/10/00	Labor	80	5120	Dir. HVAC Labor
66	HVAC	601	7/31/00	Labor	106	7208	Dir. HVAC Labor

(continues)

Figure 6-5 *(continued).*

67	HVAC	603	7/31/00	Labor	20	1640	HVAC Supervision
68	HVAC	605	8/5/00	Labor	20	1540	HVAC Subcontract
69	HVAC	601	8/14/00	Labor	80	5440	Dir. HVAC Labor
70	HVAC	603	8/15/00	Labor	20	1680	HVAC Supervision
71	HVAC	605	8/21/00	Labor	20	1610	HVAC Subcontract
72	HVAC	601	8/31/00	Labor	60	4080	Dir. HVAC Labor
73	HVAC	605	8/30/00	Labor	10	680	HVAC Subcontract
74	HVAC	601	11/8/00	Labor	40	2720	Dir. HVAC Labor
75	HVAC	603	11/12/00	Labor	10	1680	HVAC Supervision
76	HVAC	651	7/15/00	Equip	0	10600	Perm. Equipment
77	HVAC	652	7/16/00	Equip.	0	800	Equip. Consumables
78	HVAC	651	8/5/00	Equip.	0	2100	Perm. Equipment
79	HVAC	652	8/3/00	Equip.	0	600	Equipment Supplies
80	HVAC	651	8/16/00	Equip.	0	2300	Perm. Equipment
81	HVAC	652	8/9/00	Equip	0	450	Equipment supplies
82	HVAC	651	8/31/00	Equip.	0	9300	Perm. Equipment
83	HVAC	652	11/2/00	Equip.	0	3020	Equip. Consumables
84	Painting	601	7/5/00	Labor	68	2448	Dir. Painting Labor
85	Painting	602	7/5/00	Labor	20	880	Ind. Painting Labor
86	Painting	603	7/7/00	Labor	10	460	Painting Supervision
87	Painting	601	1/3/01	Labor	100	3600	Dir. Painting Labor
88	Painting	602	1/7/01	Labor	20	840	Ind. Painting Labor
89	Painting	603	1/6/01	Labor	10	470	Painting Supervision
90	Painting	601	1/24/01	Labor	40	1440	Dir. Painting Labor
91	Painting	601	2/3/01	Labor	148	4884	Dir. Painting Labor
92	Painting	602	2/5/01	Labor	40	1680	Ind. Painting Labor
93	Painting	603	2/10/01	Labor	20	910	Painting Supervision
94	Painting	632	6/14/00	Material	0	3400	Paints & Thinners
95	Painting	651	6/22/00	Equip.	0	2200	Jacks & Ladders
96	Painting	652	6/22/00	Equip.	0	642	Spray Equipment
97	Painting	632	1/4/01	Material	0	1440	Paints & Thinners
98	Painting	651	1/7/01	Equip.	0	581	Clean-up Equipment
99	Painting	652	1/31/01	Equip.	0	383	Brushes, etc.
100	Plumbing	601	5/24/00	Labor	40	2800	Dir. Plumbing Labor
101	Plumbing	601	6/21/00	Labor	100	7110	Dir. Plumbing Labor
102	Plumbing	603	6/24/00	Labor	20	1655	Plumbing Supervision
103	Plumbing	601	7/8/00	Labor	102	7242	Dir. Plumbing Labor
104	Plumbing	603	7/12/00	Labor	21	1722	Plumbing Supervision
105	Plumbing	601	7/24/00	Labor	72	5112	Dir. Plumbing Labor
106	Plumbing	603	7/22/00	Labor	12	972	Plumbing Supervision
107	Plumbing	631	6/15/00	Material	0	11860	Drains & Ducts
108	Plumbing	632	6/18/00	Material	0	866	Plumbing Supplies
109	Plumbing	651	6/23/00	Equip.	0	969	Plumbing Equipment
110	Plumbing	652	6/21/00	Equip.	0	685	Equip. Consumables
111	Plumbing	631	7/18/00	Material	0	10652	Toilets & Fixtures
112	Plumbing	632	7/17/00	Material	0	896	Plumbing Supplies
113	Plumbing	651	7/28/00	Equip.	0	1044	Plumbing Equipment
114	Plumbing	652	7/23/00	Equip.	0	839	Equip. Consumables
115	Roofing	601	6/22/00	Labor	40	992	Dir. Roofing Labor
116	Roofing	603	6/22/00	Labor	10	312	Roofing Supervision
117	Roofing	601	6/30/00	Labor	38	956	Dir. Roofing Labor
118	Roofing	603	7/3/00	Labor	10	298	Roofing Supervision
119	Roofing	631	6/20/00	Material	0	4779	Roofing Materials
120	Roofing	632	6/30/00	Material	0	677	Roofing Supplies
121	Sheetrock	601	11/16/00	Labor	40	1440	Dir. Sheetrock Labor

122	Sheetrock	603	11/16/00	Labor	10	461	Sheetrock Supervisio
123	Sheetrock	601	11/30/00	Labor	52	1872	Dir. Sheetrock Labor
124	Sheetrock	603	11/29/00	Labor	16	736	Sheetrock Supervisio
125	Sheetrock	601	12/12/00	Labor	78	2730	Dir. Sheetrock Labor
126	Sheetrock	603	12/15/00	Labor	12	552	Sheetrock Supervisio
127	Sheetrock	631	11/8/00	Material	0	4553	Sheetrock
128	Sheetrock	632	11/8/00	Material	0	1229	Plaster, Tape, etc.
129	Rebar	601	3/18/00	Labor	200	9400	Dir. Rebar Labor
130	Rebar	603	3/22/00	Labor	40	2040	Rebar Supervision
131	Rebar	601	3/21/00	Labor	80	3840	Dir. Rebar Labor
132	Rebar	601	3/27/00	Labor	128	3072	Dir. Rebar Labor
133	Rebar	603	4/1/00	Labor	40	2040	Rebar Supervision
134	Rebar	631	3/7/00	Material	0	4951	Rebar, Mesh, etc.
135	Rebar	632	3/14/00	Material	0	1081	Rebar Supplies

panded cost comparison reports. For instance, you could select the Cost Comparison Report from the Main Menu of the Modern Project toolset by clicking on its control button.

6.3.2 New Progress Transactions

At the end of Chapter 5, there were only ten progress transactions in the example database. These are the progress transactions that were listed in Figure 3-6 and entered during the reading of Chapter 3. The new progress transactions that have been added to the Chapter 6 version of the example database are shown in Figure 6-6.

With these new progress transactions it is now possible to produce more realistic performance charts, such as those shown in Figures 6-7, 6-8, and 6-9. Figure 6-7 is the new Earned Value (EV) chart we get from all of these new transactions. The new expenditure transactions and progress transactions that we entered were calculated to give the performance measurement charts a more realistic look. They do not necessarily represent realistic cost and progress values for a project of this size and duration. The reader will notice that in the new EV chart, the *cost curve* (expended man-hour curve) tracks the *budget curve* (project baseline curve) fairly closely. This indicates that the rate of expenditure of resources throughout the project lifetime is close to what was estimated.

Figure 6-6. Additional progress transactions for example project.

Trans No	Package ID	Task ID	Date	Qty to date	Qty this period	Percent complete
11	Concrete	1	4/5/00	0	0	100
12	Concrete	2	4/15/00	290	0	0
13	Concrete	3	4/28/00	5100	0	0
14	Forms	1	3/7/00	780	0	0
15	Forms	2	4/18/00	780	0	0
16	Rebar	1	3/17/00	760	0	0
17	Rebar	2	3/17/00	0	50	0
18	Rebar	3	3/22/00	0	100	0
19	Frame	1	5/20/00	4280	0	0
20	Frame	1	5/27/00	5000	0	0
21	Frame	2	5/27/00	760	0	0
22	Frame	2	6/5/00	1121	0	0
23	Frame	3	6/10/00	581	0	0
24	Frame	3	5/15/00	1062	0	0
25	Frame	4	6/21/00	4898	0	0
26	Frame	4	6/30/00	9879	0	0
27	Plumbing	1	5/31/00	590	0	0
28	Roofing	1	6/21/00	11	0	0
29	Plumbing	2	6/24/00	1934	0	0
30	Roofing	2	6/24/00	6087	0	0
31	Roofing	3	7/2/00	6087	0	0
32	Plumbing	3	6/29/00	21	0	0
33	Plumbing	3	7/9/00	32	0	0
34	HVAC	1	7/18/00	3	0	0
35	Painting	1	7/5/00	4230	0	0
36	Painting	1	7/21/00	11218	0	0
37	Plumbing	4	8/2/00	71	0	0
38	HVAC	2	8/4/00	841	0	0
39	HVAC	3	8/14/00	6	0	0
40	Electrical	1	8/21/00	2	0	0
41	HVAC	4	9/3/00	6	0	0
42	Electrical	2	9/7/00	73	0	0
43	Electrical	2	9/18/00	114	0	0
44	Electrical	3	10/9/00	52	0	0
45	Electrical	4	10/12/00	1075	0	0
46	Electrical	4	10/20/00	1671	0	0
47	Electrical	4	11/5/00	2377	0	0
48	Electrical	5	10/31/00	12	0	0
49	HVAC	5	11/28/00	3	0	0
50	Sheetrock	1	11/21/00	11212	0	0
51	Sheetrock	2	12/3/00	11008	0	0
52	Sheetrock	3	12/21/00	5981	0	0
53	Sheetrock	3	1/3/01	9201	0	0
54	Painting	1	1/3/01	7434	0	0
55	Painting	2	1/9/01	9990	0	0
56	Painting	2	1/21/01	13210	0	0
57	Frame	5	1/30/01	761	0	0
58	Frame	6	1/31/01	12	0	0
59	Painting	3	2/8/01	761	0	0
60	Painting	4	2/24/01	12	0	0

Figure 6-7. New earned value chart based on new transactions.

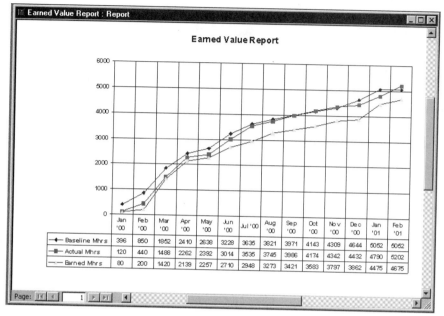

However, in this new EV chart, the earned value curve (earned man-hours curve) trails the other two curves somewhat throughout the project lifetime. This indicates that the project has been running somewhat behind schedule during the duration of project execution. So, all in all, the example project is not doing too badly, but then we calculated the cost and progress transactions so it would come out this way.

Figure 6-8 shows the new Cost Performance Ratio (CPR) trend chart. Notice that on this chart the total (cumulative) CPR curve approaches the value of 1 quickly and then stays fairly near this value. In contrast, the period (monthly) CPR curve oscillates dramatically. One month it is substantially above 1 and the next month substantially below 1, and then the following month it is substantially above 1 again, and so forth.

The oscillatory behavior of the period Cost Performance Ratio from month to month should not alarm the project manager. It often has as much to do with delays in getting expenditure and progress data into the database as it does with the

Figure 6-8. New Cost Performance Trend Chart based on new transactions.

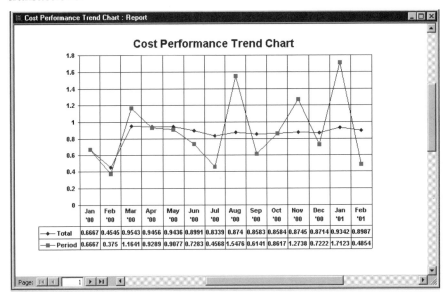

actual cost performance on a project. On very large projects, there can be thousands of expenditure and progress transactions a month. Some months the timing of the logging of these transactions causes work done in one month to be reported the following month. If, during the following month, all the work gets reported on time, it can cause the previous month to show a very low cost performance ratio and the following month to show a very high cost performance ratio.

Consequently, it is the total (cumulative) Cost Performance Ratio curve that should concern the project manager. If this curve stays near the value of 1, then chances are the cost performance on the project will continue to be good. Of course, there can be trends in the period CPR curve that indicate a deteriorating situation. For instance, if the period cost performance ratio stays low for two or more periods in a row, then there may be some cause for concern.

Another trend in the period CPR curve for which the project manager needs to watch is if the period CPR stays high for several periods in a row. This indicates that either exceptional cost performance is being achieved or that, purposely or unknowingly, the expenditures are being consistently understated or the progress is consistently being overstated. The latter of these two possibilities is the more common.

The project manager does not want to get lulled into the conclusion that everything is going well just because the reports and charts indicate high performance scores. The behavior of the two CPR curves in Figure 6-8 is very typical of real projects. If the period cost performance curve does not oscillate or if the total cost performance curve does not approach some value asymptotically, then the project manager should find out why.

Figure 6-9 is the new Schedule Performance Ratio (SPR) trend chart. Notice that for the last month (February '01) the Period Schedule Performance Ratio is zero, and yet the Total (cumulative) Schedule Performance Ratio increases during the month. How can this be? The answer is that the Period Schedule Performance Ratio for February '01 is really not zero, but rather nonmeasurable. Modern Project uses zeros in both the

Figure 6-9. New Schedule Performance Trend Chart from new transactions.

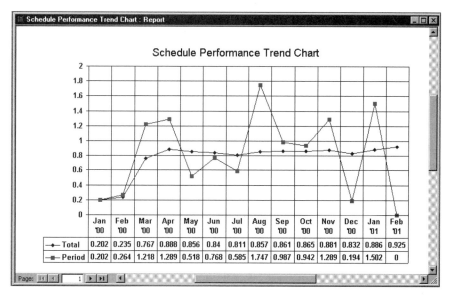

	Jan '00	Feb '00	Mar '00	Apr '00	May '00	Jun '00	Jul '00	Aug '00	Sep '00	Oct '00	Nov '00	Dec '00	Jan '01	Feb '01
Total	0.202	0.235	0.767	0.888	0.856	0.84	0.811	0.857	0.861	0.865	0.881	0.832	0.886	0.925
Period	0.202	0.264	1.218	1.289	0.518	0.768	0.585	1.747	0.987	0.942	1.289	0.194	1.502	0

Cost Performance Trend Chart and the Schedule Performance Trend Chart to indicate either a value of zero or that the ratio cannot be calculated.

The reason the Period Schedule Performance Ratio cannot be calculated for February '01 is that 200 labor-hours were earned during that month, but the control budget for February '01 does not increase over the January '01 control budget as shown by the current baseline graph (Figure 6-2). Consequently, the calculation of the Period Schedule Performance Ratio for February '01 would involve dividing 200 by zero, which is not a meaningful value. So it is not possible to calculate the Period Schedule Performance Ratio for the period February '01. Modern Project detects this and inserts a zero instead for the Period Schedule Performance Ratio for February '01.

The behavior of the Schedule Performance Ratio curves is likely to be similar to the Cost Performance Ratio curves. Often, however, it is the case that the total cost and the total schedule performance ratios do not asymptotically approach the same values. This is simply an indication that one of the two ratios is not as good as the other. It is common to see projects that have good cost performance and poor schedule performance. It is less common, but possible, to have a project with good schedule performance but poor cost performance.

Unfortunately, it is all too common to see projects with both poor cost performance and poor schedule performance. It seems that poor cost performance begets poor schedule performance, and vice versa. Only experienced project managers who understand their projects and project management techniques thoroughly stand any chance of bringing in a truly large project with good cost and schedule performance.

6.3.3 New Variance Transactions

We could, of course, expand the variance transactions. On a real project there would probably be more than just three variances as we currently have in the example project database. However, we have already devoted enough space to expansion of the database. Moreover, the new cost and progress transactions that we have already entered will be sufficient to allow us to see the different views manifest in several of the project reports.

6.4 Expanded Budget and Cost Reports

Before we construct an alternate view (hierarchy), we should produce some cost and budget reports based on these new expanded transaction lists that we can compare with the reports we will be getting with our alternate view when we create it in the next section.

Figure 6-10 shows an updated version of the Cost Comparison Report and Figure 6-11 shows the new Status Report. From the Cost Comparison Report we see that the example project has expended 112% of its total cost budget, and from the Status Report we see that the project is 93% complete. So we can assume the example project is now in its last stages with the new expenditure and status transactions we have entered.

Also from the Status Report we can see that, even though the example project has expended 112% of its cost budget, it has expended only about 103% of its labor-hour budget. Moreover, we see that it has expended only about 95% of the forecasted labor-hours, so a good deal of the labor-hour overrun is expected as there is evidently a productivity variance(s) since the forecast labor-hours for the project exceed the control man-hour budget by 400 hours. If we check one of the Qty/Mhr Variance reports, we see that indeed there is a 400-labor-hour productivity variance against Task 2 of the Siteprep work package.

We now turn our attention to creating an alternate view of the example project by constructing an alternate hierarchy for it.

(text continues on page 154)

Figure 6-10. Updated Cost Comparison Report for example project.

Cost Comparison Report

Hierarchy Position	Package ID / GL Account	Description	Control Budget	To Date Cost	% Budget Expended	Open Amount	Total Cost	Forecast Budget
0	Example Proj	5000 SF Building	$340,977	$381,280	112%	$0	$381,280	$349,377
1	Foundation	Construct Foundation	$97,898	$98,527	101%	$0	$98,527	$106,298
1.1	Siteprep	Site Preparation	$22,320	$20,640	92%	$0	$20,640	$30,720
	601	Direct Labor	$13,000	$10,400	80%	$0	$10,400	$20,200
	603	Supervision	$3,600	$7,200	200%	$0	$7,200	$4,800
	605	Sub-contract labor	$1,760	$2,320	132%	$0	$2,320	$1,760
	651	Equipment	$3,300	$600	18%	$0	$600	$3,300
	652	Equipment Consumables	$660	$120	18%	$0	$120	$660
1.2	Forms	Forms Installation & Removal	$10,670	$13,460	126%	$0	$13,460	$10,670
	601	Direct Labor	$7,480	$10,440	140%	$0	$10,440	$7,480
	603	Supervision	$1,980	$1,460	74%	$0	$1,460	$1,980
	632	Construction Materials	$1,210	$1,560	129%	$0	$1,560	$1,210
1.3	Rebar	Rebar, Mesh & Anchors	$29,290	$26,424	90%	$0	$26,424	$29,290
	632	Construction Materials	$690	$1,081	157%	$0	$1,081	$690
	601	Direct Labor	$19,360	$16,312	84%	$0	$16,312	$19,360
	603	Supervision	$3,960	$4,080	103%	$0	$4,080	$3,960
	631	Permanent Materials	$5,280	$4,951	94%	$0	$4,951	$5,280
1.4	Concrete	Concrete Pour, Cure & Finish	$35,618	$38,003	107%	$0	$38,003	$35,618
	651	Equipment	$2,728	$2,813	103%	$0	$2,813	$2,728
	632	Construction Materials	$990	$631	64%	$0	$631	$990
	631	Permanent Materials	$19,800	$18,780	95%	$0	$18,780	$19,800
	601	Direct Labor	$10,120	$12,815	127%	$0	$12,815	$10,120

Figure 6-11. Updated Status Report for example project.

Status Report

Hierarchy/Position	Package/Task ID	Description	Quantities				Man-hours			
			Percent complete	Unit of Measur	Control Qty	Qty To Date	Control Mhrs	Earned Mhrs	Actual Mhrs	Forecast Mhrs
0	Example Proj	5000 SF Building	93	SF	5000	4627	5052	4675	5182	5452
1	Foundation	Construct Foundation	89	CYC	319	283	2410	2139	2262	2810
1.1	Siteprep	Site Preparation	86	SF	25000	21471	850	730	860	1250
	1	Clear & Grub	100	SF	20000	20000	80	80		80
	2	Earth Removal	50	CY	480	240	240	120		640
	3	Grading	100	SF	25000	25000	120	120		120
	4	Excavation	100	CY	300	300	410	410		410
1.2	Forms	Forms Installation &	95	SF	750	709	460	435	400	460
	1	Forms Installation	95	SF	825	784	276	262		276
	2	Forms Removal	95	SF	825	784	184	175		184
1.3	Rebar	Rebar, Mesh & Anchors	81	LBS	1000	812	528	429	488	528
	3	Anchor Bolts	91	LBS	110	100	176	160		176
	1	Rebar Installation	91	LBS	836	761	264	240		264
	2	Mesh Installation	32	LBS	154	49	88	28		88
1.4	Concrete	Concrete Pour, Cure &	95	CYC	319	304	572	545	514	572
	3	Finish Concrete	91	SF	5588	5085	264	240		264
	1	Pour Concrete	100	CYC	319	319	264	264		264
	2	Cure Concrete	91	CYC	319	290	44	40		44
2	Structure	Build Structure	93	SF	5000	4659	1482	1381	1658	1482

6.5 The Organizational Breakdown Structure (OBS)

On many projects, the organization performing the work has an organizational structure significantly different from the WBS structure. This is especially true for companies that employ the matrix management approach. These companies are often organized around crafts, products, or technologies. For example, systems integration firms are often organized into divisions by product and within product lines (divisions), by engineering disciplines (departments), such as electrical engineers, mechanical engineers, and software engineers.

For the purpose of illustrating an alternate hierarchy in this chapter, we will assume that the company performing the work on the example project is organized primarily by craft. Furthermore, we assume that these crafts are summarized at higher levels into what we will refer to as disciplines. The OBS hierarchy we will assume is shown in Figure 6-12. Notice that the (summary-level) craft called "Pavers" appears to be a work package since there are no lower-level packages under it in the hierarchy. But this is not the case. The reason it appears this way is that there is no paving work on this project. The "real" OBS may have summary-level control packages that are not relevant to a given project. Consequently, when we enter the OBS structure into the database, we will not include the Pavers control package. This makes perfectly good sense. All this means is that only a subhierarchy of the "real" OBS hierarchy is relevant to this project.

6.5.1 Building Alternate Hierarchies

To maintain alternate hierarchies for the example project, you will need a separate database that we will refer to as the *hierarchy database* for the example project. This hierarchy database will be used to contain the various hierarchies that correspond to the different views of your project. To save you the effort of building a database in which to store different hierarchies, we

Figure 6-12. OBS hierarchy for example project.

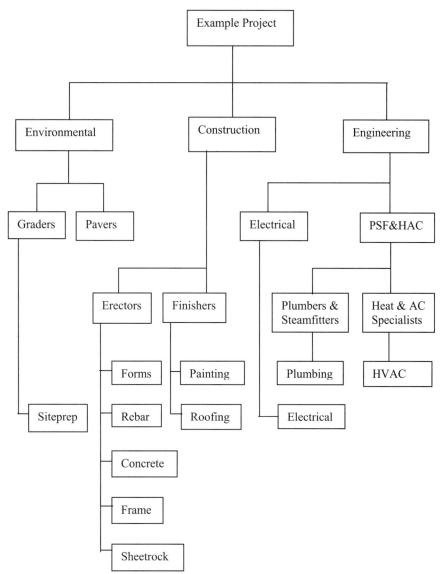

have included a database titled *Hierarchies.mdb* on the CD provided with this book. This database has two tables in it. One is named WBS, and the other is named OBS. The WBS table contains the work breakdown structure that is in the example project database, and the OBS table contains the organizational breakdown structure shown in Figure 6-12. You will probably want to copy the Hierarchies.mdb database from the CD into the directory you are using to store your example project database.

Even though you do not have to build the OBS hierarchy yourself, we will go over the process of building additional hierarchy tables, since you may want to create yet another hierarchy table for some other view in the future. We will also explain the process of how to export these different tables into the example project database in order to get reports summarized by means of an alternate hierarchy. After you have produced the project reports summarized by the alternate hierarchy, you may want to again produce reports summarized by the WBS hierarchy. To do this, you just export the WBS table into the project database, and it will replace the alternate hierarchy. You will then be back where you started and can again produce project reports summarized by the WBS.

If you have copied the Hierarchies.mdb table into your working directory, you can now open this database. When you do, your computer screen should look something like what is shown in Figure 6-13.

Notice that in addition to the *Alternate Hierarchies Menu* there is another object on the screen behind this menu. To see this object, click on its header. Your screen should then look something like Figure 6-14. This is what is called a *database window*. It allows you direct access to everything in the database. The reason you will need access to the tables in the hierarchy database is that it is much easier to copy an existing hierarchy table into the database than to create a new one from scratch. Also, you will need to export your alternate hierarchies into

Figure 6-13. Alternate Hierarchies Menu.

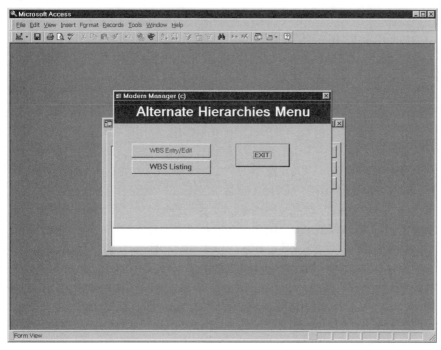

Figure 6-14. Database window showing hierarchy tables.

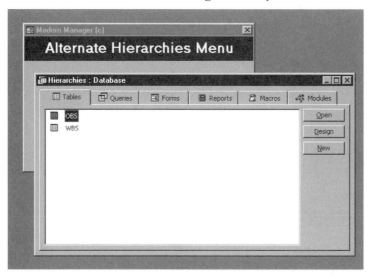

the example project database, and this process requires that the database tables be visible.

If the Hierarchies database window does not show the two hierarchy tables named OBS and WBS (as shown in Figure 6-14), then click on the **Tables** tab at the upper left corner of the Hierarchies database window. Then your screen should look like Figure 6-14.

To see what is contained in the OBS table, click on the OBS table object in the database window, and then click on the control button labeled **Open** at the right side of the database window. A spreadsheet-style table should appear that looks like Figure 6-15. To exit this table and get back to the database window, just click on the little control button at the upper right-hand corner of the OBS table window with an "X" in it.

Suppose you want to add a third hierarchy to the Hierarchy database. You could open the WBS table object and look at its structure and then create a new database with that structure. Instead, we will show you how to simply make another copy of the WBS table.

Figure 6-15. OBS Table for example project.

Hierarchy Posi	Package ID	Description	Active Flag	Unit of Measur	Original Qty	Client
0	Example Proj	5000 SF Buildin	☑	SF	5000	
1	Environment	Environmental C	☑	Site	1	
1.1	Graders	Grading Equip.	☑	Site	1	
1.1.1	Siteprep	Site Preparatior	☑	SF Land	20000	
2	Construction	Construction Cr	☑	Building	1	
2.1	Erectors	Masons, Carper	☑	Building	1	
2.1.1	Forms	Forms Installati	☑	SF Forms	750	
2.1.2	Rebar	Rebar, Mesh &	☑	LBS	1000	
2.1.3	Concrete	Concrete Pour,	☑	CY Concrete	290	
2.1.4	Frame	Framing & Misc	☑	LF Lumber	20000	
2.1.5	Sheetrock	Sheetrock, Tape	☑	SF Sheetrock	10000	
2.2	Finishers	Painters & Roof	☑	Building	1	
2.2.1	Painting	Painting	☑	SF Surface	10000	
2.2.2	Roofing	Roofing	☑	SF Roofing	6000	
3	Engineering	Engineering Cra	☑	Systems	3	
3.1	Electricians	Electrician Craft	☑	Systems	50	
3.1.1	Electrical		☑	Systems	50	
3.2	PSF & HVAC	Plumbing, Stea	☑	Systems	10	
3.2.1	Plumb & SF	Plumbing & Ste	☑	Systems	10	
3.2.1.1	Plumbing		☐	Systems	10	
3.2.2	Heat & AC	Heating & AC C	☑	Systems	2	
3.2.2.1	HVAC		☑	Systems	2	

Record: 14 ◄ | 1 ► ►I ►* of 22

To do this, click on the **File** button at the top of the Access window. Then select the **Save As Export** option on the File menu that drops down. This will cause the Save As window to appear, as shown in Figure 6-16. There are two buttons you can select from on the left side of this window. Select the lower one, titled **Within the Current Database as**, and then type "Old WBS" into the *New Name* field below. Finally, click on the **OK** button at the upper right of this window. You should now see the database window as shown in Figure 6-17 and that you now have a copy of the WBS table in the hierarchy database named "Old WBS." Clearly, the Old WBS table is merely a copy of the WBS table.

Figure 6-16. Save As window.

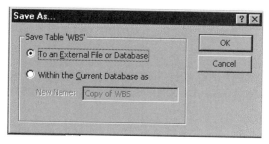

Figure 6-17. Database window showing revised hierarchy tables.

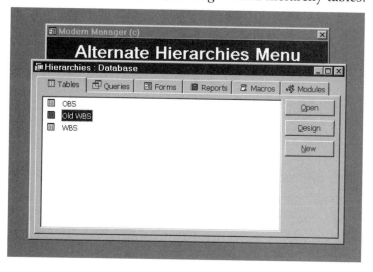

Now that you have a copy of the WBS table called Old WBS, we will explain how you can edit the WBS table to make it into yet another hierarchy table. There are two different ways. If you are familiar with Microsoft Access, you can click on the **Open** control button on the right side of the database window. A spreadsheet version of the table will appear that you can edit in much the same way you would edit a Microsoft Excel spreadsheet.

The other way is to use the WBS Entry/Edit tool that you are already familiar with. A copy of this tool is also included in the Hierarchies database. To start this tool, first click on the header of the Alternate Hierarchies Menu. Clicking on it will bring this menu to the foreground. Now you can click on the **WBS Entry/Edit Tool** control button on the Alternate Hierarchies Menu. It is important to understand that the WBS Entry/ Edit tool *can only edit a table named* "WBS." If you wanted to edit the OBS table with this tool, you would have to rename the WBS table something else and then rename the OBS table "WBS." Then you could edit it with the WBS Entry/Edit tool and then rename it "OBS" again.

To rename a database table, click on the table object in the database window and then click on the **Edit** button at the top of the Access window. You then select the **Rename** option, and Access allows you to type in a new name for the table. Now press the **Enter** key. We will not devote space here to doing this, but you can experiment on your own with copying hierarchy tables in the way that was just shown and then using the WBS Entry/Edit tool to edit them.

6.5.2 Exporting Alternate Hierarchies into the Project Database

The next thing to be demonstrated is how to *export* a new hierarchy table into the example database. Again, it is important to understand that when you export a hierarchy table from the Hierarchies database into the example database, *you must export it to the WBS table in the example database*. It does not matter that the table you want to export from the hierarchy database is named something else (e.g., OBS). What is important is that when you export a hierarchy table (e.g., the OBS table), when it gets into the example database it is named WBS.

Fortunately, the process of exporting a database table to another database allows for the renaming of the exported table as it is being exported. We will now show how this is done. First, select the OBS table by clicking on it in the database window. Now click on the **File** button at the top of the Access window. Select the **Save As/Export** . . . option on this menu. This will cause the Save As window to appear, as it did in the previous example as shown in Figure 6-16. But this time select the **To an External File or Database** option. Doing this will cause yet another window to appear, this one called "Save Table 'OBS' in. . . ." This will cause your screen to look like Figure 6-18. You may have to use the "up arrow" control button and the directory-changing capability in this window to get back to the directory where you have the example database and the hierar-

Figure 6-18. Save Table window.

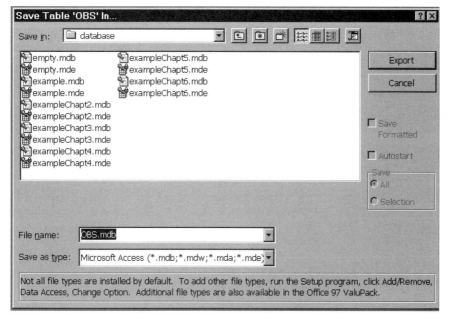

chy database stored. Access tends to lose track of what directory it is in when it gets to this window.

Change the File name in the *File name* field near the bottom of this window to *exampleChapt6.mde*, and then click on the **Export** control button on the right side of this window. This brings up one last window, called the *Export window*, as shown in Figure 6-19.

In the only field in this window, change "OBS" to "WBS," and then click on the **OK** control button on the right side of the Export window. You may have to confirm to the system that you really want to do this since a table named WBS already exists in the example database. If a confirmation window appears warning you that the table WBS already exists in the example database, just click on the **OK** control button. You have now exported the OBS table in the Hierarchy database into the WBS table in the example project database. Now close the Hierarchy database by clicking on the **Exit** control button in the Alternate Hierarchies Menu window.

Figure 6-19. Export window.

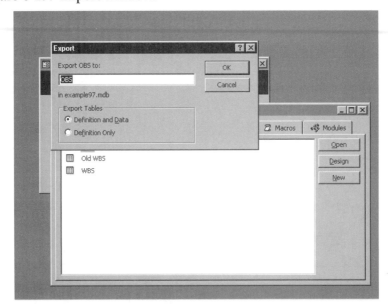

You can experiment with getting project reports in this new alternate view by reopening the example project database and displaying or printing any of the project reports that were organized in accordance with the WBS. You will see that they are now organized in accordance with the OBS, rather than the WBS. The Cost Comparison Report and the Status Report based on the OBS hierarchy are illustrated in Figures 6-21 and 6-22.

Later, when you want to produce project reports organized around the WBS, you will need to repeat the process just explained, but this time exporting the WBS table in the Hierarchies database into the WBS table in the example project database.

6.5.3 Hierarchy Maintenance

On a large project it is not unusual to want to have several views of the project. So, in addition to needing a hierarchy entry and edit tool, there is also a need for a hierarchy display tool to display (or print) the various hierarchies for comparison. Consequently, the WBS Listing tool that you are already familiar with is included on the Alternate Hierarchies Menu.

If you reopen the Hierarchies database, rename the WBS hierarchy "New WBS," and rename the OBS hierarchy "WBS," then you can display the OBS hierarchy in a WBS Listing report. To do this, simply click on the header of the Alternate Hierarchies Menu, and then click on the control button labeled **WBS Listing**. This will produce a listing of the OBS hierarchy, as shown in Figure 6-20.

Figure 6-20. OBS hierarchy in a WBS Listing for example project.

WBS Listing

WBS Position	*Package ID*	Active Indicator	*Description*	*Unit of Meas.*	Original Qty	Client Qty	Control Qty	Forecast Qty
0	*Example Proj*		*5000 SF Building*	*SF*	5000	5000	5000	5000
1	*Environment*		*Environmental Crafts*	*Site*	1	1	1	1
1.1	*Graders*		*Grading Equip. Operators*	*Site*	1	1	1	1
1.1.1	*Siteprep*		*Site Preparation*	*SF Land*	20000	25000	25000	25000
2	*Construction*		*Construction Crafts*	*Building*	1	1	1	1
2.1	*Erectors*		*Masons, Carpenters & Sheetrock*	*Building*	1	1	1	1
2.1.1	*Forms*		*Forms Installation & Removal*	*SF Forms*	750	750	750	750
2.1.2	*Rebar*		*Rebar, Mesh & Anchors*	*LBS*	1000	1000	1000	1000
2.1.3	*Concrete*		*Concrete Pour, Cure & Finish*	*CY Concrete*	290	290	319	319
2.1.4	*Frame*		*Framing & Misc. Carpentry*	*LF Lumber*	20000	20000	20000	20000
2.1.5	*Sheetrock*		*Sheetrock, Tape & Float*	*SF Sheetrock*	10000	10000	10000	10000
2.2	*Finishers*		*Painters & Roofers*	*Building*	1	1	1	1

Thursday, January 11, 2001 ***Page 1 of 2***

Figure 6-21. Cost Comparison Report based on OBS hierarchy.

Cost Comparison Report

Hierarchy Position	Package ID / GL Account	Description	Control Budget	To Date Cost	% Budget Expended	Open Amount	Total Cost	Forecast Budget
0	*Example Proj*	5000 SF Building	$340,977	$381,280	112%	$0	$381,280	$349,377
1	*Environment*	Environmental Crafts	$22,320	$20,640	92%	$0	$20,640	$30,720
1.1	*Graders*	Grading Equip. Operators	$22,320	$20,640	92%	$0	$20,640	$30,720
1.1.1	*Siteprep*	Site Preparation	$22,320	$20,640	92%	$0	$20,640	$30,720
	601	Direct Labor	$13,000	$10,400	80%	$0	$10,400	$20,200
	603	Supervision	$3,600	$7,200	200%	$0	$7,200	$4,800
	605	Sub-contract labor	$1,760	$2,320	132%	$0	$2,320	$1,760
	651	Equipment	$3,300	$600	18%	$0	$600	$3,300
	652	Equipment Consumables	$660	$120	18%	$0	$120	$660
2	*Construction*	Construction Crafts	$0	$0	0%	$0	$0	$0
2.1	*Erectors*	Masons, Carpenters & Sheetrock	$0	$0	0%	$0	$0	$0
2.1.1	*Forms*	Forms Installation & Removal	$10,670	$13,460	126%	$0	$13,460	$10,670
	632	Construction Materials	$1,210	$1,560	129%	$0	$1,560	$1,210
	601	Direct Labor	$7,480	$10,440	140%	$0	$10,440	$7,480
	603	Supervision	$1,980	$1,460	74%	$0	$1,460	$1,980
2.1.2	*Rebar*	Rebar, Mesh & Anchors	$29,290	$26,424	90%	$0	$26,424	$29,290
	632	Construction Materials	$690	$1,081	157%	$0	$1,081	$690
	631	Permanent Materials	$5,280	$4,951	94%	$0	$4,951	$5,280

Figure 6-22. Status Report based on OBS hierarchy.

Status Report

Hierarchy Position	Package / Task ID	Description	Percent complete	Unit of Measure	Control Qty	Qty To Date	Control Mhrs	Earned Mhrs	Actual Mhrs	Forecast Mhrs
0	Example Proj	5000 SF Building	93	SF	5000	1	850	730	860	1250
1.1	Graders	Grading Equip. Operators	86	Site	1	14627	5052	4675	5182	5452
1	Environment	Environmental Crafts	86	Site	1		850	730	860	1250
1.1.1	Siteprep	Site Preparation	86	SF Land	25000	21471	850	730	860	1250
	1	Clear & Grub	100	SF	20000	20000	80	80	80	
	2	Earth Removal	50	CY	480	240	240	120	640	
	3	Grading	100	SF	25000	25000	120	120	120	
	4	Excavation	100	CY	300	300	410	410	410	
2	Construction	Construction Crafts	92	Building	1	1	3042	2790	3060	3042
2.1	Erectors	Masons, Carpenters &	91	Building	1	1	2555	2324	2506	2555
2.1.1	Forms	Forms Installation &	95	SF Forms	750	709	460	435	400	460
	1	Forms Installation	95	SF	825	784	276	262	276	
	2	Forms Removal	95	SF	825	784	184	175		184
2.1.2	Rebar	Rebar, Mesh & Anchors	81	LBS	1000	812	528	429	488	528
	2	Mesh Installation	32	LBS	154	49	88	28	88	
	3	Anchor Bolts	91	LBS	110	100	176	160	176	
	1	Rebar Installation	91	LBS	836	761	264	240	264	
2.1.3	Concrete	Concrete Pour, Cure &	95	CY	319	304	572	545	514	572

Monday, January 31, 2000

Chapter 7

Interfacing Scheduling Systems

I n this chapter we discuss interfacing scheduling systems with Modern Project. We begin with an extended discussion of resource scheduling, taking up where we left off in Chapter 2. Then we discuss the advantages and disadvantages of manually interfacing a scheduling system to the rest of a project management system. It may seem surprising, but it is often best if project scheduling is not very tightly integrated with the rest of a project management system. We conclude the chapter with a demonstration of an automated interface between Microsoft Project and Modern Project.

Since every scheduling system can be manually interfaced to Modern Project, it is possible to use the Modern Project toolset with any scheduling system. Moreover, it is probably not a great deal more difficult to interface scheduling systems other than Microsoft Project with Modern Project. The fact that the only automated interface supplied on the CD that is distributed with this book is to Microsoft Project should not be viewed as an endorsement of that product. Rather, the automated interface is supplied to indicate how such an interface can be implemented simply.

7.1 Task Sequencing with Microsoft Project

In Chapter 2, not a lot of detail was given about resource scheduling. The difference between work sequencing and resource scheduling was discussed, but the details of resource scheduling were deferred to this chapter. It is now time to cover this topic in more detail. Since we entered additional tasks into the example project database in Chapter 6, we now have quite a few more tasks to schedule. We begin the discussion of resource scheduling by sequencing all the tasks we now have in the example project database.

The discussion of task sequencing and resource scheduling that follows uses Microsoft Project. Since some readers may have access to Microsoft Project but may not have actually used it before, we explain how to use this scheduling tool to both sequence and schedule the tasks in the example project. For readers who are utilizing another scheduling tool, this should not present a problem, since the same process can be followed using other scheduling tools.

7.1.1 Task-Naming Convention

To use Microsoft Project to sequence the tasks in the example project, we must first enter the tasks into this scheduling tool. In order to help you do this, we now explain a certain convention in task naming. This convention serves two purposes. The first is to overcome a limitation in the Microsoft Project task-naming convention. The second is to make the automated interface between Microsoft Project and Modern Project as simple as possible.

Microsoft Project does not allow multiple tasks to have the same name. You may be wondering why you would want to give two different tasks the same name. But having many tasks with the same name is common on many projects, and for good reason. Most project management systems are *package oriented*, but scheduling systems are often *task oriented*. In the *User's Guide* for Microsoft Project, the explanation of how to enter a task begins by explaining to the reader to "use a verb and a noun to name a task (for example, Pour concrete)." On many construction projects there may be many tasks named "Pour concrete." For instance, there may be several work packages (e.g., "Footings," "Columns," "Culverts," "Retaining Walls," and "Spans") that contain a task named "Pour concrete."

These are all different tasks, and the project management system can distinguish them as being different because it knows the relationship between each task and the work package in which it is contained. In the example project we have used an extremely simple task-naming convention by just assigning numbers to the tasks within a work package; you will recall that all of the work packages have a task named "1." This is acceptable since the Modern Project toolset supports naming tasks with alphabetical names and distinguishing tasks with the same name as being different so long as they are in different work packages.

To get around this limitation in Microsoft Project and other task-oriented scheduling systems, one must name tasks a little differently. For instance, instead of simply naming a task "Pour concrete," we could name it "Pour footing concrete" or "Pour retaining wall concrete." This keeps the names unique and allows Microsoft Project to distinguish one task from another.

Our naming convention for the example project will be to name tasks (for the purpose of entering them into Microsoft Project) as "Siteprep 1" or "Concrete 2," and so on. This allows Microsoft Project to distinguish all the tasks named "1" or "2" or "3" from one another. It also makes it easy to write a program that automatically loads the schedule dates that Microsoft Project computes into a Modern Project database. Consequently, if you use the Modern Project toolset on a real project and want to automatically transfer schedule dates from Microsoft Project to Modern Project, you must use the convention of naming the tasks within a work package with an (integer) number and then combining the work package name and the numeric task name to create its "Microsoft Project task name."

7.1.2 Task Sequencing

To use Microsoft Project to sequence the tasks in the example project, we must now enter these tasks (named in accordance with the convention explained in the previous section) into Project. To do this you must first execute Project. When you start Project, a *Welcome window* may appear. If it does, you first need to terminate it by clicking on the "cross" symbol at the upper right corner of the Welcome window. Next, click on the **File** option of the Standard menu at the top of the Project window, and then select (click on) the **New** option to create a new *project file*. When you create a new project file, Project presents you with a *new project window* that allows you to either enter the start date for the project or the finish date, but not both. It is not recommended that a finish date be entered. The start date you should enter in the **Start date** box is 01/07/00, which is the start date of the example project. There are some other boxes where additional information can be entered, but for the example project we will be using the default values Project provides.

Click on the **OK** control button on the right side of the new project window. By default, an empty project file appears after you have entered the start date. Your computer screen should now look like Figure 7-1. If it does not, you may not be in what is called *Gantt Chart View*, or you may not have the *Entry* table displayed on the left-hand side of the window. You can check this by clicking on the **View** control button and selecting **Gantt Chart**. Then click on the **View** control button again, and select **Table**. This will bring up yet another menu. Select **Entry**. Now the Project window should look like Figure 7-1.

To change a start date once one has been entered, select the **Project Information** option from the **Project** menu. Then reenter the start date in the **Start date** box.

The Project *User's Guide* calls entering tasks into the project file creating a *task list*. To enter a task from the Gantt Chart view, you simply type the task's name in the *Task Name column*, and then press the **Enter** key. Doing this causes the cursor to move down one row so you can enter the next task's name in the Task Name column.

In addition to entering a task's name, we need to enter its *duration* (how long it will take) and what the *precedence relation-*

Figure 7-1. Empty Microsoft Project Gantt chart screen.

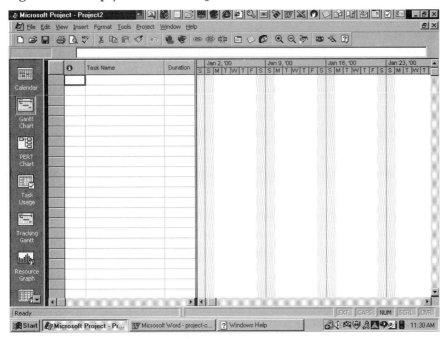

ships are with other tasks. The observant reader will notice that durations are a scheduling concept and not a sequencing concept. This is a problem in using Microsoft Project for task sequencing because it does not differentiate between the two. We will, however, show how to get around this problem. The concepts of sequencing and scheduling were explained in Chapter 2, but we will review them as we enter this information into the example project scheduling file. The Project *User's Guide* devotes a chapter to entering just the project names and durations and then another chapter to entering the precedence relationships (called *linking* and also *dependencies* in the *User's Guide*). Moreover, these two chapters describe how to do this only in the Gantt Chart View.

We will give a much more concise explanation of how to enter the task data, and we will introduce the *PERT Chart View*, which is much more useful for visualizing the task sequencing than the Gantt Chart View. Although Project supports the

PERT Chart View, it is only mentioned but not explained in the *User's Guide*. This seems curious, since most project schedulers make extensive use of PERT charts. Perhaps the reason is that the *User's Guide* does not distinguish task sequencing from task scheduling. It emphasizes displaying only the schedule that shows the relationship of the tasks to a time line. The Gantt Chart View is a more concise view for a time line, especially on a computer display.

PERT charts tend to take up more space. They are the kind of charts you often see adorning the office walls of a project scheduler. But, in the task sequencing phase, we are not yet interested in the scheduling dates; rather, we are interested in the task dependencies. If we do not require that a PERT chart be displayed with all the tasks lined up on a time line, what is called a *time-phased PERT chart*, then PERT charts can also be represented economically in a display window.

We are now going to explain how to enter tasks using both the Gantt Chart View and the PERT Chart View. We will enter the task names and durations in Gantt Chart View and then specify their dependencies in PERT Chart View. The reasons we are entering these durations now is to show how Project expects to be used. We will show how to get around entering durations during task sequencing a little later in this section. To begin with, enter the first four tasks (shown here) and their durations in Gantt Chart View by typing them into the *Task Name column* and the *Duration column* and then pressing the **Enter** key. Or you can use your mouse to move down a row.

Task Name	Duration
Siteprep 1	5
Siteprep 2	12
Siteprep 3	13
Siteprep 4	13

Your screen should now look like Figure 7-2. Notice that for each task you enter, Project draws a *task bar* proportional in

Figure 7-2. Entering tasks on a Gantt chart.

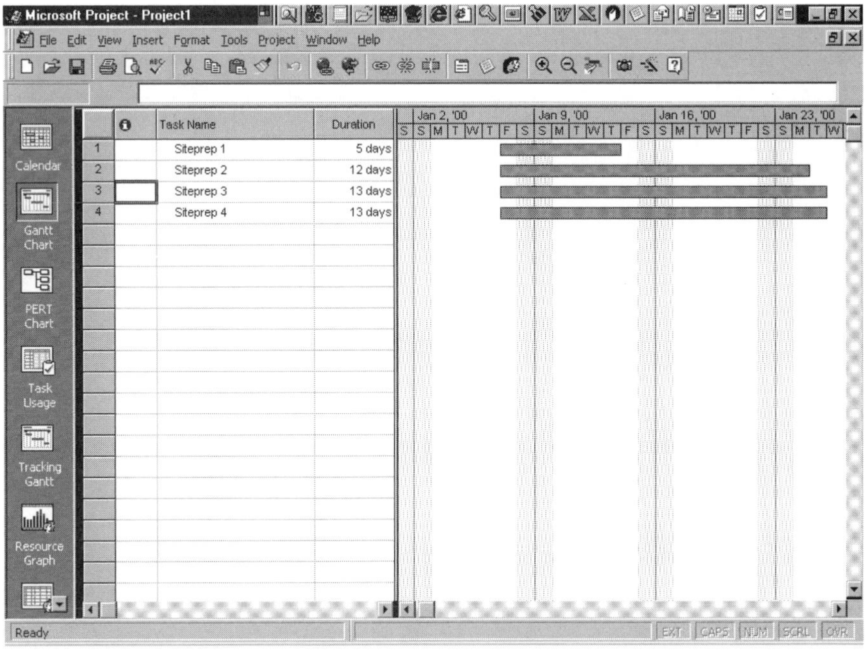

length to the task's duration to the right of the task data you entered. Now click on the PERT Chart View icon on the left side of the Gantt Chart View window. This will cause your screen to look like Figure 7-3. You may have to reduce the viewing size of the Pert Chart View in order to make it look like Figure 7-3. To do this, select the **Zoom** option from the pull-down menu that appears when you click on the **View** button at the top of the Project window.

Some of the boxes in the PERT Chart View are red, and some are black. The reason for this is that, without any further information, Project considers tasks 3 and 4 to be on the *critical path*. It does not yet have enough information to conclude that tasks 1 and 2 are also on the critical path. The concept of the critical path has not been explained yet, but it will be shortly.

Now click on the first box (Siteprep 1), and, while holding the right mouse button down, drag the mouse until the cursor is over the second box (Siteprep 2). This will cause an arrow to

Figure 7-3. The PERT chart screen showing entered tasks.

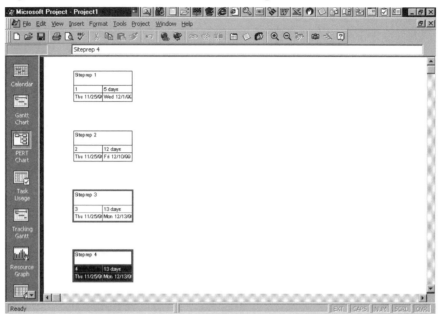

be drawn from box 1 to box 2 as shown in Figure 7-4. By default, this causes Project to consider boxes 1 and 2 to be connected by a finish-to-start relationship, as defined in Chapter 2. In constructing the task sequencing for all the new tasks introduced in Chapter 6, we assumed that most of the dependencies were finish-to-start relationships. There are, however, a couple of start-to-start relationships in the sequencing. If you want to make one of the dependencies another type, such as a start-to-finish relationship, you can double-click on the arrow that depicts the dependency, and a *Task Dependency window* will appear that will allow you to choose one of the other dependency types. Also, you can repeat this process on this same task (Siteprep 1) to create other arrows (dependencies) to other tasks.

Since there are now a total of 42 tasks, you probably do not want to take the time to enter all of them, although it is a good exercise for those who have the time to spare. Instead, we have included a list of all the tasks, their durations, and their dependencies in Figure 7-5 and a copy of what such a sequencing

Figure 7-4. PERT chart showing task dependency relation.

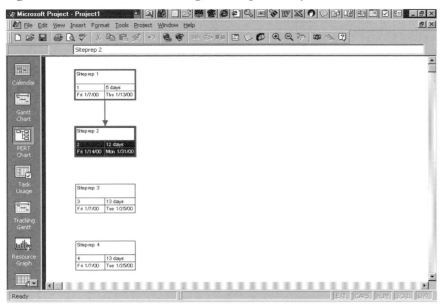

looks like in Figure 7-6. Also, for those who have access to Project, we have included a copy of the example project scheduling database on the CD included with this book. It is in the file named *example.mpp*.

Most of what appears in the table in Figure 7-5 is self-explanatory, but the way the dependencies are expressed may need a little explaining. What is shown in Figure 7-5 is part of the *Entry* table from Project. The Entry table is one of several tables that can be obtained from Project. As previously mentioned, it can be seen by clicking on the **View** control button at the top of the Project window and then selecting the **Table** option. Thereafter, select the **Entry** option.

Project displays the dependencies in a column labeled *Predecessors*. It does this because the way Project displays a dependency is to list the *dependent task* and then, in the dependent task's Predecessors column, lists all the preceding tasks on which the dependent task depends. It also describes the type of dependency for each of the predecessor tasks. For instance, the

Figure 7-5. Task list for example project.

ID	Task Name	Duration	Predecessors
1	Siteprep 1	5 days	
2	Siteprep 2	12 days	1
3	Siteprep 3	13 days	2SS+5 days
4	Siteprep 4	13 days	3FS+1 day
5	Forms 1	4 days	4FS+3 days
6	Forms 2	4 days	12
7	Rebar 1	6 days	5FS+2 days
8	Rebar 2	6 days	7FS+1 day
9	Rebar 3	9 days	8FS+1 day
10	Concrete 1	8 days	9FS+1 day
11	Concrete 2	4 days	10FS+2 days
12	Concrete 3	6 days	11FS+1 day
13	Frame 1	5 days	12
14	Frame 2	10 days	13
15	Frame 3	8 days	14
16	Frame 4	8 days	15
17	Frame 5	8 days	38FS+1 day, 18FS+2 days
18	Frame 6	20 days	38FS+1 day
19	Roofing 1	3 days	15
20	Roofing 2	3 days	19
21	Roofing 3	4 days	20
22	Plumbing 1	4 days	6
23	Plumbing 2	12 days	22,14
24	Plumbing 3	12 days	23FS+1 day
25	Plumbing 4	8 days	24
26	Electrical 1	5 days	33FS+2 days
27	Electrical 2	12 days	26FS+1 day
28	Electrical 3	15 days	27FS+1 day
29	Electrical 4	15 days	28
30	Electrical 5	4 days	29FS+1 day
31	HVAC 1	7 days	16FS+3 days
32	HVAC 2	12 days	31FS+1 day
33	HVAC 3	9 days	32FS+1 day
34	HVAC 4	8 days	33FS+1 day
35	HVAC 5	7 days	30FS+1 day,34
36	Sheetrock 1	5 days	16,29, 35FS+1 day
37	Sheetrock 2	6 days	36FS+1 day
38	Sheetrock 3	10 days	37FS+1 day
39	Painting 1	7 days	16
40	Painting 2	15 days	38FS+1 day
41	Painting 3	6 days	42SS+8 days
42	Painting 4	20 days	40FS+1 day

third dependency listed is for Siteprep 3. Its Predecessor column contains the cryptic symbols "2SS + 5 days." This means Siteprep 3 depends on the second task in the list (the one labeled 2, that is, Siteprep 2), and the dependency is a start-to-start dependency (denoted "SS" in the table). In addition, there is a five-day lag time before Siteprep 3 can be started after Siteprep 2 is started. Adding the lag time part of the dependency is done at the same time you specify the dependency type in PERT Chart View, as explained earlier. The same window that allows you to choose the dependency type (e.g., start-to-start) allows you also to specify the lag time associated with a dependency.

Some tasks, such as Task Number 17 (Frame 5), depend on more than one other task. Task Number 17 is also an example of a task that depends on two other tasks that were added to the task list after Task Number 17 was entered. Project assigns sequence numbers to the tasks as they are entered. Since Task Number 17 depends on tasks 18 and 38, it is clear that these tasks were entered after Task Number 17 was entered.

Figure 7-6 shows what the task sequencing looks like when all the information in Figure 7-5 has been entered into the example project database. The reader may be wondering how to get around entering all these durations at this time, since this is not part of task sequencing. Task sequencing is concerned only with determining which tasks precede which other tasks. The lag time constraints for dependencies, however, can properly be considered part of task sequencing. The reason for entering the durations in this example was to show how Project prefers to operate. It is difficult to use Project strictly for task sequencing. Project does not have the concept of task sequencing and is eager to schedule the tasks. Here is what happens.

When you enter information about an individual task into Project, it wants to schedule that task as soon as it is entered. Consequently, if you leave the task's *Duration* column blank, Project automatically enters a duration of one day. This allows Project to go ahead and schedule the task—perhaps with the

Figure 7-6. Task sequencing for example project.

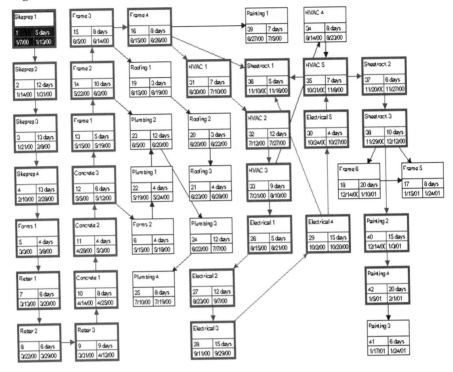

wrong duration, but it gets the task scheduled. This may produce a meaningless Gantt chart, but the PERT Chart View will
be the same as what you would expect to get if you did not
enter durations.

It is possible to zero out these one-day durations that Project automatically inserts when you leave the duration column
blank. You might think that this would be the thing to do to
cause Project to produce a pure task sequencing. This can be
done, but it will not change the way the PERT Chart View will
look. It will, however, cause the Gantt Chart View to look very
strange because of the way Project deals with tasks of zero duration.

For this reason, it is best to just leave the duration column
for each of the tasks blank and let Project put in the one-day
durations when you are doing task sequencing. This is essen-

tially how you get around entering the duration information at this time.

7.2 Resource Scheduling

At the time the tasks are sequenced, as discussed in Chapter 2, the tasks should not yet have been estimated. The reason for this is that the sequencing of the work should be taken into consideration when estimating the task budgets (e.g., man-hours, dollars). And an attempt to schedule the tasks should not be undertaken until the estimates have been made so that the resources needed to complete the tasks can be taken into consideration in the schedule.

It is common for projects to schedule tasks without knowing the resources needed to accomplish each task, but it is not a good idea. Project allows this, and it is common for projects using Microsoft Project to schedule projects this way. We discuss this method of scheduling a project first. Project also provides the capability to do resource scheduling, and we discuss that next. The difference between *simple scheduling* (without knowledge of the resources) and *resource scheduling* is that with simple scheduling, you attempt to guess the duration of each task, whereas with resource scheduling, the scheduling system computes the duration based on the resources required.

7.2.1 Simple Scheduling

There was a time when simple scheduling was the only kind there was. In the early 1960s, draftsmen were employed to draw PERT schedule diagrams manually. They would manually move the boxes around on a large drawing, trying to construct an optimum schedule by trial and error. By the mid-1960s, draftsmen still drew schedules, but computer programs were beginning to appear that would calculate the optimum dates. The draftsman was now faced only with placing the boxes on the drawing in such a way as to minimize the number of arrows that crossed each other or that crossed over or behind boxes. This made the charts more comprehensible to humans.

The history of how scheduling came to be done on computers is an interesting one that we do not have time to develop. However, a few paragraphs that summarize this period of development are in order to help the reader understand the meaning of the frequently used acronyms CPM and PERT. In the mid-1950s, E. I. Du Pont de Nemours & Company formed a working group with Remington Rand Corporation to study the planning and management of construction work for chemical plants. This team developed a mathematical theory of network planning and control called the Critical Path Method (CPM). The working group understood that for large projects this method required considerable computational capabilities. Dr. John Mauchly, of UNIVAC Corporation, one of the early researchers with electronic computers, joined the working group for the purpose of adapting the method to the digital computer.

Concurrently, the Bureau of Naval Weapons set up a program evaluation office to provide senior management with continuous appraisals of the POLARIS submarine program. This office sought proposals from industry for the development of a program evaluation system, and in 1957 contracts were awarded to Booz, Allen, & Hamilton and Lockheed. This effort resulted in another mathematically oriented technique that has come to be known as the Program Evaluation and Review Technique (PERT). Although both of these efforts were undertaken independently, they both were based on computing the critical path, a concept that is discussed in the next section. The concepts of CPM and PERT form the basis of what we refer to as simple scheduling.

Also during this period, papers were beginning to appear in the literature that described a technique that has come to be called *resource leveling*. Since that time, better algorithms have been discovered for resource leveling, but in general the problem is known to be intractable. However, it is often possible to restrict the problem under a suitable set of assumptions to allow its solution or at least to find a schedule that meets the requirements even though it may not be optimal. A discussion of what resource leveling means and how it is accomplished is presented later in this chapter.

Also during this time, computer programs were beginning to be put forward that could do resource leveling under certain assumptions. But these programs were not in general use. By the mid-1970s, though, an extensive literature on the subject had developed, and a number of commercial software products were available that could do resource scheduling (scheduling based on the concept of resource leveling). However, for large projects it could be computationally expensive to try to resource level a schedule in those days. So, for many years, resource leveling was possible but not widely used because of the time and expense involved in producing a schedule that was resource leveled. Even today it is not always used because of the effort required to set up a scheduling system to do the resource leveling. For smaller projects or under certain conditions, simple scheduling may still be appropriate. We discuss resource leveling in Section 7.2.3.

During the mid-1960s, most companies that used any form of scheduling charts, including PERT charts, developed their own computer programs if they wanted automated assistance with computing schedules. At Texas Instruments, in 1968, the author produced what we believed to be the first scheduling program that automatically drew precedence-diagramed PERT charts on a plotter while automatically minimizing the number of lines that intersected. There may have been earlier programs that drew arrow-diagramed charts, but at the time we were unable to locate any such computer program described in the literature.

Simple scheduling is characterized by the defining of the expected duration for each task to the scheduling system (in addition to the dependency types and lag times already mentioned in the previous section). The scheduling system then performs two types of algorithms, known as the *forward pass algorithm* and the *backward pass algorithm*, to produce the schedule. What is obtained in this process is two different sets of dates for each task. The first set of dates is known as the *early date set*, and the second set of dates is known as the *late date set*. The early date set consists of the *early start* date and the *early finish* date. The late date set consists of the *late start* date and the *late finish* date.

The early dates are the earliest possible dates that a task can start and finish based on the dependencies and lag times specified to the scheduling system. Of course, it is possible for the task to start later and finish later. The question is: How much later can they start and finish without causing the overall project to finish late? The answer is the late dates. The late start date is the latest date the task can start without jeopardizing the project schedule, and the late finish date is the latest date the task can finish without causing the project to finish behind schedule.

There are many papers and books that the interested reader can refer to that describe these algorithms in detail. Their presentation is far beyond the scope of this book. What we are interested in here is how the durations are estimated. Even if simple scheduling is to be used on a project, the estimate of the duration of a task *should not be made until the budgeting of the task has been completed*. Without an understanding of the man-hour budget for the task, it is difficult, if not impossible, to determine how long it will take to accomplish the task.

Sometimes it is possible to determine the duration of many of the tasks in a straightforward manner, but more often it is a complex, time-consuming job, because the estimate of the duration of a task depends not only on the amount of work to accomplish (man-hours to complete) but the conditions under which the work can be undertaken. For instance, workers may not be allowed to work on weekends in order to reduce overtime expenses. Or some tasks might require the workers to have a certain skill and there may be a limited number of workers with this skill, which prevents multiple tasks requiring this skill to be performed at the same time.

Sometimes, there are other sources of information that can be used to assist the project planners with their estimates of the durations of the tasks. Large companies that engage in specific types of tasks regularly often gather statistics on the average durations for certain types of tasks. Also, the experience and judgment of the project planners plays a role in deciding what the durations should be. Determining the durations of tasks is very much an estimating function, just as determining the budgets of the tasks is an estimating function.

For the example project, the durations were given in Figure 7-5. These durations have already been entered into the example project scheduling database that is included on the CD at the back of this book. If you use Microsoft Project to open this schedule database (*example.mpp*), it should produce a Gantt Chart View that looks like Figure 7- 7.

You can use the scroll bar on the right side of the Gantt Chart View window to scroll backward and forward to view the whole schedule, as it does not fit entirely within the window. Also, you may need to suppress a table on the left side of the Gantt chart or scale the chart to fit the window in order to get your Gantt Chart View to look like the one shown in Figure 7-7. To scale the chart to fit the window, click on the **View** button at the top of the window, and then select **Zoom** at the bottom of the menu that drops down. This opens a *zoom window* so you can specify the scaling you desire. Select the **Entire project** option, and then click on **OK**. This will scale the chart to fit your Gantt Chart View window.

From this view of the schedule it can be seen that the project can be completed in a little over a year from the time it is started. What is not as obvious is that the tasks are arranged on the time line in accordance with their early date set. This is characteristic of simple scheduling. Later, when we discuss resource leveling, we will find that the schedule may have tasks

Figure 7-7. Gantt chart of example project schedule.

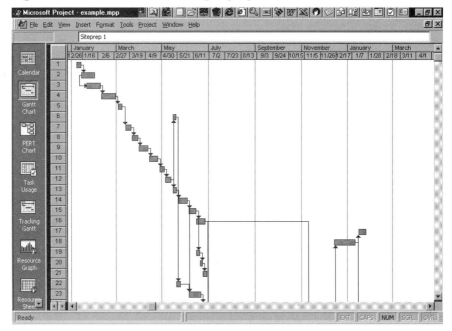

starting and finishing at intermediate times between their early date set and their late date set.

It is important to understand what types of dates you are getting from your scheduling system. The dates you get determine the time phasing of the control budget and consequently the shape of the baseline labor-hour curve on the Earned Value Chart. This, in turn, influences the performance evaluation of the project in each time period. When you do simple scheduling, you usually get early start dates, and these may not always be appropriate to enter into your project management system. *Early start and end dates are always optimistic.* On real projects, most tasks do not start or finish on the earliest possible dates for them to start and finish. Consequently, if you use these early dates, you may find that your performance evaluation measures are constantly showing you behind schedule.

Experienced project managers usually weigh the dates produced by the scheduling system and then choose the dates they think are the most likely, given all the information that they have at hand about the project and about the individual task. Of course, the dates they choose for the plan should be somewhere between the early dates and the late dates for each task.

7.2.2 The Critical Path

If you click on either the *Tracking Gantt* icon at the left of the Project window or the PERT Chart icon, you will get a chart that has some of the boxes colored red. You are already familiar with the PERT Chart View from our discussion in the previous section and know that the red boxes refer to those tasks that are on the *critical path*, but you may not fully understand what the critical path is. To understand the concept of the critical path you must first understand the concept of *float* (sometimes referred to as *slack* or *slack time*). The float for a task *t* is the difference between the late start date and the early start date:

$$float_t = latestart_t - earlystart_t$$

The float for a task is the amount of time you have to play with in scheduling the task. As long as you do not plan to start the task later than the late start date, theoretically it will not affect the completion date of the project. There are other types of float that can be calculated from the early and late start dates that are used on some projects, but we will not devote any space to them here. These other float concepts can be useful on large projects, but they are not essential. Schedulers who use these other float concepts often refer to the type of float we have just defined as *total float* because it is the amount of float available to a task without affecting the finish date of the total project.

From a practical point of view, you would like to have large amounts of float for all tasks because the float is sort of an "insurance" that tasks will be able to be completed in time even if unforeseen delays occur in getting the task started. However, it should be clear that it is impossible for all tasks to have a nonzero float, because then the time when the last task completes could be reduced by some time period. This would mean that the end date for the project could be shortened, which in turn would mean that the scheduling system had not really found the optimal set of dates after all. Consequently, some tasks will have floats with a time value of zero. These are the tasks that are colored red in the PERT Chart View and the Tracking Gantt View.

The collection of all the tasks with zero float is called the *critical path*. The term *path* suggests that the boxes that represent the tasks on the critical path form a sequence, each box of which is connected to its successor, such that the first box in this sequence has the same start date as the project start date and the last box has the same finish date as the project finish date. This is rarely the case since there may be more than one task on the critical path whose start date is the start date of the project or whose finish date is the finish date of the project. Therefore, it would be more suggestive if the critical path were called a *critical subnet* or a *critical spanning set*, since, usually, there will be a family of "paths" that are all critical rather than a unique one.

The concept of the critical path has proved to be a very useful concept. Since it consists of a family of tasks within the project that have zero float, it must be dealt with very carefully because there is no room for delay in getting any of the critical tasks started or in completing them. If any one of them finishes even a day late, the total project schedule will slip by at least a day, unless a way is found to complete at least one of the other critical tasks a day early. Conversely, it is clear that if we concentrate our attention on reducing the durations of the critical tasks, then we might be able to reduce the time it takes to finish the project, or at least "buy some insurance" that the project will finish on time.

When project staff talk about using CPM, they often are referring to periodically analyzing the critical path. On many large projects, the project schedulers periodically prepare an analysis of the critical path for presentation to the program manager. As tasks are completed, the actual finish dates can be inserted into the scheduling system. The scheduling system can use these new dates to compute new start and finish dates for all the tasks that have not yet completed. This may cause the critical path to change for better or worse. If the duration of the total project as computed by the scheduling system continues to grow, it is a bad sign. Some growing and contracting is to be expected. A normal situation is for the total duration to grow a little, and then project management, through analysis and by capitalizing on opportunities that arise, then figures out how to resequence the work and reduce the critical path a little. As a result, the scheduling system can compute a total duration back in the range of where it was before. Then the total duration grows a little more, and again project management finds a way around the problem such as reducing duration of some of the critical tasks, and so on throughout the life of the project.

But unrestrained growth of the total project duration is un-acceptable. Experienced project managers know they need to be constantly aware of the critical path if they want their per-formance evaluation and productivity measures to remain ac-ceptable. One of the questions that arises naturally is: How often should the project schedule be recomputed? Clearly, major changes in the scope of the work, major quantification variances, and major productivity trends are reasons for recom-puting the schedule. However, experience has shown that peri-odic recomputation of the schedule is the best policy, because, even in the absence of variances, tasks can complete late for various reasons, and this tendency alone generally causes schedule growth. Many programs reschedule monthly, but shorter or longer periods may be more appropriate. As a gen-eral rule of thumb, the frequency of rescheduling should in-crease if schedule growth is increasing and can be reduced if the total duration is contracting.

Just as different parts of an organization need to see differ-ent views of the performance and productivity reports, they may also only want to see the part of the scheduling network for which they have responsibility. Scheduling systems like Microsoft Project have the capability to produce subsets of the schedule, sometimes referred to as subnets. Often, these crafts or departments will want to do a critical path analysis of a subnet, but we will not discuss all of the possible variations here. The point to be made is that managers on the project need to be aware of the part of the project schedule that applies to them and of the intersection of the critical path with this part of the schedule.

7.2.3 Resource Scheduling

So far, all of our discussion of scheduling has centered on simple scheduling. We have seen that a simple scheduling system usually computes two sets of dates for each task. For tasks on the critical path, these two sets of dates are the same. For all those tasks that are not on the critical path, it is possible to schedule them between these two sets of dates. By scheduling these noncritical tasks later than their early start dates, it is possible to reduce the demand for resources for all tasks that need these resources.

For example, suppose we have two tasks t_1 and t_2 such that t_1 is on the critical path but t_2 is not. Further suppose that both t_1 and t_2 need resource R during their entire duration, but there is only enough of R to fulfill the needs of one of the tasks. If by chance t_1 and t_2 have the same early start date, it would be possible, but unwise, to start t_1 and t_2 at the same time, because the demand placed on R by t_2 would take away from its ability to serve t_1, possibly causing t_1 to finish late. Since t_1 is on the critical path, finishing late will cause the total duration of the project to slip. Consequently, we see that *resources should always be allocated to critical tasks before they are allocated to noncritical tasks.*

Originally, the process of scheduling the noncritical tasks to minimize the demand on all resources was called *resource leveling*. Somewhat later, it was realized that guessing at the durations of tasks also produced less than optimal schedules. If the scheduling system knew how much of each resource it needed to complete each task, it might be possible for it to compute an optimal schedule consisting of the best duration set possible for all the tasks that both minimized the schedule and the consumption of resources.

Unfortunately, in general, this task scheduling problem has been shown to be intractable (i.e., requires impossible compute times), even with the most powerful computers. On the other hand, heuristic algorithms are known that can produce very good schedules that are generally better than what can be produced by simply minimizing resource demand. The reason for this is that these heuristic algorithms often compute shorter average durations for task sets than can be arrived at by human trial and error. Consequently, resource leveling now usually refers to the process of computing the best possible schedule by taking resource utilization into account.

During the late 1970s, the author and colleagues at Brown and Root studied some of the algorithms employed by some popular commercial scheduling products and found them to be excessively expensive and very suboptimal. During this period W. Douglas Tiner (later professor emeritus at Texas A&M University) put forward a very good heuristic algorithm for resource leveling that was not only fast but produced better resource leveling than we had previously seen.

The author is not certain if Tiner's algorithm ever found its way into any commercial scheduling packages, but today most commercial scheduling systems have good resource leveling capabilities. The drastic increases in computational power and memory size have, of course, helped make this technique much more practical today.

While labor is often one of the most expensive resources, on many projects equipment and materials resources account for a substantial percentage of project costs. For small projects, resource leveling is inappropriate if the main cost is labor and all the laborers available to the project have similar skills. This is often true for software development projects. But, as projects grow larger and more complex, there is a strong financial incentive to know what a nearly optimal resource leveled schedule might be.

Near-optimal schedules can save money in two ways. First, by getting a project completed as soon as possible, it is often the case that a company can begin earning money using the project's output. For instance, if the project is to construct a refinery, every day the new refinery is not available may cost the company a million dollars in lost revenue. Second, by minimizing resource utilization, it is possible to cut the cost of the project substantially. For example, many high-tech defense projects are labor intensive, but they require a vast array of expensive skills. They may require physicists, computer scientists, electrical engineers, mechanical engineers, etc., in addition to quality control personnel, assemblers, and supervisors. Usually, an electrical engineer cannot replace a mechanical engineer on a task; a chemist cannot replace a computer scientist.

7.2.3.1 How Resources Are Communicated to the Scheduling System

For tasks that require diverse skill sets, project schedulers usually deal with labor resources by considering these skill sets to be *labor pools* (e.g., the physicist labor pool, the mechanical engineer labor pool). The defining assumption for a pool is that, for scheduling purposes, all members of the pool are alike in the sense that any physicist can perform a physics task and any electrical engineer can perform an electrical engineering task. These labor pools are the individual labor resources for the project.

If a number of tasks have simultaneous requirements for a given labor pool, it is possible that at any given time the pool will not be large enough to supply all the requirements for its particular skill category. Decisions then need to be made as to which tasks get the available resources. Project management relies on resource leveling scheduling systems to compute the best schedule, not only in terms of duration but also in terms of which tasks are scheduled to have which resources at any given time.

Although labor is often the most significant cost on a project, there are other resources that may have insignificant cost but a big impact. On information technology (IT) tasks, meeting rooms are often a problem. IT projects often involve various design reviews, interface reviews, code walk-throughs, training classes, and so on. There often are not enough conference rooms in a building during various phases of an IT project to conduct all the necessary meetings. Some major reviews take several days to accomplish, tying up limited conference room space for extended periods. Consequently, something as seemingly insignificant as a conference room can become a significant resource.

Construction projects usually have significant materials content. As much as 40% of the cost on a construction project may be allocated to materials with which to build. Moreover, the materials need to be available at the time they are needed. Often, materials purchases for a project are transacted by a materials management division of a company and are not under the direct control of project management. In such cases, the materials management function usually provides the project with a schedule of when various classes of materials will arrive at the job site. These classes of materials are also treated by the project schedulers as resources.

We can see from this example that materials resources can be dynamic, as opposed to static. Labor resources are often somewhat static, although there are periods at the beginning and ending of a project when labor pools are expanding or contracting. Some materials resources are constantly expanding and contracting as new shipments of materials arrive and then are drawn down for use on individual tasks. The dynamics of resources also need to be taken into account.

Just as schedulers have a task list to schedule, they need to have a *resource list* to construct the schedule and a relationship between tasks and resources (i.e., how much of each resource is needed by each task). For instance, suppose a task needs 100 labor-hours from labor pool A and 200 labor-hours from labor pool B and a conference room 25% of the time and various materials resources C, D, and E to complete. Further, suppose only one person from resource A can work on the task at a time, and no more than three persons from resource B can work on the task at a time. Then the scheduling system should be able to compute the duration for the task given that the materials are available. But, when there are many tasks competing for the same resources, the computation of a near-optimal schedule becomes very difficult.

Scheduling systems like Microsoft Project allow you to define a resource list and specify which tasks need these resources. They also provide even more esoteric refinements such as *working time calendars*. Working time calendars allow different labor pools to have different calendars for when workers are available to work. Engineers may only work a 40-hour week, but tradesmen may be available to work overtime for an additional cost. Resource leveling scheduling systems can take these sorts of project details into consideration when computing their schedules.

7.2.3.2 *Using Microsoft Project to Produce the Resource List*

According to the *User's Guide* for Microsoft Project, creating the resource list for a project includes the naming of each resource and specification of the maximum amount of time per day a resource is available. To create a resource list, you click on the *Resource Sheet* icon on the left side of the Project window. The Resource Sheet (table) shown in Figure 7-8 should then be displayed.

You will notice that there are a number of columns in the Resource Sheet in Figure 7-8. These columns reveal that there can be a lot more to specifying a resource than just giving it a name and specifying the maximum amount of time per day it is available. In the **Resource Name** column, you can begin en-

Figure 7-8. Blank resource sheet screen.

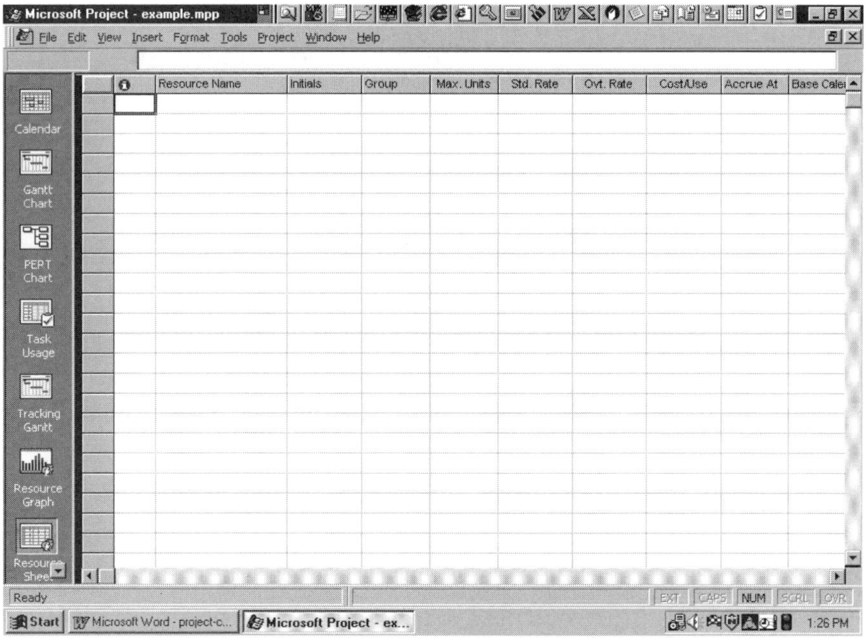

tering the list of labor resource pools determined by the labor categories depicted in Figure 6-12 from Chapter 6. These are the labor pools included:

1. Graders
2. Pavers
3. Concrete workers
4. Framers
5. Sheetrockers
6. Electricians
7. Painters
8. Plumbers
9. Roofers
10. HVAC specialists

After entering ''Graders'' in the **Resource Name** column, use the **Enter** key to move the cursor to the next row and then enter "Pavers" in the **Resource** column of the second row and so on until you have entered all ten of these labor resource pools. Your Resource Sheet should now look like Figure 7-9.

You will notice that Project fills in most of the columns for you, since you left everything but the **Resource Name** column blank when you entered the names of the labor resource pools. It is not important for our purposes that you understand the meaning or utility of all these attributes of a resource that you can specify when using Project. The reason for this is that, when using Modern Project to manage a project, you already have other means of entering some of these data into your project database. But some of these attributes should now be discussed.

Notice that Project has automatically entered 100% in the **Max. Units** column of each resource pool. If you do not specify how many laborers there are in a resource pool, Project assumes there is only one person in the resource pool who is

Figure 7-9. Resource sheet showing labor pools.

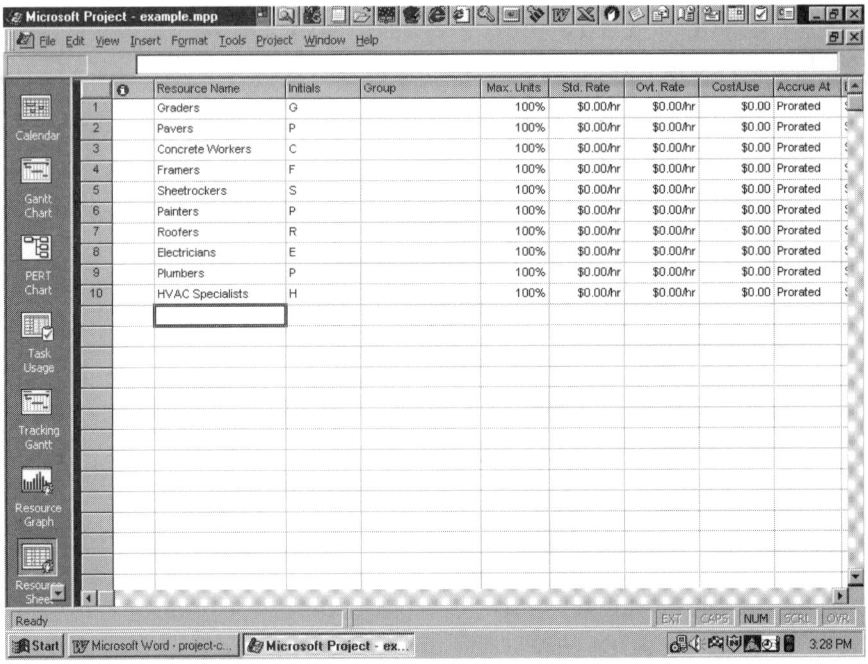

available to work on any task 100% percent of his or her time. If, for instance, there are three laborers in the labor pool that are available to work on project tasks 100% of their time and three other laborers in the pool that are each available 50% of their time, this is specified to Project by entering 450% in the **Max. Units** column for the resource pool.

Project has also automatically added "Standard" in the **Base Calendar** column of each resource pool. Project supports defining individual working time calendars, as mentioned in the last section, for each different resource pool. Project provides a default working time calendar called the *Standard* working time calendar. We will not take time to explain how to define different working time calendars for individual resource pools. How to do so is explained in Chapter 7 of the *Project User's Guide*. On our example project, for simplicity we will use the default Standard working time calendar for all our resource pools. It is of interest to know what periods of time the default working time calendar is assumed to cover.

The default Standard working time calendar assumes that resources that utilize this calendar are available on weekdays but unavailable on weekends and that they are available from 8:00 A.M. until 5:00 P.M. with a break from 12:00 P.M. until 1:00 P.M. If you define a different working time calendar, you do so by modifying the default working time calendar.

You will also notice that Project automatically assigns zero dollar amounts for labor-hour rates and overtime rates, or cost per usage rates for the resource pool. Project can do some simple cost accumulations for planning purposes, but they are usually inadequate for the type of detailed cost estimating discussed in Chapter 2 of this book. Therefore we will not devote time to discussing this capability. The interested reader can pursue this topic in Chapter 9 of the *Project User's Guide*.

What is of interest to us is how to define the relationship between tasks and resource pools. To assign a resource pool to a task, click on the Gantt Chart icon on the left side of the Project window. Then, select the task you want to assign a resource pool to by clicking on the **Task Name** field in the *Task Name* column for the task. If you have the standard toolbar enabled, you can click on the **Assign Resource** icon, which looks like two small heads of two different persons. If not, click on the **Tools** control button at the top of the Project window. A pull-down menu will appear. Click on the **Resources** selection, and another pull-down menu will appear. Click on the **Assign Resources** selection, and an Assign Resources window that looks like Figure 7-10 will appear.

Next, select the resource pool by clicking on the appropriate resource pool in the *Name* column of the Assign Resources form. If more than one unit of the resource pool is to be assigned to a task (e.g., if more than one person from a labor pool is to be assigned to the task), enter that information in the *Units* column for the resource pool. Then, click on the **Assign** control button in the Assign Resources window. You can assign multiple resource pools to a task. You can do this by clicking on another resource pool in the *Name* column and then specifying the number of units in the *Units* column if necessary. If, for instance, you needed 1 1/2 graders from the Graders labor resource pool and 1/2 of a paver from the Pavers resource pool, after selecting both of these resource pools, your Assign Resource window would now look like Figure 7-11.

If you now click on the **Close** control button, the Assign Resources windows will close, and your Gantt Chart View of

Figure 7-10. Assign Resources window showing labor pools.

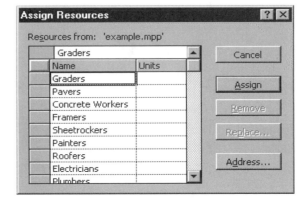

Figure 7-11. Assign Resources window showing size of two labor pools.

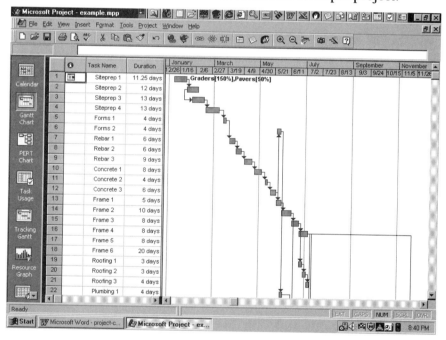

Figure 7-12. Updated Gantt chart schedule for example project.

the project should look like Figure 7-12. Notice that the Gantt Chart View now shows a bold-faced caption by the side of the Siteprep 1 task bar showing that we have assigned 1 1/2 graders and 1/2 paver to it.

But also notice that something has gone wrong. The duration has been changed from five days to 11.25 days. Why did this happen? It happened because we have not yet specified to Project how much work is involved in the Siteprep 1 task. Recall that the man-hour budget for Siteprep 1 is 80 man-hours. We need to convey this to Project. What we are assuming is that we have the equivalent of two persons working on the task. The Standard calendar assumes each worker puts in 40 hours per week (five working days). Consequently, the duration for the task should be five days, which is what we entered for the task originally. What has happened is that since we have not yet specified to Project the man-hour budget for the task, there are some random *work data* for this task in Project's database. We need to correct this.

To specify the man-hour budget to Project, we do the following. From Gantt Chart View we click on the **Window** control button at the top of the Project window. We then select **Split**. This gives us a split-screen display as shown in Figure 7-13. In the upper half of the split-screen we click on the Siteprep 1 task to select it. Then we click somewhere in the lower half of the split-screen to indicate that we want to make a change to the table displayed in the lower half of the split-screen. Next, we click on the **View** control button at the top of the Project window and select the **More Views** option. This brings up a *More Views* window. Now, scroll down to the **Task Form** option, and click on the **Apply** control button. This should make the Project window look pretty much like Figure 7-13. The only thing that remains to be done is to specify the man-hour budget for the Siteprep 1 task to Project. We do this as follows. In the *Work* column we enter 60h (60 hours) for the Graders labor pool and 20h for the Pavers labor pool. This is the 80 man-hour budget for Siteprep 1. The assumption clearly is that two graders will work on the task for a week, putting in 150% of a man-week between them, and that one paver will work on the task 50% of the time for a week.

Notice that this procedure returned the duration to five days, as we would expect. We will not take the time to enter all

Figure 7-13. Split screen for specifying man-hours by labor pool.

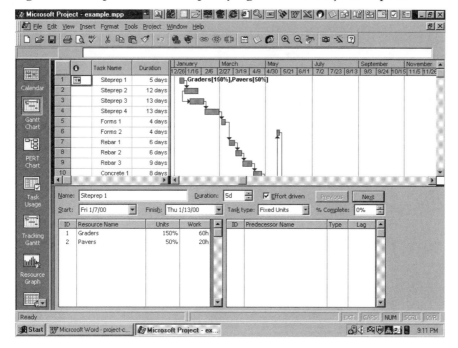

the man-hour budgets for all the tasks into Project. Nor will we use Project to produce a resource leveled schedule for our example project. But from what has been shown, it is clearly possible to produce a resource leveled schedule using Project. There is, however, one more thing we need to cover before we leave this section. Let us return to the Resource Sheet View of the example project, as shown in Figure 7-14. Notice that now the Graders labor pool shows up in red. What does this mean? It means that the Grader resource pool is *overallocated*. By this we mean that the requirement placed on this resource pool by the Siteprep 1 task is greater than what the resource pool can deliver.

The reason for this is that when we defined the Graders resource pool, we left the *Max. Units* column blank, so Project automatically inserted 100%. What this means is that there is only one person in the Graders resource pool, and hence it is impossible to supply 150% for the five-day duration that we

Figure 7-14. Revised resource sheet view of labor pools.

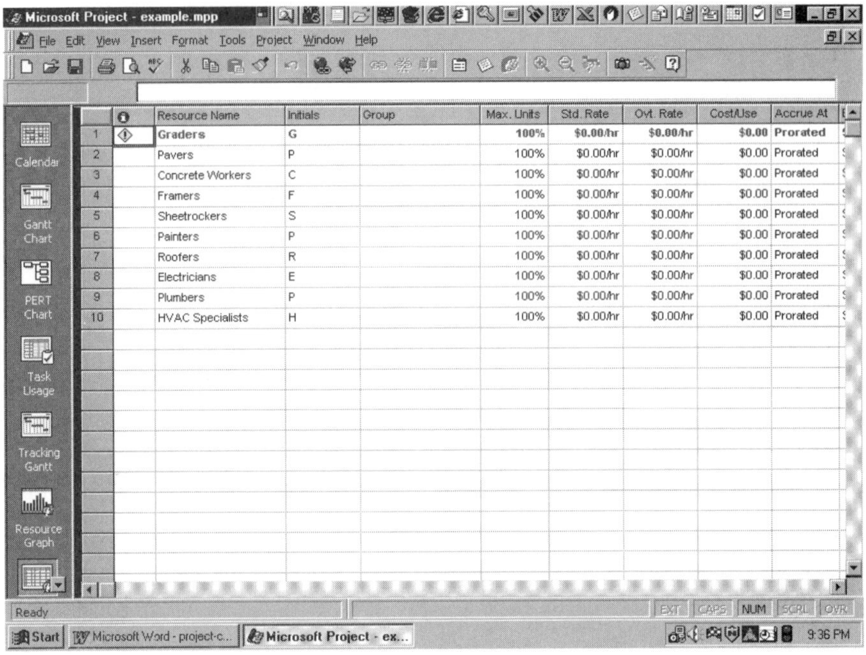

envision. To fix this, we assume that there are two graders in the Graders resource pool. Making this change will cause the Graders resource pool to no longer appear in red.

7.3 Pros and Cons of an Automated Interface

On a large project, if the scheduling system and the project management system are separate systems, which is often the case, then there can clearly be a significant amount of redundant data entry. It is natural to desire an interface that allows the sharing of data between the two systems. From a technological point of view, this is not a big problem, but from an operational point of view it can often be insurmountable.

Many small to medium-size projects circumvent this problem by not using a project management system, getting by with only a scheduling system. Many of these projects may not even know they are not using a project management system, thinking that their scheduling system is a project management system. Also, most scheduling systems have incorporated a few project management functions in addition to just scheduling, but usually only in a limited manner.

One of the most serious disadvantages of an automated interface between a scheduling system and a project management system is the risk of corruption or even loss of critical project information. The problem is that serious project management systems provide the capability to maintain multiple project budgets, as explained in Chapter 3. These budgets, like the Original Budget, Client Budget, Control Budget, and Forecast maintained by Modern Project all should be time phased by different schedules if they are used for project control or client communication. Yet it is rare for even the largest of projects to maintain multiple schedules. In fact, the version of Modern Project provided with this book only time-phases the control budget in order to keep the toolset as simple as possible.

Consequently, as the schedule changes, great care needs to be taken regarding which schedule dates are applied to which budgets. This is especially true with respect to the control budget, since its time phasing directly affects all the performance and productivity measures for the project. There does not exist an algorithm that can figure out under what circumstances to apply which dates to which budgets. There are some operational policies, under which it is possible to operate, that allow for reasonably safe interoperation between a scheduling system and a project management system. In most cases, these operational policies are deemed unfeasible, and, instead, a manual interface between the systems is used even though it means entering some of the project data into both of the systems.

We now discuss two of these operational policies that allow an automated interface between a scheduling system and a project management system. The first policy is to *time phase only the control budget*. This is the policy that enables the automated interface between Microsoft Project and Modern Project. Since at the very beginning of a project the control budget is the same as the original budget, the original time-phased budget can be obtained (and archived) by saving a copy of the project database under a different name that will never be altered.

Operating under this policy allows us to keep the control budget, which is used for most purposes, updated with the dates produced by the scheduling system. If the project manager requires that the other budgets be time phased, then the client budget and the forecast dates will still have to be maintained manually, and, since they are often different from the control budget dates, they will require management discretion in their entry.

Project managers often do not like this policy for a variety of reasons. The current project schedule often does not have a close correlation with any of the budgets or the forecast. Scheduling systems produce schedules that can tell you the most optimal dates you can hope for if everything goes right, and they can also tell you the most conservative dates under a variety of assumptions. The problem is how to pick the *most likely* dates that are somewhere in between. These are the dates that are needed to time phase the control budget. Most project managers believe this is done with discretion, based on experience. They tend to rely on project schedulers to tell them what the range of possibilities is. Then, together with the project management staff, they make decisions on what they believe can reasonably be accomplished.

Consequently, project managers often reason that even if there is an automated interface for loading dates from the scheduling system into the project management system, it is not reasonable to assume these dates are the ones you really want to time phase the control budget. Therefore, they usually reject this operational policy, since most project managers believe that the maintenance of schedule dates takes an individual periodic review of each of the start and end date pairs for each task. However, even if this policy is rejected, most project managers do not mind using an automated interface to make the initial bulk move of schedule dates over to the project management systems at the beginning of a project, because it saves a lot of time and effort in the beginning, and they know that all of these dates are going to be periodically reviewed (and possibly updated) anyway.

The second operational policy that might allow automated transfer of schedule dates from the scheduling system to the project management system is to *maintain a separate schedule for each budget and for the forecast.* In this way, each of the individual schedules can be tuned to the budget that it is used to time phase, rather than having a single schedule for all purposes. This option is universally unpopular with project managers because it requires increasing the scheduling effort by approximately 300%.

Change orders and quantity variances often cause dependencies among tasks to change. They also cause the amount of resources needed from the resource pools to change. So even if all the schedules had the same tasks, they would still be intrinsically different schedules. Also, change orders often create new tasks and eliminate old tasks, so these individual schedules will probably not contain the same tasks. The effort required to maintain four schedules (or even two or three) makes this policy unworkable. Furthermore, all the objections to moving dates automatically from the scheduling system to the project management system without individual review still hold to some degree for this second policy as for the first.

We will allocate a significant amount of space in the following section explaining how the automated interface between Microsoft Project and Modern Project works. Our recommendation, however, is to use it only to move the initial set of dates from the scheduling system during the project planning phase into the project management system. Thereafter, you can make manual changes to the dates on the basis of the current schedule, the nature of the variances that cause the schedule changes, and project management judgment.

It is also recommended that the schedule that is maintained by the scheduling system correspond to the control budget. This way the resources needed for the tasks will be the same in the scheduling system as in the project management system. This, of course, necessitates a strict separation of variances between quantification variances and productivity variances, because productivity variances cause changes in the timing of a project that in turn cause changes in the time phasing of the budget to which the variances correspond. If the time phasing is not correct, the schedule performance ratio will not be correct in each of the reporting periods.

There is a tendency on many projects to be careless about separating quantification variances and productivity variances. On the surface, it may seem reasonable because eliminating the distinction will cause the schedule to be more "realistic" in the sense that it will more closely reflect when the project might finish. But what needs to be kept in mind is that the schedule needs to represent what the project manager is trying to manage to and *not* the time phasing of the forecast.

7.4 The Automated Interface to Microsoft Project

Now that you are aware of the risks involved with importing schedule dates from a scheduling system into a project management system, we are ready to discuss an automated interface to transfer Microsoft Project schedule dates into Modern Project. The plan for this interface was to utilize the existing import/export features of Microsoft Access and Microsoft Project as far as possible to keep the interface simple, both for the user's ease and to keep the amount of custom code to a minimum. To transfer the schedule dates from the Microsoft Project schedule, you should be in Gantt Chart View with the Entry table visible as shown in Figure 7-15.

If your screen does not look like Figure 7-15, you can get to Gantt Chart View by clicking on the Gantt Chart icon at the left side of the Project window. You can get the Entry table displayed by clicking on the **View** control button at the top of the Project window and then selecting **Table** from the pull-down menu that appears. Finally, select **Entry** from the next menu that appears.

You are now ready to export the Entry table. To do this, first click on the **File** control button at the top of the Project window. Then select **Save as HTML** from the pull-down menu. This causes a *File Save* menu to appear, as shown in Figure 7-16. This window shows that it is prepared to save the Entry table in a file named *example.html* in the *Schedule* directory. Since this File Save menu is common to Microsoft products, you probably already know how to use it to change the name of the

Figure 7-15. Entry table in Gantt chart view.

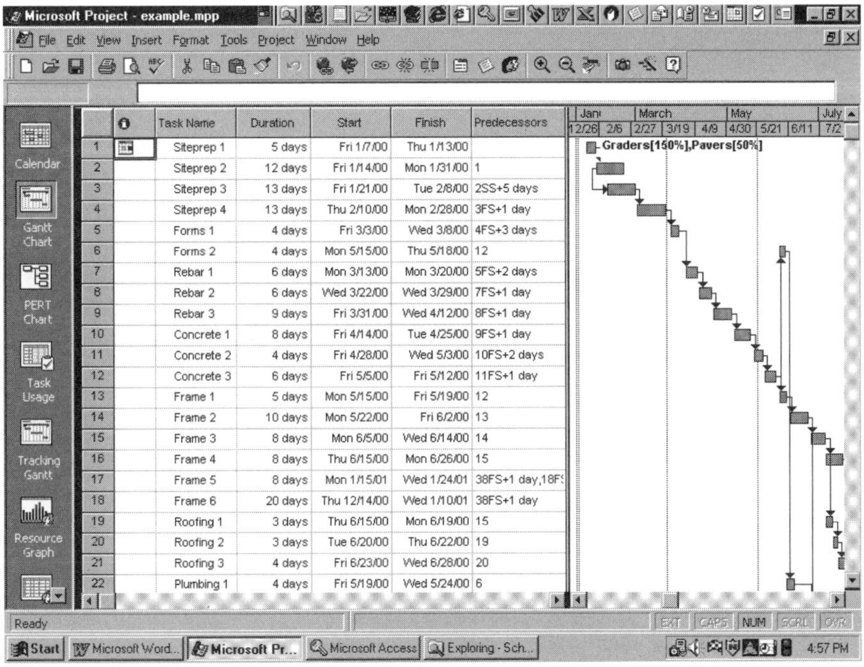

Figure 7-16. File Save window.

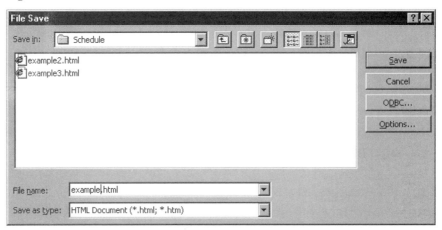

Figure 7-17. Export Format window.

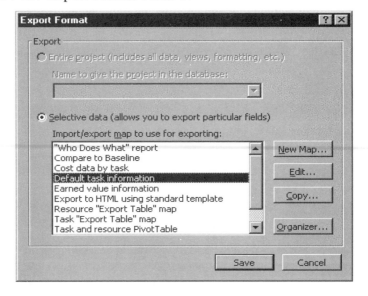

file or the directory to a location of your choice. It does not matter where you save this HTML file. What matters is that you remember where you saved it so you can later import it into Modern Project.

Click on the **Save** control button on the right side of the File Save window, and the Entry file will be saved as an HTML file. This causes the *Export Format* window to appear as shown in Figure 7-17. You should click on the **Default task informa-tion** selection in this window. When you do, it will be backlit in blue, as indicated by the highlight in Figure 7-17. Now click on the **Save** control button at the bottom of the window. This causes the Entry table to be saved in HTML format in the file location you previously specified in the File Save window.

The next step is to import this file into Modern Project. You do this from within the example project database into which you want the imported schedule dates to be received. So open the *exampleChapt6.mde* version of the example project database. Then click on the **File** control button at the top of the Access Window and select **Get External Data**. Then select **Import** from the next menu that appears. This causes the *Import* window to appear, as shown in Figure 7-18. Move to the directory where you saved the file *example.html*. In the example shown in Figure 7-18, this is the *Schedule* directory. Next, select the **HTML Docu-ments** option from the *Files of type* field at the bottom of the window. Then click on the *example.html* file in the main part of

Figure 7-18. Import window.

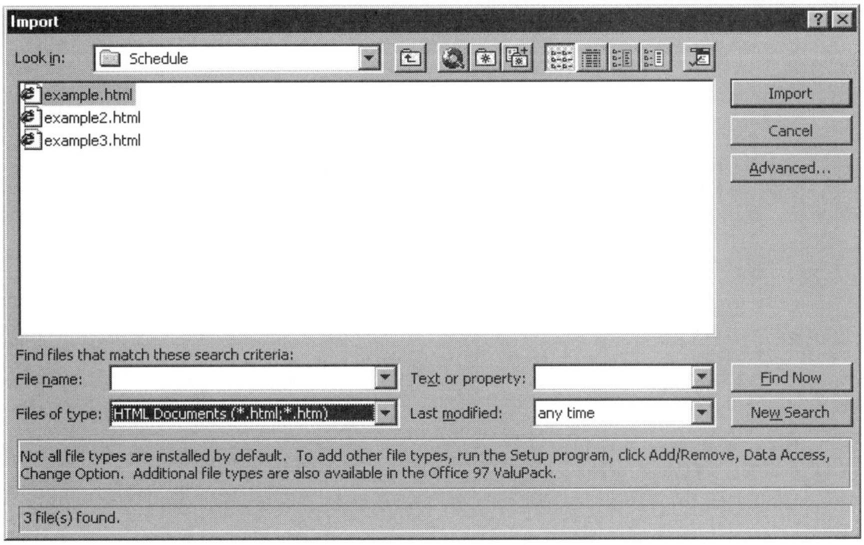

the window. This prepares the Modern Project to receive the *example.html* file.

Now click on the **Import** control button on the right side of the Import window. This causes the *Import HTML Wizard* to appear, as shown in Figure 7-19. Make sure the *First Row Contains Column Headings* box is checked, as shown in Figure 7-19.

You will now use the Import HTML Wizard to import only the relevant columns of information into Modern Project. To start the wizard to work, click on the **Next** control button at the bottom of the wizard's window. The wizard will ask you if you want to store this data into a new table or an existing table. Make sure that the **new table** option is selected. Then click on **Next** again. The wizard now changes the upper half of its window. You can now click on the various columns of data in the lower part of the wizard's window, and they will be backlit in

Figure 7-19. Import HTML Wizard.

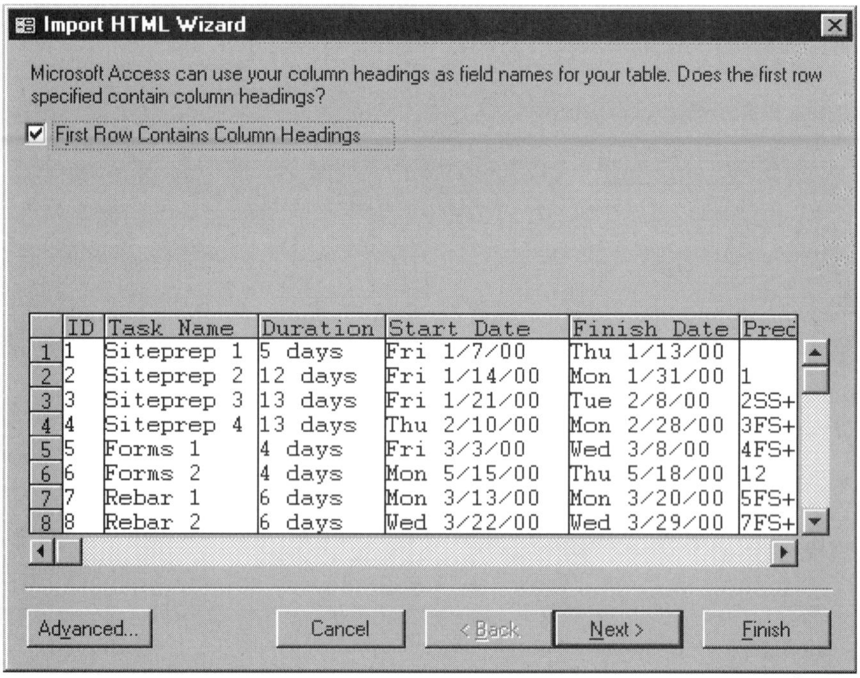

black. Each time you select one of these columns, the wizard gives you the choice of importing that column of data. You specify your choice to the wizard by either checking the *Do not import* field (Skip) box or leaving it blank. Only the columns for which you leave the box blank are imported.

The only columns of data we want to import from the *example.html* file are the *Task Name* column, the *Start Date* column, and the *Finish Date* column. Select the various columns sequentially, and put a check in each of the other boxes. Then click on the **Next** control button at the bottom of the wizard's window again. The wizard now asks you whether you want this new table to have a key. Select the **No Primary Key** option, and then click on the **Next** control button again.

The wizard now gives you the opportunity to name this new table that is going to be imported into Modern Project. It is important that you name it "Schedule Dates." Type "Schedule Dates" into the *Import to Table*: field in the center of the wizard's window. Finally, click on the **Finish** control button at the bottom of the wizard's window. You should now have successfully imported the schedule dates that you saved from Microsoft Project into Modern Project.

There is one last thing to do. Even though you have imported the schedule dates into Modern Project, you have not told Modern Project to actually use these dates as opposed to some other set of dates. These new dates, as we already know, are stored within Modern Project in a database table called Schedule Dates, but they have not yet been moved into the individual tasks in Modern Project. To do this, you must click on the **Transfer Schedule Dates** control button on Modern Project's Main Menu. This will cause the *Transfer Schedule Dates* form to appear, which allows you to choose which schedule you want to update. Choose the control schedule by clicking on the **Update Control Schedule** control button. Modern Project should now confirm that it has successfully transferred the dates.

If you display the Earned Value Chart again after the dates have been transferred from Microsoft Project, you will see that the shape of the baseline labor-hours curve has changed somewhat. This is because the schedule data produced by Microsoft Project is a little different from the control schedule dates we entered manually in Chapters 2 and 6.

Chapter 8

Government Projects

The management of large government-funded projects has had a profound impact on the project management profession. In general, it can be said that project management for government projects and for commercial (nongovernment) projects has progressed along two separate tracks. On the surface, these tracks appear to be considerably different, but upon closer inspection it can be seen that they run parallel to each other. Each project management profession (government and commercial) has developed its own vocabulary. In this book, up until now, we have restricted our vocabulary to that of the commercial project managers, primarily because there are a lot more of them out there.

But now it is time to turn our attention to the government project management sector. This is not for the purpose of making government project managers feel they have not been left out but to understand the significance of their contribution to the project management field and their particular philosophies of project management.

8.1 Historical Perspective

Government project managers could argue that, in a sense, most of the significant project management technical innovations of the past forty years have originated in government projects. Commercial project managers who have come in contact with government project management techniques often feel they are overly restrictive, with an emphasis on techniques and form rather than on end results. Commercial project managers also find the vocabulary of government project managers arcane, filled with cryptic acronyms that, when expanded, translate into overly complicated technical names for simple concepts.

Before we can mine the gold that is hidden within the government project management profession, we must first learn its vocabulary. The language government project managers speak is actually not a complicated one. Unlike human language translation, translation from the government project management language to the commercial project management language is a simple, one-to-one correspondence. During the course of this chapter we introduce most of the relevant government project management terms and phrases and explain what they mean with respect to the concepts we have already developed in this book. Along the way, we also try to give a little of the rationale behind their philosophies that should justify, to some extent, why things have evolved in the way they have.

Before proceeding with this task, we first say a few words of an historical nature to put some of their accomplishments in perspective. Perhaps two of the most significant project management innovations were associated with government projects. World War II, directly or indirectly, generated more technical innovations than any previous period. The war had a profound impact on our social structure and values, and the nation emerged with the view that technology held the solution to many of the world's problems.

For at least two decades after the war, the nation struggled to stay ahead of the emerging Soviet technology threat. During this period, the government undertook colossal technology programs. Government programs being undertaken today are still growing larger and more complex, but, in comparison to what had preceded it, this period was unprecedented. A new generation of engineers and scientists was bred, and there was great pressure to succeed in accomplishing large-scale technological leaps. One of these gigantic undertakings was the development of the Polaris submarine.

This project was a huge technological undertaking, and the engineers, scientists, and managers who accomplished it had, in general, technological backgrounds and technological outlooks. With this project is associated the two key project management techniques of earned value analysis and PERT chart-type scheduling analysis. We discussed the emergence of PERT chart scheduling analysis in Chapter 7. It is not clear exactly to whom we should credit the earned value analysis concept, but it appears that either the idea itself or at least its widespread employment came out of this project.

But this was not the whole of the government project management contribution to the profession. Many of the details of cost and schedule variance analysis and of other technical project management techniques seem to have either originated on government projects or at least been developed through them.

Consequently, technical excellence and innovation have characterized the government project management profession. But, on the practical side, the commercial project managers have made their own contribution, and it is equally significant, if not more so. Unfortunately, the government, as it is wont to do, has spent a great effort trying to codify and pass down its style of project management to the government project managers of the future. In so doing, it has tended to overlook some of the most significant project management developments in the commercial sector. For instance, the government has been slow to adopt the multibudgeting approach explained in Chapter 3 or to place much importance in productivity analysis as explained in Chapter 5.

So, while the project management emphasis in the government has tended to be on the analysis of performance, the commercial project managers have tended to emphasize the analysis of productivity and cost containment and accountability. This is exactly the opposite of what you would expect when you listen to the rhetoric of commercial and government project managers. Government project offices constantly complain that commercial companies do not provide them with the productivity, accountability, and cost containment that they require. Yet they do not require this sort of emphasis on government projects. Commercial companies that do business with the government complain that government management and reporting requirements are too restrictive to allow them to perform at their highest levels.

The reader is, we hope, beginning to appreciate that much of the difference between commercial and government project management is an issue of vocabulary and emphasis. The basic ideas are the same. The difference is in how these ideas are put into practice.

8.2 Government Project Management Models

To learn both the vocabulary and the viewpoint of (official) government project management, it is helpful to understand their *abstract model* of a project. This is shown in Figure 8-1. It is also helpful to understand their *format* for charting the performance of a project. This is shown in Figure 8-3. While this format is similar to the Earned Value chart you can get from Modern Project by clicking on the Earned Value Chart button on the Main Menu, there are some important differences that we will explain.

The summary presented with these two figures will introduce the reader to enough of the government project management vocabulary and viewpoint to be able to communicate freely with government project management personnel. However, readers should not think they have mastered government project management by simply reading this chapter. Government project management methods and policy are defined in various government regulations and directives. One of the most

Figure 8-1. Abstract model of a government project.

```
                      ┌─────────────────┐
                      │ Contract Price  │
                      └────────┬────────┘
              ┌────────────────┴────────────────┐
    ┌─────────────────┐              ┌─────────────────┐
    │ Total Allocated │              │   Profit/Fees   │
    │ Budget          │              └─────────────────┘
    └────────┬────────┘
        ┌────┴───────────────────────┐
┌─────────────────┐        ┌─────────────────┐
│ Performance     │        │ Management      │
│ Measurement     │        │ Reserve         │
│ Baseline        │        └─────────────────┘
└────────┬────────┘
    ┌────┴──────────────────────────┐
┌─────────────────┐        ┌─────────────────────┐
│ Control Accounts│        │ Undistributed Budget│
└────────┬────────┘        └─────────────────────┘
    ┌────┴──────────────┐
┌─────────────────┐ ┌─────────────────────┐
│ Work Packages   │ │ Planning Packages   │
└─────────────────┘ └─────────────────────┘
```

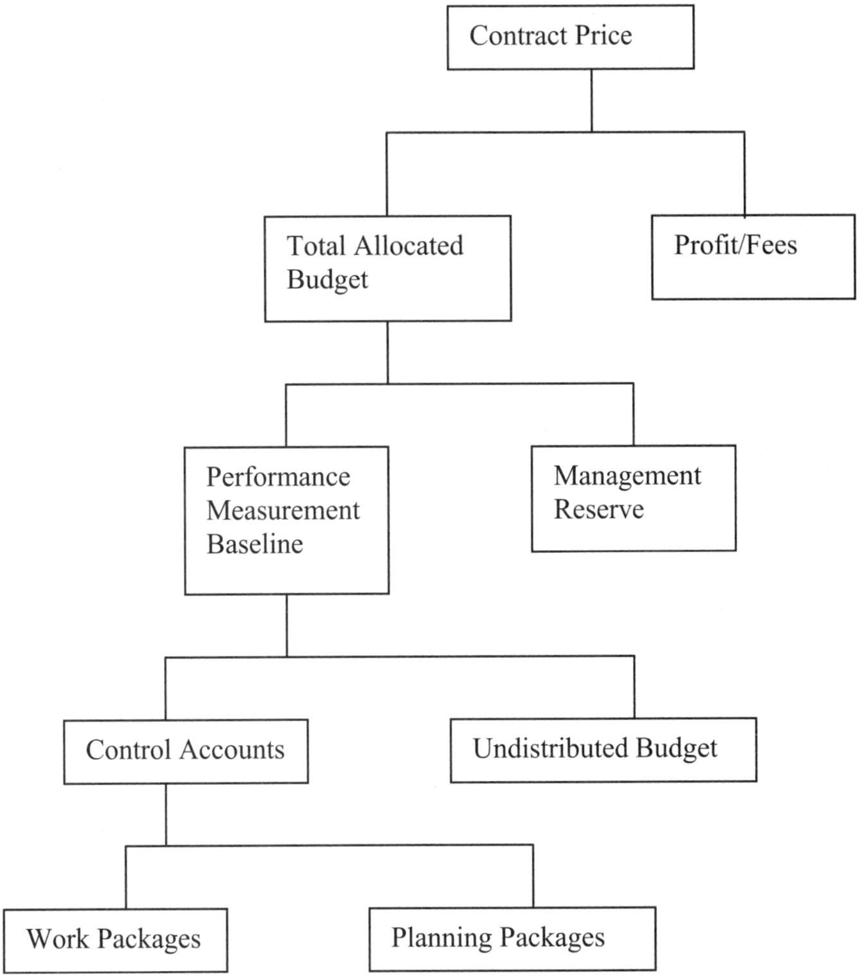

relevant in our context is the government Earned Value Management (EVM) policy, which is documented in DoD 5000.2-R. Perhaps more accessible is the government's EVM homepage, located at *http://www.acq.osd.mil/pm/*. The Defense Systems Management College (DMSC) has an e-mail address to which you can forward requests for information. It is *evm@dmsc. dsm.mil*.

From Figure 8-1, one sees that the abstract model of a government project is a hierarchy that depicts the Budget for the project and its allocations to different cost accounts. The root (top) of this hierarchy is labeled "Contract Price." At the lowest level of the hierarchy there are "Work Packages" and "Planning Packages."

This hierarchy is similar to the Cost Breakdown Structure (CBS) that is supported in Modern Project in parallel to the WBS. But, in accordance with government terminology, the government version is called the WBS. In fact, it is not entirely a CBS but rather a hybrid cost, organizational, and product breakdown structure, as we explain a little later. Commercial usage of the term *WBS*, on the other hand, is as explained in Chapter 2. This difference in the meaning of the term *WBS* between commercial practice and government practice leads to many misunderstandings.

As one might expect, project managers do not always stay put. Project managers often switch from the commercial sector to the government sector or vice versa. It is common for a project manager to gain experience in one sector and then switch to the other. These displaced project managers often do not understand that there is a big difference in the meaning of terms, and they try to continue operating under their own interpretations and in accordance with their past experience. It is remarkable, and possibly a credit to their flexibility, that such managers often go for years without understanding the differences themselves. Of course, they find it necessary to make modifications to their interpretation of terms along the way in order to survive. This leads to all sorts of mixed meanings of terms and private or perhaps "minor" project management philosophies.

Because the commercial sector is so much larger than the government sector, and less rigid in management style, these minor approaches in the commercial sector tend to be ignored. Project managers in the commercial sector usually know they have to define their terms when they are communicating with other project managers or with project management staff. In the government sector, everything is supposed to be standardized, and, as a result, private interpretations are often hidden. It is not common to ask government project managers to define their terms. In this arena one learns to figure out what is really going on, on a project, by observation, and one pays lip service to many of the government policies while practicing something else.

Having issued all these warnings about how careful we must be in understanding how a term is being used, let us now try to examine what all the terms mean in the hierarchy of Figure 8-1.

8.3 Government Project Management Vocabulary

In Figure 8-1 there are two boxes (hierarchy elements) under the top box. One is the "Total Allocated Budget," commonly represented by the acronym TAB, and the other is the "Profit/ Fees." Together, the TAB plus the Profit or Fees constitute the "Contract Price." The TAB is the thing to be managed, the Profit or Fees often being linked to how well the TAB is managed.

The TAB is further decomposed, as shown in Figure 8-1, into the "Performance Measurement Baseline," represented by the acronym PMB, and the "Management Reserve." A discussion of management reserve, often called *contingency* in the commercial sector, is postponed until the chapter on risk management. Again, the PMB is that part of the TAB to be managed, the management reserve being a portion of the TAB held in reserve for certain contingencies.

The PMB is then decomposed into a number of "Control Accounts" that correspond to the control packages with which we are already familiar, plus the "Undistributed Budget." The undistributed budget is that part of the PMB that has not yet been allocated to work packages. You will notice in Figure 8-1 that the work packages are at the lowest level of the hierarchy, just as in the WBS structures with which you are already familiar. You will also notice that there are "Planning Packages" in addition to the work packages. You can think of the planning packages as being work packages that are not yet activated, that is, closed work packages that have not yet been opened.

But the planning packages can also be a receptacle for planning type work conducted by project personnel. On many large government projects, there is a large component of research and development that needs to be accomplished to enable the actual construction of the output of the project. Consequently, large government projects are often begun without an understanding of how they will be completed. There are commercial projects of this nature, also, and it is useful to understand how to build a WBS that accounts for this phenomenon.

8.3.1 Multibudgeting vs. the TAB

The emphasis in the model in Figure 8-1 is on the cost budgets, rather than on the work. In the next section, when we discuss the government version of a WBS, we will see that this emphasis makes a government WBS something different from a commercial WBS, but there are parallels. Before we discuss the government concept of a WBS, let us look a little closer at this cost emphasis of the model. The government has not embraced the concept of multibudgeting, but it understands the problems multibudgeting tries to solve. The concept of multiple budgets on a project seems to the government to be a contradiction in terms. In discussions at the Pentagon's project management office, the author has heard it asked: "How can a project have more than one budget?" In an attempt to treat change orders and variances as part of a single budget, they have devised the following subdivision of the TAB shown in Figure 8-2.

The TAB is viewed as being composed of more basic budgets. First, there is the Negotiated Contract Cost (NCC), which corresponds to our Original Budget. This is the budget based on the cost originally negotiated with the contractor. Then there

Figure 8-2. The Total Allocated Budget (TAB) model.

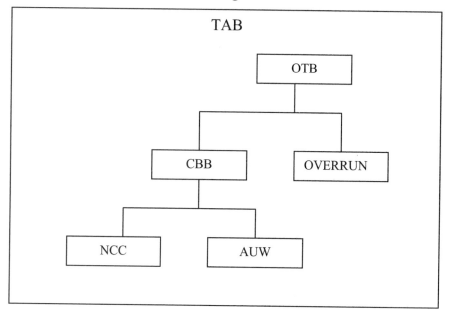

is the "Authorized Unpriced Work" (AUW), which can include government-authorized changes. This is additional work that has been authorized by the government that is not covered in the NCC and the price of which has not yet been negotiated with a contractor.

The sum of the NCC and the AUW is what is called the "Contract Budget Base" (CBB). This corresponds roughly but not exactly to the Client Budget, as explained in Chapters 2 and 3. The government also realizes that it is unlikely that the CBB will be met because there is something called "Overrun." The overrun is, of course, the end result of what we recognize as quantification deviations and productivity deviations. In fact, the overrun is essentially the sum of all the quantification and productivity deviations.

Rather than attempt to document the most significant of these deviations as variances and attempt to manage them as described in Chapters 3 and 4, the government managers prefer to lump them together as overrun and insert them in their cost model as one of the components of the TAB. This gives the appearance of a single budget, but it hides the detail of the variances that need to be managed. The author views this as a significant weakness in this project management philosophy. This is one of the places where the government could learn a practical lesson from commercial-sector best practices.

The sum of the CBB and the overrun is the "Over Target Baseline" (OTB). The OTB corresponds roughly to the Forecast, rather than the Control Budget, even though it is used like the Control Budget in Chapters 3 and 4. The failure to differentiate between quantification overruns and productivity overruns does not allow government managers to compute the control budget. By now the reader has no doubt realized that if they do not compute the control budget and instead base their earned value performance calculations on something that is more like a forecast, they are corrupting their earned value computations.

The result of all this is that commercial earned value computations and government earned value computations (what is called Budgeted Cost of Work Performed—BCWP) are usually not the same. Theoretically, they use the same formula, but in practice the formula is applied to budgets that have been calculated differently. The unfortunate effect of this miscalculation is that it encourages cost overruns for productivity reasons. Since the productivity deviations are not factored out of the budget calculations before the earned value formula is applied, the government method of earned value computation gives credit for productivity deviations. In other words the government method of computing earned value results in a larger amount of earned value than would have resulted from the calculations presented in the rest of this book.

8.3.2 The Meaning of WBS

As pointed out in the previous section, the model depicted in Figures 8-1 and 8-2 emphasizes the cost, rather than the work. We now need to consider what this emphasis leads to in government work breakdown structures. The WBS hierarchy consists of *control accounts* (equivalently *cost accounts* in their vocabulary), which in turn contain *work packages*. This is similar to the relationship between control packages and work packages that we explained in Chapter 2. But there is a significant difference, as shown in Figure 8-3.

Figure 8-3 shows what is called a *Contract* WBS. The hierarchy at the upper right of Figure 8-3 that begins with the "Fire Control" box is what is called a *Program* WBS. A Program WBS is to be *product oriented*. The Defense Department's work breakdown structure handbook states that "In order to use the work

Figure 8-3. The contract WBS for a government project.

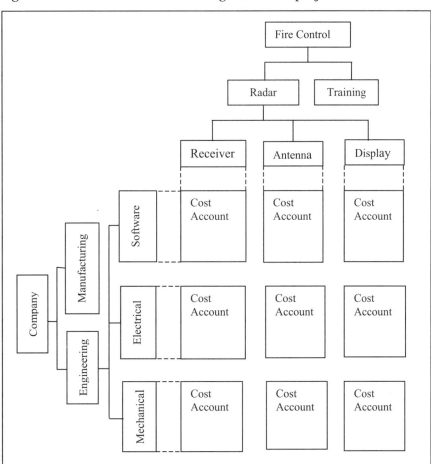

breakdown structure as a framework for the technical objectives of a program, the work breakdown structure must be product oriented." In the example shown in Figure 8-3, the Product WBS is for a Fire Control System. Figure 8-3 is a simplification of Figure 3-3 of the handbook.

The product orientation of a government WBS is not always bad. Often the product-oriented breakdown structure reflects the way the product will be built and therefore coincides with the definition of a WBS that was given in Chapter 2. The problem with this concept is that the product orientation does not always coincide with the way the work will be performed. The government project management officials recognize that this often presents a problem for contractors, and the Contract WBS is their view of how to solve this problem. Shortly we will consider why it often does not.

Why does the government want to make a WBS product oriented? There was a time when government program offices and labs were more involved in the design and engineering of the facilities and systems that they purchase. Today, government program offices primarily oversee the work of contractors who build these facilities and systems. The emphasis now is on requirements definition and on the monitoring of the contractors. Since program offices today have proportionally smaller staffs, and since the contractors deliver products, it is easier for them to focus on the things they are getting from the contractors than on how the contractors actually build the products they deliver.

Moreover, contractors prefer not to have the government program office staff monitoring the details of their work, so they are, for the most part, happy with the solution the government has proposed. The government solution is to take the Program WBS hierarchy and the OBS of the organization performing the work and to form what in mathematical terms is called the *cross-product* of these two structures. This cross-product is what they call the Contract WBS. It is that part of Figure 8-3 that appears in the lower right part of the figure.

According to the DOD handbook, the Contract WBS consists of cost accounts or control accounts, each one of which is determined by a *(sub)product* in the Program WBS and an organizational unit in the contractors OBS. These cost accounts in turn contain work packages. The handbook gives little guidance on the relationship of these work packages to each other or on the relationship of the tasks within them, other than to acknowledge that within a cost account, budgets, schedules and responsibility come together.

Section 3.1.3 of the handbook begins by stating, "To provide the responsible contract manager with technical, schedule, and other needed resource information, the management control system must be keyed to the same work breakdown structure element and organization unit." So one way of using the Modern Project toolset on a government project is to build your WBS in a different way, as shown in Figure 8-3. This is the type of structure that you will have to enter into your Modern Project WBS, using the WBS Entry/Edit tool.

When used in this manner, you will not have separate WBS and OBS structures as explained in Chapter 6, since they will be merged into the Contract WBS. You can still have lower-level control packages in the Modern Project WBS under a given cost account, as well as the work packages if you need to specify the relationship of some of the work packages within a cost account. When Modern Project is used in this way, it is probably better to use the term *control account* rather than *cost account* to specify these summary-level WBS elements, since the term *cost account* is used in a different sense within Modern Project.

Government project management policy requires that the government program offices define the Program WBS hierarchy three levels deep and that further subdivision of the control packages be left up to the contractors who perform them. This level of decomposition usually yields control packages that are rather large. They are not necessarily intended to be performed by a single contractor. The handbook gives a little guidance in Section 3.1.2 on how these Contract WBS structures can be further decomposed into Subcontract WBS structures in a few circumstances.

A contractor who is responsible for a work package in turn treats the package as a project and constructs a WBS that describes the project of implementing the government-defined work package. This often leads to difficulties in matching up contractor work breakdown structures and the government work breakdown structures. The reason for this is that a single contractor is often responsible for a number of government work packages and wants to treat the work in this collection of government work packages as a single project.

Furthermore, contractors often want to subdivide this work in accordance with the way the work is to be accomplished, but the product orientation of the government work packages frequently does not lend itself well to doing this. A good example of this is in the area of software. Often a single contractor provides the software for a number of subsystems within a larger system. Several of the software components that are developed can be used in a number of these subsystems, so the contractor wishes to organize the work around these components and not around the subsystems. This is a long-standing problem that has never been solved in an entirely satisfactory manner. Clearly, this problem would not occur if the work breakdown structures were always constructed in accordance with how the work is actually done.

8.3.3 Government Performance Reporting

We now turn our attention to government earned value reporting. The number of different reporting formats the government uses depends upon the size of the contract. As of the writing of this chapter, there are two cases. If the contract is not a firm fixed price contract and its price exceeds $70 million (in 1996 calendar year dollars) in RDT&E, or if it exceeds $300 million in procurement, then the contractor is required to utilize a project management system that meets 32 criteria. It is also required that Cost Performance Reports (CPRs) be provided in five different formats. These five formats include a WBS format, an Organizational format, and a Baseline format.

If the contract price is less than these limits but exceeds $6 million in calendar year 1996 dollars, and if the project is to last longer than 12 months, then there is a less restrictive requirement that requires a "reasonably objective" project management system and Cost/Schedule Status Reports (C/SSRs) in two different formats, one of which is the WBS format.

The Earned Value Chart shown in Figure 8-4 contains some acronyms that have not been explained yet. You are already familiar with the TAB and the Management Reserve shown on the chart. The PMB is represented by the amount (of dollars) below the Management Reserve line. At the upper right of the chart is the acronym "BAC." This stands for "Budget at Completion." It is the same as the PMB, but the emphasis here is on what the PMB component of the TAB will be at completion.

You no doubt have already noticed that the actual expenditure curve, the baseline curve, and the earned value curve are

Figure 8-4. Earned Value Chart for a government project.

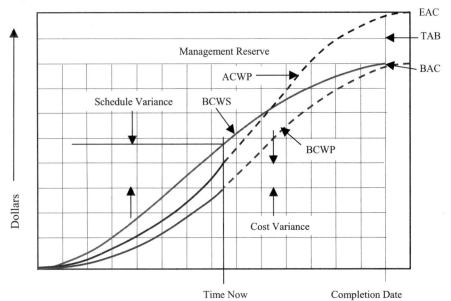

labeled differently in the government version of the Earned Value chart. The actual expenditure curve (labeled ACWP) also runs past the completion date and exceeds the sum of the BAC (PMB) and the Management Reserve. The acronym ACWP stands for "Actual Cost of Work Performed." That the ACWP exceeds the budget is not surprising, but that it runs past the completion date may appear strange. The reason for this is that the "Completion Date" is the planned completion date, not the real completion date.

On government projects, the ACWP is measured in dollars, rather than labor-hours, because the government project offices belong to the customer rather than to the contractor and are more interested in the actual cost than in the actual labor-hour expenditure. The ACWP curve ends at a point labeled EAC. The EAC acronym stands for "Estimate at Complete."

The EAC is a type of forecast that is computed by dividing the BAC by the Cost Performance Ratio. This computation can be thought of as modifying the baseline budget by the current productivity ratio. As computed forecasts go, this is one of the better projections. However, using computed forecasts, no matter what the algorithm, does not tend to give nearly as accurate forecasts as treating the forecast as a budget and managing it accordingly.

When using Modern Project on a government project, if you want to get a more accurate estimate of the EAC, you can do so as follows. First, use the Forecast to get the managed forecast of labor-hours. Then apply the appropriate labor-hour rates to get the "EAC labor costs." Finally, add in the planned nonlabor-hour expenditures. Of course, this is considerably more time-consuming than using the EAC computation, and, no doubt, this is one of its attractions on large projects. The author has found, however, that it is often worth the extra effort to get an accurate estimate at completion by computing it from the Forecast as outlined earlier. The computed estimate at complete can often be fairly inaccurate, especially during the early phases of a project.

The reason for this is twofold. First, modifying the materials and equipment expenditure budgets by the productivity ratio is not an accurate way to get an estimate at complete for the materials and equipment cost. Often, the materials and equipment are purchased by a purchasing department over which the project manager has little control, and the deviations from the original estimates of these costs tend to be related to market conditions, and not to productivity on the project. Second, cumulative productivity rates tend to change a lot during the life of the project. All forecasting methods tend to get better as you get closer to the end of the project, but the calculated ones are often unreliable until fairly late in the project lifetime.

The baseline curve in Figure 8-4 is labeled "BCWS," which stands for "Budgeted Cost of Work Scheduled." It is essentially the time-phased PMB. Like the ACWP curve, the BCWS curve is a time-phased cost budget, as opposed to a time-phased labor-hour budget. When using Modern Project on a government project, the labor-hour component of the PMB corresponds to the Control labor-hour budget. But on most government projects it is very difficult to tell what the PMB corresponds to theoretically.

The reason for this difficulty is the TAB theory of accounting for change orders and variances, as explained earlier in the chapter. At any point in time, it depends on how many of these deviations from the plan have been incorporated into the OTB and how much of the Management Reserve has been allocated into the PMB to cover these deviations. If all of the deviations to date have been incorporated into the OTB and the necessary budget to cover them has been allocated from the Management Reserve into the PMB, then the labor-hour component of the PMB corresponds to the Forecast in Modern Project.

When using Modern Project on a government project, you get the baseline cost budget (BCWS) from the Cost Comparison Report for any level of the WBS (or any alternate) hierarchy.

The earned value curve in Figure 8-4 is labeled "BCWP," which stands for "Budgeted Cost of Work Performed." Again, it is the earned cost, rather than the earned labor-hours. When using Modern Project on a government project, you can get the earned cost (BCWP) by multiplying the Control cost budget (from the Cost Comparison Report) by the percent complete.

8.3.4 Additional Performance Measures

All of the performance measures used on government projects can be obtained from Modern Project. Most of them are performance measures already included in Modern Project that have names different from those commonly used on commercial projects. In this section we discuss most of them.

The cost and schedule variances used on government projects are computed in dollars, rather than in man-hours. While the variance analysis techniques taught in this book involve computing the cost and schedule variances at every level in the WBS hierarchy to assist the project manager in isolating problem control packages, government program managers are often interested only in the cost and schedule variance for the total project.

There are several reasons for this that are beyond the scope of this section, but one of the reasons has to do with the product orientation of the government work breakdown structures. Government project offices are often more interested in the cost or schedule variances for a product or subproduct than for work packages. Also, because the materials, equipment, and other costs consumed by a work package are not always allocated to that work package or to the control account that contains it, whereas they usually are for products, makes the extra work of computing these variances for work packages appear unnecessary to them.

In any event, computing the total cost and schedule variances in dollars is easy once the ACWP, BCWP, and the BCWS have been computed for the project. In fact, the government defines them as follows:

$$\text{Cost Variance: } CV = BCWP - ACWP$$
$$\text{Schedule Variance: } SV = BCWP - BCWS$$

In addition to the cost and schedule variances for the project, they define the "Variance at Completion" (VAC), the "Cost Variance Percentage" (CV%), and the "Schedule Variance Percentage" (SV%). These are all usually computed at the total project level but theoretically make sense at any level of the WBS hierarchy. They are defined as follows:

$$\text{Variance at Completion: } VAC = BAC - EAC$$
$$\text{Cost Variance Percentage: } CV\% = CV/BCWP$$
$$\text{Schedule Variance Percentage: } SV\% = SV/BCWS$$

The CV% is simply the percentage of the BCWP the CV represents, and the SV% is the percentage of the BCWS the SV represents. Notice that the denominators in the last two definitions are different. The BCWP is how much cost has been *earned* at "time now," whereas the BCWS is how much cost has been *scheduled* at "time now." Clearly, the CV applies only to how much cost has been earned, not to the total cost, and the SV applies only to how much cost has been scheduled. As time progresses, the BCWP and the BCWS will grow, and so will the CV and SV. Therefore, the CV% and the SV% will continually change.

In addition to the different variances that have been defined, there are other performance measures that can be divided into performance indices and status measures. The performance indices, like the variances, are usually computed only at the total project level. The first two, the cost performance index and the schedule performance index, correspond to the cost performance ratio and the schedule performance ratio with which we are already familiar. All of these performance indices are considered to be good if they are greater than one and bad if they are less than one.

Cost Performance Index: $CPI = BCWP/ACWP$
Schedule Performance Index: $SPI = BCWP/BCWS$
To Complete Performance:
$TCPI = [BAC-BCWP]/[EAC- ACWP]$

The *TCPI* represents the ratio of the "work remaining" to the "cost remaining" to complete the project, which is the productivity ratio projected to complete the project. The status measures are the percent complete, with which we are already familiar, and the "Percent Spent." They are also usually computed only for the total project. They are defined as follows:

Percent Complete: $PC = BCWP/BAC$
Percent Spent: $PS = ACWP/BAC$

The Percent Spent is sometimes calculated using the alternate formula: $PS = ACWP/EAC$. Finally, there is the EAC, which has already been discussed; there are two ways of calculating EAC, referred to as the *CPI* method and the *composite* method. They are defined as follows:

$EAC_{CPI} = BAC/CPI$
$EAC_{COMPOSITE} = ACWP + [BAC - BCWP]/[CPI * SPI]$

We have already discussed the EAC as computed via the CPI method. The second method involves adding what has already been spent to a computation of what may be spent if the present trends, as measured by the CPI and the SPI, continue.

Chapter 9

Risk Management

A s we saw in Chapter 2, before the work content of a project
can be managed, it must be quantified, and before the cost
of a project can be estimated, not only the work but the materials, equipment, consumables, and so on must also be quantified. Since risk, as we use the term, relates to completing the
project on time and within the allocated budget, it should come
as no surprise that the fundamental principles that underlie
risk management are closely related to the fundamental principles of project management. Consequently, the principle that
work that cannot be quantified cannot be managed transforms
into the principle that risk that cannot be quantified cannot be
managed.

As we shall see in this chapter, the method we advocate for
risk management is very much like the method we advocate for
project management. A fortunate by-product of this relationship is that the same tools developed for project management
can be used for risk management.

9.1 Quantification of Risk

The quantification of risk must be based on an assessement of
risk in a similar manner in which the quantification of work is
based on a project design or a project definition. In Chapter 2
we did not discuss how to design a product whose production

might be the end result of a project, nor did we discuss how to specify a project definition for an internal corporate initiative. We have something to say about that kind of undertaking in Chapter 10. But, for the most part, the focus of this book has not been on how to design something or how to write a specification for some initiative but rather on how to develop a project plan, given that the specification for the project has already been decided upon.

Similarly, we do not focus on how to do risk assessment. A whole book could be written about how to do risk assessment for various project types, just as whole books can be and have been written on how to design or specify the work content of a project. What we do is show how to develop a risk management plan, similar to the project management plan, and how to manage the risk based on this plan. The process is very similar to that for developing a project management plan.

To begin with, we need a WBS for the risk. This is easy to produce because we can essentially use the WBS for the project, with some modifications. The fundamental question that is essential for a good risk management plan is, What level of the WBS is appropriate for risk management? Before we can answer this question, we need to understand the concept of *contingency* as used by project managers.

Contingency can be thought of as yet another budget that is allocated to cover the risk that has been assessed. Why is another budget necessary to cover risk? Risk is normally measured probabilistically. We might say, for instance, "There is a 50% chance of a 10% overrun on the project." But, if this is the case, then it is not the whole story. If there is a 50% chance of a 10% overrun, then there probably is a greater probability of a smaller overrun and a smaller probability of a larger overrun. The statement that there is a 50% chance of a 10% overrun may just be the guess of the project manager or someone on the project management staff. But, if a detailed risk assessment has been done, we should have a graph in the form of Figure 9-1 that quantifies the risk for the total project.

Figure 9-1. Probability of finishing on time graph.

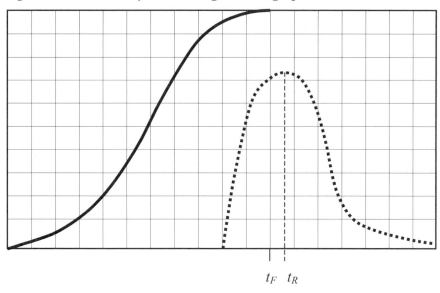

t_F t_R

Figure 9-1 shows the graph of total planned project expenditure plotted against time as a solid line. This graph shows the project completing at time t_F. Superimposed upon this graph is another graph, plotted as a dotted line. This graph is the probability density function (in different units) of the project finishing at some other time (earlier or later). The vertical line at time t_R denotes the mean of this probability density function. In other words there is about 50% probability that the project will finish before time t_R and about 50% probability that it will finish after time t_R.

If the project finishes later, it will probably cost more, and if it finishes earlier, it will probably cost less. Consequently, there is a corresponding probability density function associated with the differential cost of the project. If we take the mean of this second probability density function and add it to the total planned cost of the project, we might say that we now have the "most likely" total cost of the project at completion. Consequently, the client and/or project management may want to add this additional amount on to the budget as *contingency*. This is how the need for contingency arises.

The client and project management may agree that the nature of the project is a risky business. In fact, the contract may even acknowledge the risk, as, for instance, a cost-plus-incentive-fee contract. The incentive scheme may be something like this: the company executing the project gets 25% of any of the contingency it saves but must pay 25% of all costs above the total planned cost plus the contingency. In other words, the contractor has an opportunity to make even more profit than planned, but if the project is poorly managed it makes less profit than planned.

Now that we know what contingency is, we can return to the original question of what level of the WBS is appropriate for risk management. We can now see that this is really a question about what level of the WBS is appropriate for managing the contingency budget. But this leads to yet another question: what is meant by the phrase *managing the contingency budget*? We will leave the answer to that question to the next section. For now, we will just say that it usually does not make sense to manage the contingency budget at the work package level. The reason for this is that the contingency budget (in either labor-hours or costs) is usually considerably less than the control budget. Consequently, it does not seem reasonable to expend as much effort managing the contingency budget as the control budget. Also, if we do a good job managing the control budget, it follows that we will probably have done a good job managing the contingency.

9.2 Contingency Draw-Down

What we have seen in the previous section can be expressed in another way: *contingency is the quantification of risk*. Since contingency is a budget, it should have the same components as our other budgets—units of measure, quantities in those units, labor-hours, and costs. As a rule of thumb, the level at which the contingency budget is developed should be the lowest level at which to consider managing contingency.

Some projects for which risk must be assessed may have certain summary-level control packages that are much riskier than others. In this case, project management may want to specifically assess the risk of these risky control packages and use some other technique for assessing the risk of all the other legs of the WBS hierarchy together. On other projects, no attempt may be made to assess the risk of any summary-level control package except the root package at the top of the hierarchy. The reason for this may be that an organization engages in similar projects on a regular basis and has good historical information about the planned cost for projects and the actual cost of the projects at completion. From this an average contingency percentage might be calculated that is used for all projects of a certain type.

So the contingency may be arrived at quite differently on different projects. In one case there may be only a single contingency amount for the total project. On other projects there may be individual control packages that have contingency amounts calculated specifically for them. It often makes sense to have a work package directly under each control package for which a contingency budget is calculated specifically. We refer to such work packages as *contingency packages* because they contain the contingency budget for all the work packages under a particular control package. Figuring out a meaningful unit of measure for a contingency package is sometimes tricky.

For example, suppose we have a large summary-level control package with a labor-hour budget of 100,000 man-hours and a 10% contingency budget. The unit of measure for this control package may be systems, and the quantity budget at this level of the WBS hierarchy may be 3. On average, it is going to take about 33,000 labor-hours per system, so the 10,000 man-hour contingency budget would account for only about 0.3 systems, which may make no sense. In fact, even with the contingency the plan is still to deliver only three systems. So in this case it does not make sense for the unit of measure for the contingency budget to be systems.

One possibility in this example would be to choose a unit of measure of man-hours for this contingency package. Then the quantity budget and the labor-hour budget would be the same. If this is done, however, it is probably a mistake to use the quantity method for statusing such a package, because, as the contingency man-hours are used up (drawn down), the quantity method would indicate that the percent complete was the number of contingency labor-hours used divided by the total number of contingency labor-hours for the package. What is called for in this case is the indirect statusing method. If the control package with which the contingency package is associated is 50% complete, even if the contingency labor-hours are 85% used up, the contingency package should only be reported as being 50% complete. We postpone further discussion of statusing contingency packages until the next section.

By now the reader should have an intuitive understanding of measuring risk in terms of labor-hours or cost, and that we are referring to these risk amounts (labor-hours or dollars) as contingency. What remains to be explained is how these contingency budgets are to be allocated to the work packages associated with a control package. Since a particular contingency budget for a specific control package was generated at the control package level and not for the work packages associated with the control package, it is not immediately clear which work packages this contingency budget should be spent on.

In fact, in the best of all situations, we would like to spend none of the contingency budget. The fact is that, since contingency was derived from our understanding of the probability associated with achieving a budget, there may be some (nonzero) probability that we will not use any of the contingency budget. There may also be some probability that we will use twice the contingency budget. Since contingency is a probabilistic concept, we really do not know in advance what the final outcome will be. Consequently, contingency is to be spent at the discretion of the project manager or by a control package manager to whom the project manager delegates authority.

At any point that a work package budget is overspent, and the work package is associated with a control package to which a contingency is assigned, the project manager has the option of covering this overexpenditure with contingency resources. When that happens, the contingency is said to be *drawn down*. Contingency draw-down needs to be a disciplined procedure that is linked to the current status of the control package to which the contingency is associated.

If a control package has a significant contingency budget, it needs to be monitored, just as we would monitor a control package with a significant budget. If over time the contingency budget is being drawn down more rapidly than progress is being made on the control package with which it is associated, then corrective action needs to be taken. For instance, if the contingency budget has been drawn down by 40% but the control package with which it is associated is only 15% complete, then it may be the case that the contingency allocated to this package was inadequate or that the package is not being executed efficiently.

Another issue with contingency draw-down is how it is done. Different methods have been experimented with. The two most common are *budget transfer* and *contingency pool*. The budget transfer method is more complex, but it ensures that contingency expenditures are charged to the work packages for which the contingency was expended. The contingency pool method is easier to use, but on projects with large contingencies it is possible to complete the project with a significant portion of the work charged to contingency packages. This often makes the historical data of no value for planning similar projects in the future.

With the budget transfer method, portions of the contingency budget are transferred to the work packages on which the contingency is being expended. Then the labor-hour and cost transactions are made to those work packages. The question that arises is how to handle these budget transfers and to which budgets they should be transferred. Since we have a variance tracking system built into Modern Project, it is only natural to use it to make the contingency budget transfers. But it can be argued that an individual contingency transfer could be caused by any of the three different types of deviations discussed in Chapter 3.

Since contingency budget transfers are often made after the overrun expenditures have already been made, project managers are sometimes reluctant to count them as productivity variances. The reason for this is that productivity variances do not contribute to the control budget, and hence the overrun charges show up as poor productivity. They can argue that, since the contingency budgets are based on probabilities, it is a random thing and not something that could have been foreseen during the development of the project plan. Consequently, the argument is that contingency budget transfers should be counted as change orders and the additional work should not be considered as additional but rather an "intrinsic" part of the original budget. Moreover, if the contingency budget transfers are handled as change orders, they can still be labeled as contingency transfers. This way the original budget is still recorded, and the amount of contingency applied can be determined at a later date.

This line of reasoning does not, however, tend to categorize the contingency budget transfers by variance type. As a general rule of thumb, it is better, when using the balance transfer method, to make the transfers via the variance tracking system and to categorize contingency budget transfers in the same way that any other variances are categorized. This way, there is a uniform policy for using the variance tracking system, and the contingency budget ends up being merely a convenient way to pay for all or some portion of the variances.

The other commonly used method for contingency drawdown, the contingency pool method, leaves the contingency budget in the contingency package. All overruns on work packages associated with the control package to which the contingency is allocated are charged to the contingency package, rather than to the work packages. In a sense, this makes these overruns appear not to have occurred on the project but rather to be strictly a contingency phenomenon. This eliminates variance tracking of contingency budget transfers.

When this method of contingency draw-down is employed, a modification to where the contingency packages fit into the WBS is often in order. Since overruns covered by contingency are considered to be a contingency phenomenon, it is better to have all the contingency packages roll up to a total contingency package at the total project level. Therefore, it is better if there is a separate "leg" of the WBS hierarchy that contains all the contingency packages and at the same time mirrors the part of the WBS that consists of the control packages that have contingency associated with them.

Finally, there are issues that arise from unused contingency budgets that we will only touch on. If, during the life of the project, it appears that contingency is not being drawn down nearly as rapidly as progress is being achieved, the question naturally arises if some contingency can be released. This is really not a project management question so much as a financial question. On large projects, contingency budgets can be significant, and the contingency resources that are not being utilized may be better used on another project or on other business objectives. The question for project management is how to recognize whether surplus contingency exists and whether it is safe to release some or all of it.

For the author, the answer is simple, but there is by no means universal agreement on this. However, this simple answer is worth considering. The simple answer is that the unused contingency budgets for completed control packages can be considered surplus contingency, and it is safe to release this surplus contingency. It is surplus because it was not needed on the control package it was allocated to, and it can be safely released because all the remaining uncompleted work is still covered by the contingency that was allocated to it.

This is a conservative approach to the identification and release of surplus contingency. A similar argument can be used to support identifying contingency on unfinished control packages (and also releasing it) if the percent of contingency drawdown is less than the percent complete for the control package. But this second approach may be too optimistic. It may be that the riskiest work within the control package in question has not yet begun. It requires a judgment on the part of project management as to the relative risk of work packages within the control package. And this level of analysis regarding the relative risk of work packages was what the project managers wished to avoid when they decided to calculate and manage contingency at the level of this control package.

If contingency budgets are left (not fully drawn down) at the end of the project, then it should be considered that the project was still well managed even if the control budget was overrun. Since the existence of contingency implies the recognition of risk, and is in fact an attempt to quantify the risk, remaining contingency implies that the project was completed within the budgets in the face of this recognized risk.

9.3 Statusing Contingency Packages

There are many issues concerning the statusing of contingency packages. The indirect method is the best way of statusing contingency packages when contingency is allocated to control packages, for the reasons we have already discussed. However, while we believe this is the best way to allocate contingency, there is no consensus on this. Contingency is commonly allocated in other ways. Contingency is sometimes allocated by discipline or by craft. For instance, there may be an engineering contingency, a piping contingency, a power contingency, and so on when the project is to build a refinery. Or there may be contingency for staffing or for inflation or for getting the necessary permits in a foreign country.

All of these different contingencies are meant to cover risks that can affect the work of the project. For instance, a staffing contingency or a contingency for gaining the necessary approvals to operate in a foreign country is meant to quantify risks that can cause the work to proceed at a slower pace than envisioned in the project plan and consequently increase cost. When contingency is allocated in these other ways, it is often difficult to know how to status the contingency.

Some companies do not even place contingency in the hands of the project manager. This is probably the way it should be when the contingency is allocated to cover risks that cannot be correlated with the way the work will be done. But, if contingency is correlated to the way the work is to be done, it makes sense to have the project manager manage it. If the project manager is entrusted with managing the larger budget of the project itself, surely the project manager can be entrusted with managing the smaller contingency budget.

But some companies feel that risk management and, consequently, contingency management are general management functions, rather than project management functions. In this case, the project manager is expected to manage the project according to the project plan to the best of his or her ability in the face of risk without the benefit of contingency. General management may or may not have allocated contingency for a given project, and the project manager may or may not know whether there is any contingency. Sometimes there is the perception by management that if project management is aware of contingency, it will inevitably get expended. This is probably not a healthy view, but it is one that sometimes exists.

9.4 Risk Management Summary

Risk is a reality in every undertaking. If we knew the outcome of everything in advance, there would be no risk. Fortunately, for some undertakings, even though we do not know the details of the outcome, we can know the outcome generally speaking. This is the case for most projects we undertake. We know that we will be able to complete them, we just do not know precisely how much it will cost or how long it will take.

Consequently, we need to be honest with ourselves and to recognize that risk exists. Our plans, no matter how well conceived, need to acknowledge risk. Risk not only needs to be acknowledged; it needs to be managed. Just as we do not trust the execution of a project to luck, we should not leave risk to luck. While we may not be able to completely control risk, just as we cannot completely control the execution of a project, the attempt to control it on average will result in outcomes that are more to our liking than the outcomes we would get if we did not attempt to control risk. The methods presented in this chapter on risk management are straightforward and consistent with the methods of project management that have been presented in previous chapters. They do not begin to cover the diversity in concepts regarding risk management for projects. The intent of this chapter was not to treat this subject exhaustively but to give some practical advice that should work in the majority of cases a project manager will be faced with.

Risk management courses and seminars that the author has been exposed to often focus on organizing for risk, creating a risk plan, communicating about risk, and so on. The viewpoint here is that risk management is something like a total quality program; if you get everyone involved, you can somehow stamp out risk as you stamp out poor-quality work. While it probably does not hurt to promote an awareness of risk, the author is of the opinion that the project manager needs something a little more concrete than this. If the reader gets only one thing from the reading of this chapter, it should be that *risk can and should be quantified by contingency and that contingency budgets should be allocated consistently with the way the work is to be done so that they can be managed in the same way and with the same tools that the project is managed.*

Chapter 10

Rescuing a Failing Project

O ne of the least favorite thoughts of most experienced project managers is the prospect of taking over the management of a project that is failing. We are not talking about a
project that is simply over budget or behind schedule that
higher management thinks would benefit from a change in
project management. In this chapter we consider a project that
has been deemed a failure and that needs someone to take over
its orderly shutdown or one where the question is whether attempting to save it is worthwhile.

In both these cases, there is usually an attempt to discover
what went wrong and to document it. In the first case, problems are often documented because of the legal ramifications in
case of a dispute over damages. In the second case they are
documented so that those trying to make a decision regarding
an attempt at salvaging the project have something on which to
base their decision. In both cases, expediency is required. In the
first case, since project shutdown has already been determined,
much of the workforce can be dismissed to other projects. But,
in the case where project shutdown has not been decided on, it
is necessary for the project to continue operating in parallel
with the analysis.

10.1 Determining What Went Wrong

Often, when a project has failed or is near failure, one of the
contributing causes is that the methods discussed in the previ-

ous chapters of this book were not applied. However, just attempting to apply these methods does not guarantee a successful project. Failed projects often employ the same methods that are used on successful projects. Some companies have standardized project management methods and yet experience both successes and failures.

Consequently, in determining what went wrong, we may have to search more deeply than just the project management methods that were employed. In preparation for this search, let us first consider the possible causes for project failure. We have already discussed, in Chapter 3, the three reasons projects do not progress as planned. But, for determining the reasons for project failure, we need to go back even further. We need to consider what preceded the plan, that is, what the plan was based on. Depending on the purpose of the project, the project plan may be based upon a variety of different things. For instance, if the project is to design a computer system, the project plan may be based upon a design methodology, whereas, if the project is to build a building, the project plan may be based upon architectural and detail drawings that were produced during a previous project.

Similarly, a project to design and develop a new product may be based upon a product feasibility study that was conducted as a previous project. Or, a project to identify and streamline company operational policies and methods may be based upon a management consulting firm's report that cites operational methodology discrepancies as the cause of inefficiency.

In all of these cases, previous documents, studies, or projects determine the work content of the project at hand. This is different from determining how the work content will be performed. Determining how the project will be performed is that part of project planning devoted to developing the project WBS. Often, this is where project planning breaks down in the first place. What frequently happens is the definition of the work

content is sufficiently ambiguous as to permit multiple interpretations.

In this case, several possibilities emerge. Perhaps the worst
case occurs when the project planners, thinking they understand the intended work content, plan the work around an interpretation of the work content that is foreign to those who
attempted to document the work content. A more subtle case,
and one that is hard to detect, occurs when the project planners
build a plan that adheres to the letter of the documented work
content but not to its spirit. On the surface, the project planner's
WBS appears to preserve the integrity of the documented work
content, but the project management team's interpretation of
the WBS is substantially different from what was originally
documented.

So we can begin our list of what causes projects to fail with
the following reasons:

1. Ambiguous definitions of the work
2. Failure to communicate the meaning of the definition of
   work to the project team

To these we can add the reasons that projects do not progress
according to the project plan that we already know about from
Chapter 2:

3. Failure to translate the work content into a meaningful
   WBS
4. Improper quantification
5. Inadequate estimating
6. Poor productivity (including poor execution caused by
   inadequate project management)

We will not deal with all six of these problems in this chapter. It is assumed that the reader already understands from previous chapters how one would determine whether reasons 4
and 5 were partially to blame. Of course, if the project team is

not utilizing the variance and change tracking methods discussed in Chapters 3, 4, and 5, a determination may involve an analysis of individual control or work package cost and schedule overruns.

We now look at the remaining four reasons for project failure and make some recommendations for determining project failure and assessing the possibility of salvaging a failing project.

10.2 Project Definition

By project definition in this section we do not mean development of a project WBS or any other elements of a project plan. Rather, we mean definition of the work content of a project. The reader may be wondering why we are covering this topic at the end of the book, rather than at the beginning. The reason for this is twofold. First, the definition of the project work content is different from project management. How to define or specify a project has been the subject of previous books. The focus of this book is not on project specification but on how to manage a project (given that it is reasonably specified).

Second, we wanted the book to get into the essentials of project management as quickly as possible, assuming that this, rather than project specification, is the subject of most readers' interest. It is only because project definition and specification are relevant to assessing the possibility of salvaging a failing project that it is brought into our discussion here.

There are various views on how to define or specify projects and various methods that support these views. Our intent here is to give some advice that should work well for most project situations a reader might encounter without making any claim to an exhaustive treatment of the subject.

The approach proposed in this section is designed to deal with both problems 1 and 2 listed in the previous section, namely the problems of ambiguous project definitions and of communicating the project definition to the project team. It is an approach with which the author has had considerable experience and the one that was used for specifying the Modern Project system that is provided with this book. For many projects, the outcome is something that someone will use, such as a computer system, an appliance, a factory, or a dwelling. All of these things that people use can be explained in the context of a "User's Manual." While dwellings are not customarily described in a user's manual, presumably it would be possible to do so. The reason for including in the list of project outcomes something that could be described by a user's manual is to illustrate that we are considering outcomes that *could* be described this way, rather than things that are described this way.

A user's manual is a document about a product from which a potential user of the product can learn how to use the product. Such a description of the product conveys *what the product does* for the user and how the user interacts with the product, rather than how the product was built. In our context, how the product is built is in the domain of the project plan, whereas how the product relates to the user is in the domain of the project description or specification.

One of the advantages of the user's manual for both the user of the product and the producer of the product is that it separates the product *concept* from the product *implementation*. This separation of concept from implementation is useful in communicating the intrinsic nature of the product (via its concept) unencumbered by unnecessary details of its implementation. Consequently, a user's manual is often a remarkably good instrument for communicating a product concept from product specifier to product producer, even though this is not usually why a user's manual is produced for a product. There are some limitations in using a user's manual for this purpose, as I have described in one of the referenced papers at the end of this book, but for many projects the user's manual is a remarkably good communications vehicle.

Moreover, a user's manual can provide the necessary framework for constructing a definition of a project outcome (i.e., a product) in a short period of time. This is often precisely what is needed in assessing whether a failing project can be salvaged.

The suggested method for proceeding when taking over a failing or failed project is to first assess the description of the project upon which the project plan was built. If the description can be shown to be unambiguous and easily understood by a project team, then it can be reasonably concluded that the project description or specification is not to blame. However, it is the author's experience with failing projects he has been asked to evaluate that the root cause, more often than not, includes the project description.

Notice that, regardless of whether a project is failing or has already been deemed a failure, it usually makes sense to capture an unambiguous and easily communicated description of the project work content as quickly as possible. Conventional product specifications are often poor communications vehicles, because product specifications are often only meant to be understood by specialists. The reason for this is that product specifications are often organized to support implementation goals such as traceability, testability, functional allocation, and performance measures, which have nothing to do with communicating the concept of the product to the project management team.

We have suggested in this section that a product user's manual is a product definition mechanism that is essentially universally understandable. While this may not always be the case, it works so well in most cases that we make the assumption for use in the following sections that part of the failing or failed project takeover process is ensuring the existence of something like a product user's manual. The following sections deal with where we go from here.

10.3 Translating a Definition into a Plan

If the project is to be shut down, then what is left lies essentially in the realm of accounting, legal, materials, and personnel functions, with a minimum of direct project labor to facilitate these other functions. But, if the user's manual was produced with a view toward salvaging the project, then we need to consider how a project team proceeds from that point.

If we assume that we are proceeding down the path of developing a project plan from a user's manual, there are some fundamental questions that have to be answered. Project plans are not customarily produced from a user's manual. The development of a user's manual is often one of the work components in a project plan and is often modeled by a summary-level control package. Furthermore, a user's manual is often produced in the last stages of a project life cycle, rather than at the beginning. Producing a user's manual late in a project life cycle is usually a bad idea, but it often occurs that way. So developing a work plan from a user's manual often sounds like putting the cart before the horse.

There are a number of advantages of using the user's manual as the requirements specification for a project that I have explained in some of the papers referenced in the back of this book. One of them is that for software development projects, this approach improves control of the software development process, because on software development projects there is usually a natural flow of activity from the capabilities described in a user's manual into the high-level decomposition of the system into subsystems. The same thing also holds true for many other types of products, especially projects with a high level of technical complexity. Transition from the requirements specification into the design phase has historically been a problem, especially when the requirements specification is developed by one organization while design and implementation are done by a different organization(s).

Using the user's manual as the requirements specification emphasizes the *mode of delivery* of the product's capabilities, which can be used to extend this method of requirements specification into the design activity. This approach facilitates requirements traceability for projects that require traceability, since the mode of delivery of a capability is easier to recognize and trace in a design than is an abstract statement of the capability. Also, specification of the mode of delivery of capabilities facilitates the understanding of how the design proceeds from the requirements.

The preceding discussion indicates how this approach facilitates the translation of the product specification (of requirements) into a product design. We still need to discuss the transition of the design into a project plan. Before proceeding to the transition from a design into a project plan, it is worthwhile to reflect for a moment on the specifics of the situation we are in at this point.

The failing project may have started with a design that was produced in a manner entirely different from transitioning from a user's manual description of the project's product (outcome). In fact, this may be one of the underlying causes of failure. The production of that design may have itself been the result of a significant project. What the new project manager might be faced with is a total redesign of the product in a manner that is suitable for translation into a project plan (i.e., one that is producible). The cost involved in such an undertaking may in itself be reason to abandon the project.

10.4 Replanning

Once a validated specification of what is to be accomplished on the project is available, a new project plan can be built. A new WBS usually needs to be constructed that defines in broad terms how the work is going to proceed. Often, a reduction in the scope of the work can be achieved when the new specification is being developed, making it more feasible to continue. It is often the case that the original specification called for more than was actually required. Replanning represents an opportunity to rethink the scope of the project.

Requantification and reestimating must proceed in the same manner as explained for quantification and estimating in Chapter 2. In reestimating, we include resequencing and rescheduling the newly requantified work. When these are being redone, it is possible that some of the work will not have to be quantified or estimated, such as work that has already been accomplished that forms a useable part of the newly validated design specification. While we want to preserve as much of the finished work as possible from the failing project, it is often tempting to assume that some of the finished work will fit into the redirected project's work plan when it really will not. It is often the case that all the existing finished work should be requantified and reestimated and then the finished work should be compared to this in detail to determine if the seemingly finished work is really finished.

The requantification and reestimating should be used to produce a new project plan that begins where the failing project ended. Modifying the failing project's plan to form a new project plan is usually not a good idea. If the original plan was a good one and it can be determined that the reason for failure was inept management, then it might be possible to stick with the original plan. But project failure is usually caused by many shortcomings that add up to the failure.

Once a new or revised plan has been prepared, it can be decided if the expenditure (and risk) to save the failing project is worthwhile. Not until a new or revised plan is available can an informed decision be made. Replanning a large project in midstream can be a significant effort, and work may not be easily stopped and started again. The uncertainties associated with the cost of replanning alone, on very large projects, sometimes lead to their cancellation. It would be far better if the problems were discovered earlier and replanning could continue in parallel with the work. An experienced project manager can often turn a poor project plan into a workable plan if enough time is left in the project lifetime.

References

Boehm, B. *Software Engineering Economics*, Prentice-Hall, Englewood Cliffs, N.J., 1981.

Burgess, A. R., and J. B. Killebrew. "Variations in Activity Level on a Cyclical Arrow Diagram," *Journal of Industrial Engineering*, Vol. 13, No. 2, March-April 1962.

Galbreath, R. V. "Computer Program for Leveling Resource Usage," *Journal of Construction Division, proceedings ASCE*, Vol. 91, No. CO1, May 1965.

Howes, N. R. "Project Management Systems," *Journal of Information and Management*, Vol. 5, No. 6, pp. 243–268, 1982.

Howes, N. R. "Managing Software Development Projects for Maximum Productivity," *IEEE Transactions on Software Engineering*, Vol. SE-10, pp. 27–35, January 1984.

Howes, N. R. "On Using the User's Manual as the Requirement Specification," in *Software Engineering Project Management*, R. Thayer (Ed.), IEEE Computer Society Press, pp. 172–177, January 1988.

Howes, N. R. "On Using the User's Manual as the Requirement Specification II," in *Systems and Software Requirements Engineering*, R. Thayer and M. Dorfman (Eds.), IEEE Computer Society Press, pp. 164–169, 1990.

MIL-HDBK-881 of 2 January 1998, *Department of Defense Work Breakdown Structure Handbook*.

Thayer, R., and M. Dorfman (Eds.), *Systems and Software*

Requirements Engineering, IEEE Computer Society Press, 1990.

User's Guide for Microsoft Project 98, Microsoft Corporation, Document No. 92600.

Wiest, J. D. *The Scheduling of Large Projects with Limited Resources*, Ph.D. dissertation, Carnegie Institute of Technology, May 1963.

Index